# EMOTIONAL SATISFACTION OF CUSTOMER CONTACTS

Cover design: Mimi Sugarman
Cover Photo: Thomas Fasting

ISBN 978 90 5629 466 3
NUR 780

Observing and Registering

# Emotional Satisfaction of Customer Contacts

For Customer Satisfaction & Loyalty

ACADEMISCH PROEFSCHRIFT

ter verkrijging van de graad van doctor
aan de Universiteit van Amsterdam
op gezag van de Rector Magnificus,
prof. dr. J.W. Zwemmer
ten overstaan van een door college voor
promoties ingestelde commissie,
in het openbaar te verdedigen in de Aula der Universiteit
op woensdag 28 februari 2007, te 12.00 uur

door

Hüseyin Güngör

Geboren te Eskişehir, Turkije

Promotiecommissie:

Promotor: Prof. drs. J.W. Ganzevoort, *Universiteit van Amsterdam*

Co-promotor: Prof.dr. J.H.J.P. Tettero, *Universiteit van Amsterdam*

Overige leden: Prof. dr. W.F. van Raaij, *Universiteit van Tilburg*

Prof. dr. K. de Ruyter, *Universiteit Maastricht*

Prof. dr. E. Peelen, *Business Universiteit Nyenrode*

Dr. W.M. van Dolen, *Universiteit van Amsterdam*

Faculteit der Economie en Bedrijfskunde

# PREFACE

The inspiration for this research was provided by an unexpected telephone call in 2002 from EFMA (European Financial Management & Marketing Association). EFMA requested me, as the head of savings accounts & the call center of a Dutch Bank, to present a case in their conference on customer contact centers to be held in Paris.

While searching for a case I noticed that our customers were praising 'the human touch' while communicating with us. Indeed we had no advanced technologies like an interactive voice response system, no sophisticated product spectrum, no fancy advertisement campaigns, but just a simple customer service philosophy that aims at resolving all customer concerns with a genuine empathy and with the human touch.

After presenting 'the human touch' case to a large international audience, I was actually surprised that these 'very basics of customer relations' received a lot of positive attention. Afterwards, many other conference invitations followed spontaneously from cities like Berlin, Amsterdam and London. I was lucky enough to receive feedback from many customer service professionals who agreed with the fact that the very basics of customer relations and their 'emotional impact' were mainly overlooked in various sectors and many countries.

When the summary of these presentations appeared in the (inter)national sector media, I started reading and exploring more on customer contacts, and noticed that the customer contact industry was dominated by non-academic research and publications. Therefore, I decided to discuss this "niche" research area with Prof.drs. Wessel Ganzevoort, who subsequently agreed to be my PhD thesis supervisor, and let me search for "knowledge" akin to *The Teachings of Don Juan: A Yaqui Way of Knowledge* (Castaneda, 1968). Then my initial 'practical' ideas became an 'academic' research project which we called *the journey*. "And there I travel, looking, looking, breathlessly" (ibid.).

This journey was not only an academic adventure for me, but also a major career shift, a business plan, as well as a long-term dream that entails some lecturing in a sunny place. Probably inspired by Orhan Veli, I resigned from my full-time job on a "fine day" in May 2003 and ran a half-marathon the following year at the "age thirty-five," which according to Cahit Sıtkı Tarancı, "means half the course." Similar to the lyrics of MFÖ, perhaps I was in the middle of the road and in the middle of the run where destinations are actually nothing more than new departures…

Many people took a part in this journey. Gökhan Engin was very encouraging with his intellectual involvement when I was taking the very first steps on this journey. Wilfred Mijnhardt was also supportive especially during the literature research phase. Jan Pieters, from InHolland University, made it possible for me to start teaching as a marketing lecturer and sharing my accumulated knowledge with many students. Test firms, their customer service teams and their customers were pivotal for this research. Prof.dr.Jozef Tettero joined the journey as a thesis co-supervisor and gave a great deal of guidance especially in finalizing the conceptual framework. Initial suggestions from Prof. dr. J.G. de Gooijer were also very helpful for statistical analysis. Jet Labrie was there at the very beginning, as well as at the very end, improving the Dutch summary. Catherina Connaire took great care of the final-proof-reading and improvements in English, and Marinus Cordesius put the *puntjes op de i* in the Dutch summary.

The resources such as time, attention, and financial resources invested in this research are largely taken from the resources that should have been devoted to our children Mert and Zara. I do hope that I can make it up to them in the future.

Last, but certainly not least, I could neither start nor finish this journey without the support of my wife Ellen-Wiene who was always there for me. Therefore, I dedicate this dissertation to her with love...

Voorburg, June 2006

BRIEF CONTENTS

TABLE OF CONTENTS

## LIST OF TABLES



## LIST OF FIGURES

# 1 INTRODUCTION

## 1.1 Growing Importance of Customer Contact Centers

Parallel to the global recession in the early 2000s, managing or decreasing costs gained the utmost importance (The Economist Intelligence Unit, 2004). Banks, for instance, reduced their expensive face-to-face channels like branch offices,[1] and enlarged their remote channels like contact centers. Consequently, contact centers are considered to be one of the fastest growing industries. The number of contact centers has increased, for example, from 350 in 1996 to about 1500 in 2006 with more than 70.000 seats, employing about 170.000 people in The Netherlands.[2] It is estimated that roughly three percent of the working population in countries like the UK and the USA is employed in contact centers,[3] and about 2.5 percent in The Netherlands.[4]

The contact center industry is thus becoming increasingly a part of daily lives, not only when customers contact them,[5] but also when firms contact customers. For example, it is estimated that yearly 500 million telemarketing calls are made in The Netherlands (de Volkskrant, 4-6-05) alone, indicating about 30 calls per year per person in that country. Banks, insurance firms, manufacturing firms, telecommunication service providers, travel industry, utility firms, on-line shops, post-order firms, and even government organizations increasingly employ contact centers.

The performance of contact centers has recently gained even more importance. Consumer organizations, like *Consumentenbond* in The Netherlands, test the performance of contact centers when they analyze companies such as, Internet providers (Consumentengids, Juni 2003) or insurance companies (e.g., de Volkskrant, 5-1-2006).

Customer contact can be considered as a service encounter where the customer service representative (CSR) is unlikely to serve that particular individual again; therefore it is different from a service relationship where the employee and customer regularly interact (Grandey & Brauburger, 2002:263).

The terms 'contact center' and 'call center' are interchangeably used in popular as well as in academic literature. When the telephone was the only remote

[1] Between 1997 and 2002, the Netherlands reduced the number of bank branches by 47%, Belgium by 24%, Germany by 19% and the United Kingdom by 10% (Efma, 2004).
[2] Kroon, 2003; NCCBP, 2003; VCN (www.verenigingcontactcenters.nl) accessed on 16-2-2006.
[3] Knowledge@Wharton, 2-15 June 04; and as cited in Thompson, Warhurst & Contactaghan (2001:934), Datamonitor, 1998, *Contact Centers In Europe 1996-2001: Vertical Market Opportunities*.
[4] CBS, Net Labor Participation statistics, 2003 (Total population aged 15-64: 10.92m; Net Labor Participation: 65.1%); Kroon, 2003 (sector includes 150-200.000 workers including many part-timers).
[5] It is estimated that a contact center seat handles yearly 10 to 15 thousands of incoming calls. Therefore, it can be estimated for the Netherlands, with over 70 thousand seats, that there are about 900 million calls made to such centers.

contact channel for organizations, their service centers were named call centers. The growth in Internet, e-mail, online chats, and mobile devices have changed the nature of customer relations with call centers and as such were re-labeled as contact centers.

Although there are no strict definitions established yet, contact centers are commonly classified under two main categories: in-house and independent (*facilitair*). In-house centers are managed by the firms themselves, and independent centers are managed by specialist firms that might serve various industries or firms. Contact centers can be organized for answering incoming contacts (inbound), or for initiating marketing and sales contacts (outbound), or both. Furthermore, their tasks may be commercial or not-for-profit. Finally, they can deal with consumers directly (business-to-consumer) or they can serve businesses (business-to-business). This research primarily focuses on the business to consumer environment, and on inbound activities of in-house contact centers in commercial organizations.

## 1.2 Growing Dissatisfaction with Contact Centers

Despite their growing importance and presence, contact centers are increasingly becoming the center for customer "frustrations" and regularly associated with negative comments in the media (e.g., Jones & Farquhar, 2003; Wolfe & Raaen, 1999; Sprigg, Smith, & Jackson, 2003; HELA, 2001; Vocalis, 2003). Selected headlines from The Netherlands include: "Customers are on Hold" at insurance firms (De Volkskrant, 5-1-2006); "Stop *Telefoonterreur*!" (Consumentenbond, May-2005);[6] "0900-*Frustraties*" (Consumentenbond, Sep-2004).

Gottero (2005) identifies two main sources of customer frustration with banks. One is caused by the firm's internal complexities such as rigid and imposed procedures; and the other is the difficulty communicating with firms. For example, difficulty in contacting advisors or long waiting times on the phone which can sometimes be as long as 62 minutes.[7]

Even the interactive voice response (IVR) systems of contact centers are a cause for frustration due to their endless menus of *press one for this and press two for that...* (e.g., Grougiou & Wilson, 2003). Norman (1993:111) suggests that IVR systems can make customers annoyed, upset and even furious (see also Grougiou & Wilson, 2003). McKean (2003:287-294) states that most IVR systems break all the humanizing rules of technology by taking the control away from the customers.

---

[6] Consumentenbond started a campaign called 'stop telefoonterreur' in May 2005 and in ten days received 6772 complaints regarding unwanted telemarketing calls (de Volkskrant, 4-6-2005).

[7] In December 2003 an Internet service provider's helpdesk in The Netherlands managed to answer a call, made by H.Güngör, after 62 minutes waiting in their system-queue. The help desk CSR could not go any further than Frequently Asked Questions (FAQ) in 8 minutes. To reach a more experienced CSR, the call is put back in the same waiting queue. H.Güngör has hung-up after 5 minutes of more waiting on top of 70 minutes of frustration.

The contact center environment is comparable with fast-food restaurants where excessive rationalization leads to dehumanization (e.g., Ritzer, 2000:17; cf. Freemantle, 1999:11; Norman, 1993:13). Employees who work in fast-food restaurants, similar to contact centers, are trained to do a very limited number of tasks in precisely the way they are told to do them. Customers who eat in fast-food restaurants are also controlled, albeit more subtly: Queues, limited menus, few options, and uncomfortable seats imply to customers what the management wishes them to do -- eat quickly and leave (Ritzer, 2000; cf. Hoff, 1982).

A survey among 1021 banking customers and 50 executive managers in 6 European countries shows that "telephone-based banking" scores lower than other channels in terms of customer satisfaction" (Efma, 2005). Results of a global consumer survey[8] also illustrate the high level of frustration with contact centers: 85% of respondents have had a negative call center experience, and more than half of the consumers surveyed had stopped doing business with a company due to a negative call center experience. Another research similarly suggests "customer service problems cause half of the downward migration at mobile-phone companies" (Coyles & Gokey, 2002; see also Keaveney, 1995).

It appears thus that positive customer experiences need to be increased in the contact center environment.

## 1.3 Growing Necessity for Human Touch & Positive Experiences in Contact Centers

Information technology advances everyday and becomes available to everyone as a convenience, however, it is a human-to-machine communication like the Internet or cash dispensers (ATM). Furthermore, technology may also create customer frustration such as in IVR systems, and it does not guarantee an improved efficiency (Olazabal, 2002). Therefore, technology cannot be a solution in itself, but just an instrument. Yet, many businesses rely too much on IT and perform poorly on the front line (Beaujean, Davidson & Madge, 2006).

Firms are beginning to realize that "technology does not care for customers, but people do" (Arussy, 2002:31). For instance, a Dutch bank re-introduced personal contact for its small-business customers having recognized that telephone and the Internet were not sufficient to serve these customers (de Volkskrant, 30-1-2004). Dutch banks even want customers back into their branches due to dissatisfactory sales results through Internet and contact center channels (de Volkskrant, 21-12-2005).

[8] The study was commissioned by Genesys, a call center software company, and conducted by an independent email survey company. Some 20,000 consumers from around the world were queried. The survey elicited 2,367 responses, a 12% response rate. Responses by region break down as follows: Asia-Pacific, 18%; Europe, Middle-East and Africa, 18%; and the Americas, 64%. *www.genesyslab.com 15/9/2003*

Various studies indicate that customers, especially in elderly customer segments, want 'human touch' when dealing with their firms and are unwilling to accept interactive (electronic) services (e.g., Kshirsagar et al., 2001; Howcroft et al., 2003; Sheth & Sisodia, 1999). Grougiou and Wilson's (2003) research shows that senior citizens experience serious problems when using contact centers with complex IVR systems. The expected growth[9] of elderly people in western societies thus signifies the necessity for more human touch in service environment and contact centers in particular.

The Human Touch is the positive emotion that is created around services and work environment (Güngör, 2002). Actually, many authors underline a similar approach with different names such as 'customers are human' (McKean, 2003),[10] 'customer are people' (Arussy, 2002), 'personal touch' (LaSalle & Britton, 2003:30), 'emotional connectivity' (Freemantle, 1999:204), 'emotional value'[11] (Barlow & Maul, 2000), 'empathy' (Parasuraman, Zeithaml & Berry, 1988),[12] 'customer intimacy' (Treacy & Wiersema, 1995), and so on. Bitner, Booms and Tetreault (1990:72) note that "the human interaction component of service delivery is essential to the determination of satisfaction and dissatisfaction."

Emotions evoked during service encounters or during product usage are studied under "customer experience." Customer experience embraces the emotional aspects of customer encounters in the entire customer journey from pre-acquisition to post-sales (Güngör, 2006). In essence it aims at decreasing customer sacrifices such as waiting times at bank branches, and increasing customer rewards such as a pleasant help-desk service when needed.

As Pine and Gilmore (1999:163) suggest, "firms must recognize that goods and services are no longer enough; customers now want experiences." According to LaSalle and Britton (2003:29, 41) customer experience begins with an interaction between a customer and a product, a company, or its representative; and the result of an interaction is the formation of a feeling. Treacy and

---

[9] For example, the statistics of The Netherlands indicate that the ratio of potential working population (20-64 years old) to pension holder (65+years old) population will increase from 22:100 in 2001 to 24:100 in 2010 and 42:100 in 2040 (Biersma,R., *Nederland wordt grijzer, zwarter, maar ook geler*, NRC Handelsblad, 21-22 Dec 2002; CBS). The situation will be even worse in Europe where there are currently 35 pensioners for every 100 worker. By 2050, on present demographic trends, there will be 75 pensioners for every 100 workers; in Italy and Spain the same ratio will even be one-to-one (The Economist, July 19th 2003).

[10] According to McKean (2003), The Human Touch is about treating people with Acknowledgment, Respect, and Trust (ART).

[11] "Emotional Value refers to the feelings that customers experience or anticipate experiencing when they deal with organizations and their representatives" (Barlow & Moul, 2000:2).

[12] Parasuraman, Zeithaml and Berry (1988) identified 5 dimensions of Service Quality (SERVQUAL): 1) Empathy 2) Responsiveness 3) Assurance 4) Reliability and 5) Tangibles. First three of them actually resemble the Human Touch and 4 & 5 can also be categorized in one group. This classification resembles the work of Herzberg who categorized the 5 motivation hierarchies of Maslow under 2 categories: hygienes and motivators. [For Herzberg's work, Oliver (1997:147) cites: Benjamin Schneider and Clayton P.Alderfer, "Three Studies of Measures of Need Satisfaction in Organizations", *Administrative Science Quarterly*: 18:489-505 at p.490 (December 1973)]

Wiersema (1995:85) propose that customers desire a mix of tangible and experiential benefits, and expect the performance of breakthrough products to move their rational and their emotional selves. According to Lovelock and Wirtz (2004:345) "more than anything else, customer experience management requires customer empathy-- seeing what the customer sees, feeling what the customer feels." At British Airways, for example, they "try to think about what kind of impression or feeling each interaction between the company and a customer will generate" (Prokesch, 1995:104). Likewise, Boston Consulting Group raises the question: "Do you know what it's like to be your company's customer?" (BCG, 1999:101).

Customer experience occurs around unpredictable and immeasurable conditions, and varies anywhere between distress and delight each time customers encounter a firm's products and services. Using a bank card at an ATM, visiting a branch office, or calling contact centers are, for example, just a few building blocks of the total customer experience in banking.

Contact centers play a pivotal role in creating positive service experience in the entire customer journey from the pre-acquisition to post-sales phase. Even the customers who generally use branches, or Internet, sooner or later encounter contact centers especially in "emergency situations" such as stolen cards, internet problems, or rushed transactions "where customers have an unusual amount of emotional energy invested in the outcome" (Beaujean, Davidson & Madge, 2006). This is probably one of the reasons why contact centers are regularly associated with 'problems' and with 'customer frustrations.'

To understand the contact center dynamics it is necessary to discuss briefly the stake holders in the contact center environment.

## 1.4 Stakeholders: Top Executives, Contact Center Management, CSRs, and Customers

There are four parties identified as stakeholders in the contact center environment in this research: top executives, contact center management, customer service representatives (CSR) and customers.

To start with, *top executives* in many firms do not seem to be aware of, or are not fully concerned with, the contact center dynamics. Confirming this observation, a recent consumer survey in six European countries[13] (Efma, 2005) indicates that customers do not fully appreciate the services they receive from contact centers, whereas, the executives from the same organizations are relatively happy with their services rendered. Contact centers for many executives are a 'cost center' that must generate 'sales' and become a 'profit center' before even generating proper customer service (Güngör, 2006).

[13] France, Italy, Netherlands, Spain, Sweden, and the UK.

*Contact center management* commonly resides between conflicting goals such as improving quality, customer satisfaction, employee motivation, and profitability, with usually very limited resources given by the upper management. This delicate position urges harsh productivity standards in the contact center environment. Therefore, contact centers are commonly discerned as technological-bureaucracies with Taylorist[14] theories and standards. They are described as the factory floors of the 21st century where employees are constantly gauged against statistical performance standards (Wilk, 2002); and labeled as high-tech sweat shops (Dawson, 2001:118, 255; Sprigg, Smith, & Jackson, 2003:1, 54; see also Thompson, Warhurst, & Callaghan, 2001).

Organizations place their image and success in the hands of *CSRs* who handle the day-to-day business of thousands of customers. Robinette et al. (2001:165) argues that CSRs are "the brand builders who hold the power to attract or alienate customers with every single transaction." Indeed the performance of frontline employees determines how judgments of the entire company are made and future sales made or lost (Griffin, 2002:112; Winer, 2001).

Despite their obvious importance, contact center jobs are considered to be "low quality" and heavily routine. CSRs deal with a variety of people and issues with very short intervals, have little autonomy in planning or doing their jobs, and are severely monitored. CSRs are commonly the part-timers and the temporaries; they sometimes have no direct contact with the company they are serving, let alone with the related departments. Therefore, they sometimes do not even notice the contribution (positive or negative) they make to the whole process. Consequently, but not surprisingly, CSRs have higher job related depression or job-related anxiety, and lower job satisfaction than most other jobs (Holman, 2002; Sprigg, Smith, & Jackson, 2003:19, 22; HELA, 2001).

CSR's job image in general is also not very positive due to "poorly organized cold telesales actions" (Bach, 1998:18). As a Dutch telemarketing CSR recently stated: "it's better to say that you are a prostitute" (De Telegraaf, 20-3-05). Therefore, CSRs seem to be the "Achilles' heel" (vulnerable part) of contact centers. (Güngör, 2002).

*Customers* enjoy the immense supply and increased amount of information that shifts the balance of power from seller to buyer. This trend affects all lines of business from telephone companies and retail businesses to financial institutions (Teerling, Plagborg, & Gragg, 2003; see also LaSalle & Britton, 2003). Surprisingly, at the same time contact centers are increasingly becoming centers of customer "frustrations" with negative comments in the media, long waiting times, problematical IVR systems, and more like fast food restaurant treatment.

---

[14] Frederick Taylor in *The Principles of Scientific Management* (1911) tried to rationalize and standardize the production processes so that repetitive actions without thinking would lead to production increase. His ideas have been implemented in the assembly lines of the car manufacturer firm Ford, such processes therefore also known as Fordism.

In short, while customers have many choices in a very competitive market place, they frequently experience frustration in contact centers and they even switch firms due to negative call center experiences, companies do not seem to entirely comprehend this problem. One of the reasons for this incomprehension seems to be the traditional customer satisfaction measurements that do not adequately capture such frustrations.

## 1.5 Problems in Measuring Customer Dis/Satisfaction

Customer satisfaction surveys can generate valuable information that enables an organization to compare its performance in different time periods. Organizations do not only benefit from satisfied customers, but also from the satisfaction measurement itself. An aspect often forgotten is that customer satisfaction measurement can provide a sense of achievement and accomplishment for the employees involved in the customer service process (Mihelis et al., 2001). Finally, satisfaction measurements can make customers more satisfied as they receive positive attention and feel that they are listened to. There are, however, some concerns that challenge the power of typical customer satisfaction measurements.

### *1.5.1 Satisfaction Measurements Are Not Adequate To Capture Customer Dissatisfaction*

According to Birgelen, Ruyter and Wetzels (2000:2) "in the modern context of tremendous information availability through advances in information technology and research practice, use of customer satisfaction-related information does not always appear to be optimal." Referring to Mulder (1999)[15] they note that "decision-makers get frustrated when it turns out that, despite of repeated measurement and attention for quality-related issues, no changes in customer satisfaction levels are evident."

There are several reasons for these unchanged and positively-scored satisfaction survey results. First of all, many companies have millions of customers, and many of them measure customer satisfaction only with several hundred customers. Secondly, response rates of customer satisfaction surveys among unsatisfied customers are quite doubtful. It is questionable whether unsatisfied customers are still the customer of such companies when they receive satisfaction surveys. It is also questionable whether these customers would like to cooperate and spare some time for such companies. Thirdly, an invitation to complete a satisfaction survey may positively influence customers. They might therefore give "socially desirable" or more positive answers (e.g., Nancarrow & Brace, 2000).[16] Hence, customer satisfaction surveys not only miss the majority

---

[15] As cited in Birgelen, Ruyter and Wetzels (2000): Mulder, P. (1999). 'Er verandert geen moer!': Frustraties met continu-klanttevredenheidsonderzoek. *Tijdschrift voor Marketing*, (April), 20-24.

[16] They also refer to: Kalton & Schuman (1991). The Effect of the Question on Survey Responses: a review. *Journal of the Royal Statistical Society,* 145, Part 1, 42-73.

of unsatisfied customers, but also receive an "exaggerated" satisfaction picture about customers. Furthermore, there usually is a considerable time lag between dissatisfaction-survey-analysis- and improvement (if any).

Customer satisfaction surveys, therefore, are not guaranteed tools for understanding customer dissatisfaction and the bottlenecks in a firm's product and processes. As a result, firms usually realize and manage dissatisfaction reactively, namely when customers complain. Nevertheless, there are also some concerns that challenge the power of complaints.

### *1.5.2 Majority of Dissatisfactions Do Not Become a Complaint*

"ANSWER: To do nothing, absolutely nothing. QUESTION: What is the most frequent consumer response to both satisfying and dissatisfying consumption outcomes?" (Oliver, 1997:359). Confirming this, Kotler (1996:442) argues that 25% of purchases result in consumer dissatisfaction, but less than 5% of unsatisfied customers complain (see also, Engel, Blackwell, & Miniard, 1990:548). Tax and Brown (1998) suggest that on average, only 5 to 10 percent of the customers who have been unhappy with a service actually complain. For example, British Airways customer services hear only from 8% of all customers who have reason to complain (Heskett, Sasser, & Schlesinger, 1997:179).[17]

Iacobucci (1999) argues that in the vast majority of instances, a customer receiving poor service simply complains to friends, family and colleagues, but *not* to the related companies. Stone, Woodstock and Wilson's (1996:679) research suggests that even when customers are dissatisfied and defection is imminent, "companies often fail to recognize that this is happening." As Oliver (1997:361) similarly notes, many of a firm's unsatisfied customers are not identifiable to management.

In short, rather than filling in satisfaction surveys or complaint forms, many customers simply switch to a competitor when they are unsatisfied; and firms usually realize and manage customer defection on customers request to close accounts, or after the defection.

Proactively identifying customer dissatisfaction thus appears to be a necessity in marketing literature as well as in marketing practice.

## 1.6 Capturing Customer Dis/Satisfaction Information in Contact Centers: A Model Proposal

On the one hand, as discussed in previous sections, customer dissatisfaction increases especially with contact centers, but firms are not able to fully capture such information with traditional satisfaction measurement tools. On the other

[17] As cited in Heskett et al. (1997:179): Klein, N. & Sasser, W.E, Jr. (1994). *British Airways: Using Information Systems to Better Service the Customer*, Case No. 395-065. Boston: Harvard Business School. p.13.

hand, customer service representatives (CSR) in contact centers continuously observe whether or not customers are satisfied. It is, therefore, envisaged that CSRs can observe, evaluate and instantly register information about customer satisfaction.

Frontline personnel involvement in the customer satisfaction process and utilizing their feedback is already analyzed in the service marketing literature. Bitner and colleagues suggest that frontline personnel are a critical source of information about customers, and they have better understanding of customer needs and problems than others in the firm (Bitner, Booms, & Mohr, 1994:96; Zeithaml & Bitner, 2003:152). Indeed, a CSR on average can handle 8 calls per hour, 60 calls per day, and over 15.000 customer contacts a year. This is much more than any other type of employee, as well as, more than many customer satisfaction surveys.

Reichheld (1996:56-57) suggests that it is difficult to conceptualize and set up the mechanisms that turn the analysis of customer satisfaction and defection into an ongoing system, closely supervised by top managers and quickly responsive to changing circumstances. He emphasizes thus the need for creating "an ongoing mechanism that keeps senior managers permanently plugged into frontline customer feedback" (ibid., p.68, 69). Heskett, Sasser and Schlesinger (1997:91) suggest that feedback from frontline can be used for customize service to customer satisfaction. Hegebarth (2001) similarly argues that if contact centers capture and analyze customer interactions and share them throughout the organization, an enormous opportunity exists in understanding customer needs and expectations, identifying opportunities, and proactively addressing improvement areas. Jones and Sasser (1995:93) propose that "to take full advantage of frontline employees' interactions with customers...a company must train them to listen effectively and to make the first attempts at amends when customers have bad experiences."

Observing customers and registering some information about them is also not an uncommon practice. United Airlines, for example, use the "note fields" in reservation systems to describe specific (negative or positive) incidents or observations. Such notes give agents a more complete picture of passengers and "this practice is common throughout the industry" (Brady, 2000; see also E.Piphany, 2003:5). Ritz-Carlton hotel employees observe and report customer likes and dislikes for a guest preference database. The guest historians in each hotel then review the database and suggest "extra touches" that might delight each guest (Armstrong & Kotler, 2003:239). USAA, a large insurance firm, uses its frontline staff to collect sensitive information on customers and the market, such as complaints, market trends and new products, called: ECHO (Each Contact Has Opportunity). The Information is then forwarded to internal action representatives and related units. Low scores in satisfaction are automatically routed to senior management (Tax & Brown, 1998; Reichheld, 2001b:165).

These examples thus indicate that it is desirable as well as realistic to involve frontline personnel such as CSRs into the customer satisfaction (measurement) process.

*Therefore, this research will attempt to analyze customer satisfaction and loyalty process and will propose a model that can be used in the customer contact environment for observing customer satisfaction through the eyes of frontline employees (CSRs). As customer contacts can be a source of frustration (negative emotions), and as it appeared to be necessary to increase positive experiences (positive emotions) in contact center environment, this research will focus on emotional aspects of customer satisfaction, and emotional satisfaction of customer contacts (ESCC) in particular. It is envisaged that these observations would provide timely and tangible information for recovering service failures by following up dissatisfactions, for increasing sales productivity by following up satisfactions, and for organizational learning by continuous improvement actions. It is also envisaged that these actions would increase internal and external quality and satisfaction, which in turn would increase customer loyalty (and profitability) as described in "the service profit chain" by Heskett et al. (1997).*

## 1.7 Organization of the Text

Organization of the text will be parallel to the conceptual model as sketched in Figure 1-1. The model has three segments and each segment has two chapters. The first segment will cover the customer satisfaction (and loyalty) process; the second segment will cover the observation of customer satisfaction by frontline employees (CSR); and the third segment will cover the implementation issues and next steps in the proposed model.

In Part-I, chapters 2, 3, and 4 will describe these segments with literature research, and will set research questions. In Part-II, chapters 5, 6, and 7 will attempt to answer the research questions with the information gathered through customer surveys.

In chapter 2, six elements in customer satisfaction (and loyalty) will be examined, namely: Price, Product, Convenience, Service quality, Service treatment, and Positive feelings towards the firm or brand. Also, four dimensions in customer satisfaction (and loyalty) will be studied: Emotional, Cognitive, Transactional, and General Satisfaction. Cognitive satisfaction will represent the rational and thinking side of the satisfaction, whereas, emotional satisfaction will represent the experiential and feeling side. General satisfaction will represent the overall satisfaction of customers, whereas, transactional satisfaction will represent the satisfaction with the last contact with firms. Finally, customer loyalty will be investigated with the intention to stay as customer in positive cases, and defection in negative cases. Chapter 5 will reveal the relationship among these elements and dimensions.

Chapter 3 will basically examine the definition, measurement and the role of emotions in the satisfaction process, in contact centers, and in organizations. This chapter will also propose a simple methodology for observing Emotional Satisfaction of Customer Contacts (ESCC) by customer service representatives (CSR). In the ESCC model, a color range of 'red-orange-yellow-green-blue' will represent CSR observations on customer's emotional state ranging from very negative to very positive. Chapter 6 will describe the basic implementation of the ESCC methodology in the test firms, will examine the accuracy of the ESCC observations, and will explore the relationship between observed ESCC, customer satisfaction, and loyalty intentions.

Chapter 4 will explain possible next steps in using the ESCC information which will include following up positive ESCC for more sales, and negative ESCC for service recovery; learning from failures; and consequently increasing satisfaction and loyalty. Chapter 7 will describe suggested steps within the ESCC framework with some empirical evidence.

Figure 1-1: Research Model

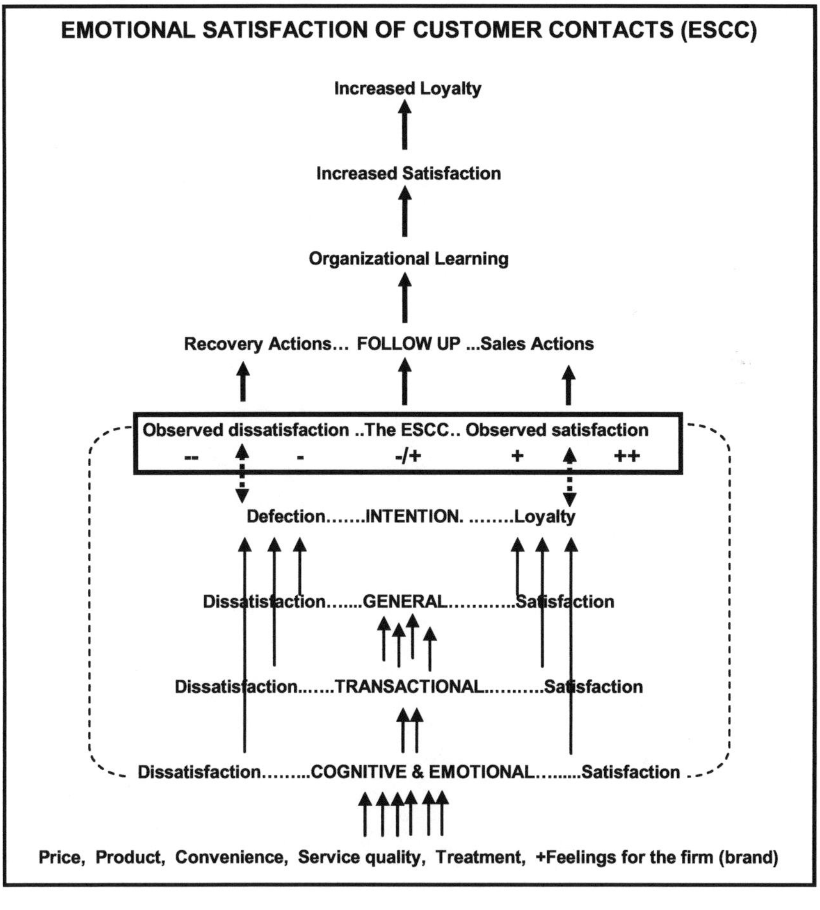

**PART I: Conceptual Model, Literature Review and Research Questions**

# 2 ELEMENTS AND DIMENSIONS OF CUSTOMER SATISFACTION AND LOYALTY

This chapter will explore the definition, elements and dimensions of customer satisfaction and loyalty that are used in this research. Literature review will lead to the research questions and these questions will be answered, as presented in chapter 5, based on the results of customer surveys in test firms.

## 2.1 What is Customer Satisfaction and Loyalty

Customer satisfaction is one of the most popular phrases in business, with over 72 million links on the Internet[18] and also a very broad subject that is interpreted in many ways in business practices and in academic literature. The word "satisfaction" seems to derive from Latin words *satis* (enough) and *facere* (to do or make) (Oliver, 1997).

Expectation is an important part of the satisfaction process and is the "anticipation of future consequences based on prior experience, current circumstances, or other sources of information."[19] Expectation can be many things varying from wishes to hopes (Oliver, 1997:69; Bolton & Drew, 1991[20]). Katona (1975:381) notes that satisfaction "depends not only on the quality of the product, but also what the person whose satisfaction is studied expects from the product." Mihelis et al. (2001:357) argue that customer satisfaction is a dynamic parameter of the business organization and is affected by the changes in customer's preferences and expectations. Similarly, Anderson and Sullivan (1993) suggest that "customer satisfaction is the overall or global judgment regarding the extent to which product or service performance matches expectations". According to Oliver (1997:11), "satisfaction is the consumer fulfillment response. It is a judgment that a product or service feature, or product or service itself, provided (or is providing) a pleasurable level of consumption-related fulfillment, including levels of under- or overfulfillment." Consumer Satisfaction is also defined as a post-consumption evaluation that a chosen alternative at least meets or exceeds the expectations. Dissatisfaction, on the other hand, is the outcome of negatively confirmed expectations (Engel, Blackwell, & Miniard, 1990:545).

---

[18] "Customer satisfaction" is searched in Google.com, accessed on 1-5-2006.

[19] As cited in Oliver (1997:68): Warren W. Tyron (1994). Expectation. In Ramachandran (Ed.), *Encyclopedia of human Behavior,* vol.2, pp.313-319 at p.13.

[20] As cited in Parasuraman, Zeithaml, Berry (1994:112): Bolton, R.N. & Drew, J.H. (1991). A Longitudinal Analysis of the Impact of Service Changes on Customer Attitudes. *Journal of Marketing*, 55 (January), 1-9.

Giese and Cote (2000) identify three common elements in different consumer satisfaction definitions: "1) consumer satisfaction is a response (emotional or cognitive); 2) the response pertains to a particular focus (expectations, product, consumption experience, etc.); and 3) the response occurs at a particular time (after consumption, after choice, based on accumulated experience, etc.)."

"Loyalty is another concept that is easy to discuss in everyday conversation, but becomes more obtuse when it is analyzed for meaning" (Oliver, 1997:389). Oliver (1997:392) suggests that "customer loyalty is a deeply held commitment to re-buy or re-patronize a preferred product or service consistently in the future, despite situational influences and marketing efforts having the potential to cause switching behavior." Jones and Sassers (1995:90) argue that there are two types of loyalty: "true long-term loyalty" and "false loyalty" in which customers seem to be loyal until certain benefits are exhausted like using all frequent-flier miles. According to Reichheld (2001b:44) "loyalty is not bribery or hostage taking. It is about earning people's enthusiastic commitment to a relationship that will improve their lives over the long term." After all "loyalty is about the future, and not the past" (ibid., p.97).

As widely agreed (e.g., Reichheld, 1993, 1996, 2001; Oliver, 1997; Heskett, Sasser, & Schlesinger, 1997) there are many positive effects of customer loyalty such as revenue growth due to repurchases as well as referrals, cost decline due to lower acquisition costs and serving experienced customers, and increase in employee retention due to job satisfaction and pride.

The relationship between customer satisfaction and loyalty will be elaborated in section (4.3).

## 2.2 Selected Elements in Customer Satisfaction

To determine the elements of customer satisfaction in this research, among many others, the following resources are used. These sources are actually a combination of different angles like services marketing (Zeithaml & Bitner, 2003), emotion marketing (Robinette, Brand, & Lenz, 2001), strategic marketing (Rust, Zeithaml, & Lemon, 2000), and (marketing) strategy (Treacy & Wiersema, 1995).

Zeithaml and Bitner (2003:85) in *Services Marketing* identify three major dimensions of customer satisfaction: Price, product quality, and service quality. Service quality has also three sub dimensions (ibid.): interaction quality, outcome quality, and physical environment quality. Also these sub dimensions are analyzed by five other dimensions known as SERVQUAL: Responsiveness, assurance, empathy, tangibles, and reliability (Parasuraman, Zeithaml, & Berry, 1988; Zeithaml & Bitner, 2003).

Table 2-1: Dimensions of SERVQUAL

| Dimensions of Service Quality (SERVQUAL) (Parasuraman, Zeithaml, & Berry, 1988; Zeithaml & Bitner, 2003) | |
|---|---|
| *Responsiveness* | Willingness to help customers and provide prompt service. |
| *Assurance* | Employees' knowledge and courtesy and their ability to inspire trust and confidence. |
| *Empathy* | Caring, individualized attention given to customers. |
| *Tangibles* | Appearance of Physical facilities, equipment, personnel, and written materials. |
| *Reliability* | Ability to perform the promised service dependably and accurately. |

Robinette, Brand and Lenz (2001:22) in *Emotion Marketing* identify five customer satisfaction and value dimensions. In their definitions the rational value dimensions are product and money; and the emotional value dimensions are equity (trust), experience (relationship), and energy (convenience).

Rust, Zeithaml and Lemon (2000: 9-10, 55-56) in *Driving Customer Equity* define customer equity in three areas. Firstly, value equity is the customers' objective evaluation of the firm's offerings, and includes quality, price, and convenience. Secondly, brand equity is the customer's subjective view of the firm and its offerings, and includes awareness, attitudes, and perceptions toward the brand. Finally, retention equity or relationship equity is the customer's view of the strength of the relationship between the customer and the firm, and it includes loyalty, special recognition, affinity, community, and knowledge programs. The focus of the firm, however, may vary among industries. For example in telephone service industry the value equity may be the key driver, in consumer package goods the brand equity, and in banking the retention equity (ibid.).

Treacy and Wiersema (1995) in '*The Discipline of Market Leaders*' set three value disciplines: 1) Operational excellence (best total cost): providing customers with reliable products or services at competitive prices, delivered with minimal difficulty or inconvenience; examples: McDonalds, Wal-Mart, AT &T Universal Card Services. 2) Product leadership (best product): providing products that continually redefine the state-of-the-art; examples: Starbucks, Intel. And 3) Customer intimacy (best total solution): selling the customer a total solution, not just a product or service, by building bonds with customers like those between good neighbors; examples: Ritz Carlton, Airborne Express. Treacy and Wiersema (1995:20) designate the following dimensions that matter for customers: Price, product quality, product features, service convenience, service reliability, expert advice, and support services.

As the sources analyzed above use a different combination of satisfaction elements/dimensions, the following six items are selected (judgmentally) for this research: *Price, Product, Convenience, Service Quality, Service Treatment, and Positive feelings* towards the firm or brand. These items are not only common denominators of the four main sources used here, but also frequently used, albeit with different combinations, in many sources (see Figure 2-1) as well as being widely used in common customer satisfaction questionnaires.

*Price* or money or cost item is used by all the sources analyzed above and by many others (Oliver, 1997: 392,394-395; Rust, Zeithaml, & Lemon, 2000:77; Treacy & Wiersema, 1995:49; Robinette, Brand, & Lenz, 2001:22). In this research price also covers the attractiveness of interest rates in banking or fees paid for services.

*Product* is another item that is used by all sources analyzed (Rust, Zeithaml, & Lemon, 2000:74; Treacy & Wiersema, 1995:87; Robinette, Brand, & Lenz, 2001:22). In this research product also covers the features or conditions of service products.

*Convenience* (accessibility and ease of being customer) is used in Rust, Zeithaml and Lemon (2000:78), Robinette, Brand and Lenz (2001:22), Treacy and Wiersema (1995:20), and in Parasuraman, Zeithaml and Berry's (1988) service quality.

*Service Quality* (reliable, accurate, and timely services) is one of the five dimensions used in SERVQUAL (Parasuraman, Zeithaml & Berry, 1988) and is also regarded as an important attribute of customer satisfaction (Oliver, 1997:397; Zeithaml & Bitner, 2003). Treacy and Wiersema (1995:20) also use this item. According to Bitner, Booms and Mohr (1994:103)[21] service reliability is considered as the single most important dimension used by consumers to judge service quality.

*Service Treatment* (the way firm treats customers) is used as empathy and responsiveness in SERVQUAL, as experience in Robinette, Brand and Lenz (2001:37), and as customer intimacy in Treacy and Wiersema (1995:125). Also Pine and Gilmore (1999), Freemantle (1998:8, 23), Barlow and Maul (2000:2) describe similar concepts under the experience framework. As a recent survey among 1021 banking customers in 6 European countries indicates "53% of the respondents believe that the image and character of the bank primarily resides in its telephone manner" (Efma, 2005:29). Similarly, a Belgian GSM network provider[22] survey reveals that "friendliness" is still the most important 'customer satisfier.'

---

[21] With reference to: Parasuraman, Zeithaml & Berry, 1988; and Parasuraman, Berry and Zeithaml (1990). *An Empirical Examination of Relationships in an Extended Service Quality Model.* Marketing Science Institute Research Program Series, Report No. 90-122.

[22] (Mobistar, Orange, Belgium) Adapted from panel discussions during the "European Contact Center Exchange" event in Amsterdam, 1-2 March 2004.

*Positive Emotions* towards the firm is analyzed as 'brand attitudes' by Rust, Zeithaml and Lemon (2000:8, 88, 93), as 'trust' by Robinette, Brand and Lenz (2001:37), and as 'customer intimacy' in Treacy and Wiersema (1995). Parasuraman, Zeithaml and Berry (1988) cover similar issues under the 'empathy' dimension in SERVQUAL. Moreover, Oliver (1997:395) and Freemantle (1998:6, 22) also underline the importance of this dimension. Jones and Farquhar (2003:72)[23] relate customer attitudes towards a company with customer loyalty. Gobe (2001:xxiv, 62) argues that "the biggest misconception in branding strategies is the belief that branding is about market share when it is really always about mind and emotions share."

The relation of these items to satisfaction and loyalty will be further analyzed in chapter 5 with empirical data obtained through customer surveys from different industries.

Figure 2-1: Satisfaction & Loyalty Dimensions Used in the ESCC Research

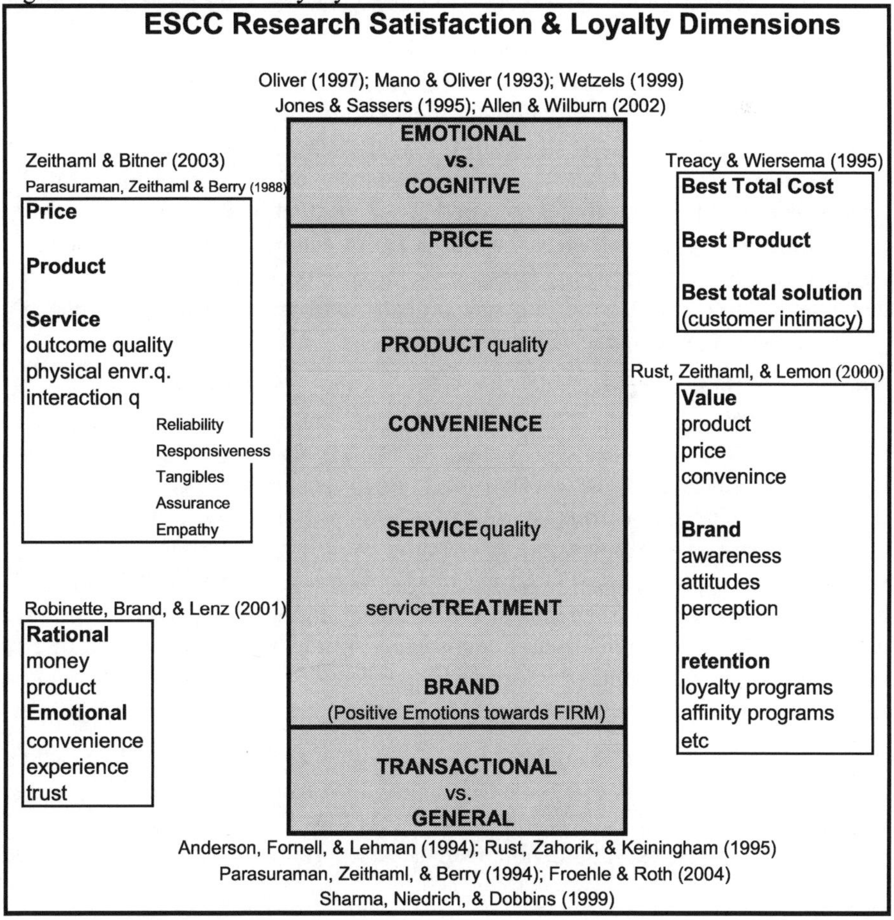


[23] With reference to: Dick & Basu (1994).

## 2.3 Cognitive vs. Emotional Dimensions in Customer Satisfaction and Loyalty

Oliver (1997:353) suggests that "...the overly simplified question "Are you satisfied?" does not tap into the complexity of the satisfaction response. Because satisfaction can mean a variety of things, researchers are advised to determine the *cognitive* (processing states) and *affective* (the emotions) substrata of the satisfaction response" (see also, Allen & Wilburn, 2002). Wetzels (1999) also distinguishes satisfaction in two similar dimensions: affective and calculative.

*Cognitive satisfaction*, to begin with, is how customers rationally calculate the product or services they are receiving. This dimension has many similarities with the concept of (perceived) value or utilitarian benefits, which are mostly related with the objective product attributes like product quality and price. Customers, based on their experiences with the product or services, evaluate constantly whether or not they receive a good value for what they gave up (or paid).

*Emotional satisfaction*, conversely, is the hedonic or experiential benefits that customers cannot calculate rationally or objectively. It is about trust and relationship (cf. Robinette et al., 2001). It is the ambiance of a restaurant. It is the sense of belongingness to a firm, or happiness of being a customer of the firm. It is the feeling that indicates whether the product or service received is 'a good choice'. It is, for instance, the way a firm treats its customers, or positive customer emotions towards the firm. It is similar in definition to the "cult of the customer", "you will know it when you see it, and you will miss it when it's gone" (Treacy & Wiersema, 1995:184).

Oliver (1997:316) suggests that satisfaction in consumer contexts responds to both cognitive knowledge of the outcomes of purchasing, and the emotions that accompany these outcomes and related events. As shown in Figure 2-2, when both are present and similarly valenced, synergy occurs such as in the form of customer loyalty. Numerous studies confirming this suggest that a strong customer loyalty is only possible if customers are cognitively and emotionally satisfied (e.g., Wetzels, 1999; Oliver, 1997; Mano & Oliver, 1993; Jones & Sassers, 1995; Robinette, Brand, & Lenz, 2001). Mano and Oliver (1993:451) argue that, "both conceptually and empirically, product satisfaction is naturally tied to cognitive judgments [thinking] and to affective [feeling] reactions elicited in consumption."

Emotions and cognition is interrelated, although there are debates[24] on which one comes first or which one is more important. Wetzels (1999) study indicates that calculative commitment is somewhat weaker than affective commitment. In other words, functional satisfaction such as good pricing or convenient location

---

[24] As cited in Oliver (1997:281): See R.B.Sajonc (1984). On the Primacy of Affect. *American Psychologist*, 39:117-123; and R.S.Lazarus (1984). On the Primacy of Cognition. *American Psychologist*, 39:124-129.

creating calculative commitment may quickly disappear as soon as an alternative supplier emerges. On the other hand, a balanced and honest [even emotional] relationship with the customers will create affective commitment and this would create more satisfied customers which in turn create a long-lasting profitable relationship for both parties.

Figure 2-2: Cognitive & Affective Satisfaction in Loyalty

| Cognitive & Affective Satisfaction in Loyalty (cf. Oliver 1997, Wetzels, 1999) | | | |
|---|---|---|---|
| *Cognitive* (e.g., price) | Satisfaction | Partial satisfaction; vulnerable to competitive offers | Full satisfaction; strong loyalty |
| | Dissatisfaction | Disappointment; likely to switch | Partial satisfaction; vulnerable to competitive offers |
| | | Dissatisfaction | Satisfaction |
| | | *Affective* (e.g., service friendliness) | |

As affective (emotional) and cognitive factors are widely accepted in the customer satisfaction and loyalty process, it would also be valuable to analyze them in customer contact settings. Therefore, the following research questions are formulated:

1) What are the elements of emotional and cognitive satisfaction?

2) What is the role of emotional and cognitive satisfaction in:

2a) Customer contacts (transactional satisfaction)? (See section 2.4)

2b) General satisfaction? (See section 2.4)

2c) Customer loyalty (intentions)? (See section 2.5)

## 2.4 Transactional vs. General Dimensions in Customer Satisfaction and Loyalty

When the time horizon is taken into account, there are two different conceptualizations of customer satisfaction: transaction specific satisfaction and general (cumulative) satisfaction (e.g., Oliver, 1997:174; Sharma et al., 1999; Rust, Zahorik, & Keiningham, 1995:59; Anderson, Fornell, & Lehman, 1994; Parasuraman, Zeithaml, & Berry, 1994:121). The former is event specific and can be defined as the post consumption evaluative judgment of a particular transaction. The latter form of satisfaction is about all previous transaction experiences over time. General satisfaction is thus the outcome of a learning process where the customer learns from (or remembers) all previous transaction experiences over time.

Anderson, Fornell and Lehman (1994:54)[25] argue that 'cumulative satisfaction', rather than 'transaction-specific satisfaction', is a more fundamental indicator of the firm's past, current, and future performance. Rust, Zahorik and Keiningham (1995:64) suggest that "there are good reasons to select either option" and argue that 'cumulative focus' better correlates with retention, but 'transactional focus' better reflects quality improvements and provides a more accurate picture of the current performance of the company. According to Parasuraman, Zeithaml and Berry (1994:121), components of transaction-specific evaluations that lead to 'transaction satisfaction' are the evaluations of 'service quality', product quality' and 'price'. Components of global evaluations are the aggregation of transaction experiences (ibid., p.122).

In this research, *'transactional satisfaction'* refers to the customer satisfaction with regard to the last transaction with firms' contact centers (i.e., satisfaction with the last contact). Froehle and Roth (2004) use a similar construct in their new measurement scales for evaluating perceptions of the technology-mediated customer service experience: "Attitude towards contact episode... [which] reflects the customer's overall attitude towards the entire contact" (ibid., p.6). *'General satisfaction'* on the other hand, refers to the 'overall satisfaction' of customers with all satisfaction elements and dimensions (i.e., satisfaction with being a customer of the firm).

The term *'cumulative satisfaction'* is reserved for a future longitudinal research which will analyze the aggregation effect of 'transactional satisfactions' on the 'general satisfaction' and 'loyalty intentions.'

As transactional and general factors are widely accepted in the customer satisfaction and loyalty process, it would also be valuable to analyze them in customer contact settings. Therefore, the following research questions are formulated:

3) What is the role of transactional and general satisfaction in customer loyalty (intentions)?

4) What is the role of transactional satisfaction:

 4a) in general satisfaction?

 4b) in customer loyalty (intentions)?

5) What is the role of time in evaluating transactional satisfaction?

---

[25] For the terms 'transaction-specific and cumulative satisfaction' Anderson, Fornell, and Lehman (1994) refer to: Boulding, W. et al. (1993). A Dynamic Process Model of Service Quality: From Expectations to Behavioral Intentions. *Journal of Marketing Research,* 30, 7-27.

## 2.5 Loyalty intention

In this research customer loyalty is investigated with the "*intention to stay*" as customer. This "behavioral intention" or "commitment" is the "conative" dimension of loyalty (Oliver, 1997:390, 393). In positive cases it refers to loyalty, whereas, in negative cases it is an indicator of customer defection (churn) where customers switch to a competitor.

Commitment, intention to repurchase, and intention to stay as customer are frequently analyzed in various marketing studies (e.g., Wetzels, 1999; Luarn & Lin, 2003).

It is however, also very important to consider the relationship between customer intentions and their future behavior. According to Katona (1975:82) "attitudes and expectations themselves do not represent forecasts. They are but the ingredients of forecasts. Consumers' discretionary demand is a function of both ability and willingness to buy. Attitudes and expectations indicate the changes in the latter." In Fishbein and Ajzen's (1975:382) framework, intentions are viewed as the immediate antecedents of corresponding behaviors. Ajzen and Fishbein (1980:62) propose that behaviors are determined by intentions to perform the behavior and that this intention is, in turn, a function of attitudes toward the behavior and subjective norms of individuals (see also Ajzen, 1991).

The extent to which attitudes provide accurate forecasts of behavior depend on a number of factors. According to Engel, Blackwell and Miniard (1990:323), the attitude-behavior relationship should grow stronger when (1) attitude measurements specify correctly the action, target, time, and context components; (2) the time interval between attitude measurement and behavior becomes shorter; (3) attitudes are based on direct experience; and (4) behavior becomes less affected by social influences.

Previous sections already formulated research questions about the relationship between customer loyalty intentions and customer satisfaction dimensions.

The relationship between loyalty intentions and actual behaviors is outside of the main focus of this research, nevertheless, may be a subject for a further (longitudinal) research.

## 2.6 Summary

Based on the literature review, the following six items are selected as the elements of customer satisfaction for this research: Price, Product, Convenience, Service quality, Service treatment, and Positive feelings towards the firm or brand.

Also four dimensions are identified as part of the customer satisfaction and loyalty process: Emotional, Cognitive, Transactional, and General Satisfaction.

Cognitive satisfaction represented the rational and thinking side of the satisfaction, whereas, emotional satisfaction represented the experiential and feeling side.

General satisfaction represented the overall satisfaction of customers, whereas, transactional satisfaction represented the last transactions, namely the satisfaction with last contact with firms.

Finally, customer loyalty is investigated with the intention to stay as customer.

# 3 EMOTIONAL SATISFACTION OF CUSTOMER CONTACTS: THE ESCC MODEL

The previous chapter investigated elements and dimensions of customer satisfaction and loyalty process. This chapter will now attempt to design a methodology that will help customer service representatives (CSR) to observe, evaluate and register customer satisfaction during customer contacts.

Attention will particularly be paid to the emotional aspects. It is expected that customer contacts would be better represented by emotional elements such as service friendliness rather than cognitive elements such as price.

Therefore, this chapter will basically[26] explore the definition of emotion, its relationship with satisfaction, customer contact environment, related organizational aspects, its measurement methodologies, and will draw a practical methodology for observing and registering the Emotional Satisfaction of Customer Contacts (ESCC).

## 3.1 Definition of Emotion

"Everyone knows what emotion is, until asked to give a definition."[27] According to Parrot (2001:1) a widely-accepted definition of 'emotions' has proved elusive, with "over ninety different definitions" (Larsen, Diener & Lucas, 2002). Cowie (2000a) argues that "the word emotion is semantically treacherous. In everyday use, its reference shifts according to context. That makes it a very flexible tool, but it creates havoc when the word is taken out of context and used to describe a field research."

Affect, emotion and mood are close concepts and even used interchangeably. *Affect* is a psychological state that is felt and in some way is evaluative or valenced (positive or negative) and "refers to the feeling side of consciousness, as opposed to thinking, which taps the cognitive domain" (Oliver, 1997:294). *Emotions* are generally associated with a short-duration and with a specific stimulus. Emotion includes arousal, various forms of affect, and cognitive interpretations of affect that may be given a single description. Thus emotion is more cognitively involved than affect (Oliver, 1997:294). *Moods*, in contrast, are more enduring, more diffuse, and less related to specific stimuli (Frijda, 1993).[28] Mood refers to transient feeling (e.g., sadness, anticipation) that exists

---

[26] Adding an emotion factor to customer relations does not mean that observers (CSRs) should make a scientific psychological analysis of customers. Therefore, the use of emotions and related analysis in this research are intentionally kept shallow.

[27] As cited in Parrott (2001:28): Fehr, B. & Russel, J.A. (1984). Concept of Emotion viewed from a prototype perspective. *Journal of Experimental Psychology: General*, 113, 464-486.

[28] Frijda (1993:399) considers "duration and intensity not to be the most profitable basis for distinction between emotion and moods. Rather, 'diffuseness' appears as the most consequential difference between these affective states."

at a particular time and place.[29] The difference between emotion and mood is that emotion is directed toward something, but mood is a general state (Frijda, 1993). For instance, "a person in an irritable mood is not necessarily angry about anything in particular – he or she is just generally grumpy" (Parrot, 2001:3).

Major forms of emotions are similarly classified in cross-cultural researches by different authors. Plutchik (1980)[30] proposed eight basic emotions derived from psycho-evolutionary framework: joy, acceptance, fear, surprise, sadness, disgust, anger and anticipation. Ekman and colleagues (1987)[31] defined *big six emotions*[32] as happiness, sadness, fear, disgust, anger and surprise. Similarly, Schaver and colleagues (2001:34-35, 52) cluster analysis listed them as love, joy, surprise, anger, sadness and fear; although they exclude the 'surprise' when they discuss *five prototypes of emotion.* In his Differential Emotions Theory, Izard (1972)[33] conceptualised (Izard's typology) *ten fundamental emotions* (joy, surprise, anger, disgust, contempt, shame, guilt, fear, interest, and sadness), and has also initiated research on emotions in a variety of consumer research contexts (Laverie, Kleine, & Kleine, 1993).

Research[34] indicates that emotions can be categorized differently, however similar, in different language and cultures. However, 'display rules'[35] which are the constraints that govern socially acceptable expression of emotion may vary among cultures and genders. For example, women are more emotional than men is a common stereotype of Western culture. Nevertheless, "when people report past emotions or general tendencies on emotions, then... the stereotype is accurate; however, when people report specific emotions that are ongoing or very recent, then stereotypic gender differences disappear" (Parrot, 2001:140).[36]

---

[29] As cited in Engel, Blackwell, Miniard (1990:450): Gardener, M.P. (1985). Moods States and Consumer Behavior: A Critical Review. *Journal of Consumer Research,* 12, 281-300.

[30] As cited in Oliver, Rust & Varki (1997:316): Plutchik (1980). *Emotion: A Psychoevolutionary Synthesis*. New York: Harper Row.

[31] As cited in Cornelius (2000): Ekman, P, et al. (1987). Universals and Cultural Differences in the Judgments of Facial Expression of Emotion. *Journal of Personality and Social Psychology,* 53 (4), 712-717.

[32] As cited in Cornelius (2000): Cornelius, R.R. (1996). *The Science of Emotion. Research and tradition in the psychology of emotion*, Upper Saddle River (NJ): Prentice Hall.

[33] As cited in Laverie, Kleine & Kleine (1993): Izard, C.E. (1972). *Patterns of Emotions*, NY: Academic Press.

[34] As cited in (Oliver, 1997:296): J.A.Russel (1991). Culture and the Categorization of Emotions. *Psychological Bulletin,* 110:426-450 p.444.

[35] E.g., as cited in Cowie (2000): Ekman , P. & Friesen, W. (1969). The Repertoire of non verbal behavior: categories, origins, usage and coding. *Semiotica* 1, 49-98.

[36] As cited in Parrott (2001:140): Fisher, A. (1993). Sex Differences in Emotionality: Fact or Stereotype? *Feminism and Psychology*, 3, 303-318. LaFrance, M. & Banaji, M. (1992). Toward a reconsideration of the gender-emotion relationships. In: M.S.Clarck (Ed.), Review of personality and social psychology: Vol.14. *Emotion and social behavior* (pp.178-201). Newburry Park, CA:Sage Pulications; Shields, S.A. (1991). Gender in the psychology of emotion: A selected research review. In: K.T.Strongman (Ed.), *International review of studies on emotion* (Vol.1, pp.227-245). NewYork: Wiley.

## 3.2 Emotions and Customer Satisfaction

Emotion is a fairly new topic in consumer behavior and the role of emotion has gained a major role in understanding the consumption experience in the last decade (Oliver, 1997:291). Emotion is also linked to consumer's satisfaction response and indirectly to repurchase intent (ibid., p.292). Edwardson (1998:18) argues that "customer satisfaction measurement and research, as commonly applied, needs to now move to the next stage and consider the specific and unique consumer emotions and emotional knowledge structures that comprise the variety and richness of the consumer experience."

Liljander and Bergenwall (1999:8) identify three main research streams dealing with emotions and satisfaction: "1) satisfaction is in itself seen as an emotional response to a product… 2) emotions are treated as a mediator between cognitive evaluations… and 3) emotions are modelled as an independent factor contributing to the level of perceived satisfaction." As their research indicates, emotions that consumers associate with the service play an important role in forming satisfaction, and positive emotions enhance satisfaction (ibid., p.2).

Zeithaml and Bitner (2003:42) analyze emotion and mood as part of the service purchase and consumption stage and note that: 1) Customers with positive moods are more willing to participate in behaviors that help service encounters succeed.[37] 2) Moods and emotions enhance and amplify experiences making them either more positive or negative.[38] 3) Moods and emotions affect the way the service is consumed and how it will be remembered. Van Dolen and colleagues' (2001:369) research similarly indicates that "positive emotions contribute positively, while negative emotions contribute negatively to satisfaction."

Oliver investigated (1997:315) the emotions that would likely be associated with an expectancy disconfirmation framework (Table 3-1). In this framework, higher expectations require higher performances for creating positive effects and emotions. Expectations thus play an important role in forming the satisfaction (e.g., Anderson & Sullivan, 1993; Oliver, Rust & Varki, 1997; Anderson, Fornell, & Lehman, 1994) as well as in forming the associated emotions. In Oliver's words, "positive encounters will create positive expectations which, in turn, will enhance the likelihood of interpreting the next encounter as positive" (Oliver, 1997:389).

[37] As cited in Zeithaml & Bitner (2003:44): M.P. Gardner (1985). Moods States and Consumer Behavior: A Critical Review. *Journal of Consumer Research,* 12, 281-300.
[38] As cited in Zeithaml & Bitner (2003:44): S.S.Tomkins (1980). Affect as Amplification: Some Modifications in Theory. In: R.Plutchik & H.Kellerman (Eds.), *Emotion: Theory, Research, and Experience,* (pp. 141-164). New York: Academic Press.

Table 3-1: Likely Emotions in the Expectancy Disconfirmation Framework

| (Oliver, 1997:315) | DISCONFIRMATION | | |
|---|---|---|---|
| EXPECTATION | *Negative* | *Zero* | *Positive* |
| *Low* | Disgust, anger, withdrawal | Tolerance, resignation, despair | Hope, promise, gratitude, relief |
| *Average* | Disappointment, dismay | Contentment, unemotion, indifference | Glee, pleasant, surprise |
| *High* | Disappointment to anger, resentment, betrayal | Happiness, pleasure | Delight, elation, ecstasy |

Oliver's research (1997:318) concludes, however, that the questions of "whether satisfaction is an emotion" and "the emotional role of satisfaction in consumption" have not been answered due to the contradictory findings in the literature. As he suggests "...the overly simplified question "Are you satisfied?" does not tap into the complexity of the satisfaction response" (ibid., p.353).

### 3.3 Emotions and Customer Contacts

Chase and Dasu (2001:79-80) suggest that practitioners have not carefully considered the underlying psychology of service encounters -- the feelings that customers experience during these encounters, feelings so subtle they probably could not be put into words. As Edwardson (1998:4) similarly asks, "has anyone bothered to ask customers how they actually feel?"

Anderson and Sullivan (1993) propose that "quality which falls short of expectations has a greater impact on satisfaction and repurchase intentions than quality which exceeds expectations." They further (ibid., p.141) argue that "an important component of managing satisfaction is the ability to control the impact of negative disconfirmation through complaint handling and effective customer service."

A recent study (Beaujean, Davidson, & Madge, 2006) shows that "a big prize awaits companies that can develop deeper and more lasting relationships with their customers. Yet many businesses rely too much on IT and perform poorly on the front line. The key to correcting frontline performance is the consistent handling of moments of truth -- those few interactions (for instance, a lost credit card, a cancelled flight, a damaged piece of clothing, or investment advice) where customers have an unusual amount of emotional energy invested in the outcome."

Chase and Dasu (2001:84) note that behavioral science, applied with equal doses of empathy and imagination, can improve service delivery. More importantly, it can change the impressions that customers remember, refer back to, and pass on to future customers. Barlow and Maul (2000:23) propose that there is a chance of creating positive emotional value when frontline staff is aware of customer's emotional state. Van Dolen and colleagues (2001:375) suggest that training, motivating, and rewarding CSRs to evoke positive emotions in customers has the potential for raising overall customer satisfaction and profits. Freemantle (1999:3) argues that if customers like a company and its people, there is a higher probability that they will buy from that company. Therefore, "the degree to which customers like your company (and its people) is a function of the emotional value you add to the relationship" (ibid.). For example, an insurance company tripled the success of referral requests by creating emotional relationship with its customers. After a positive contact CSR were just sending a postcard, saying "good clients are appreciated," with a reply card asking if the client has a friend or relative to refer (Robinette, 2001).

It appears thus that emotions play an important role in creating stronger relationships with customers, and that it is desirable to evoke positive emotions when customers are dealing with firms frontlines such as contact centers.

## 3.4 CSRs, Emotions and Moods

According to Pugh (2001), "...very few studies have examined customer emotions as an outcome of the service encounter, although a link between employee and customer emotions often has been suggested (e.g., Hochschild, 1983)."

Indeed, customer emotions in a contact center also depend on CSR emotions due to the fact that emotions are contagious and thus may spread from one person to another. Contagion of emotions has actually been examined in the ancient times "when Hippocrates coined the term "hysteria" to refer to the passing of an agitated state from unmarried women to other unmarried women."[39] Coyne's (1976/2001) research revealed the fact that female students, who made a 20-minute telephone call to depressed patients, reported to be more depressed, anxious, and even more hostile after their telephone conversations than did other female students who made similar calls to non-depressed patients as well as to normal people. Junge (1968)[40] also argued that therapists "feel" the feelings of their clients. Similarly, it can be presumed that CSRs also share the feelings of the customers they are helping. As Barsade (2001:38) puts it "people are 'walking mood inductors,' continuously influencing the moods and the judgments and behaviors of others." And "thus, emotional contagion, through its direct and indirect influence on employee and work team emotions, judgments, and behaviors can lead to subtle but important ripple effects in groups and organizations" (ibid., p.42).

---

[39] As cited in Barsade (2001:7): Veith, I. (1965). *Hysteria: The history of a disease*. Chicago: University of Chicago Press.
[40] As cited in George (2002:191): Jung, C.G. (1968). *Analytical Psychology: Its theory and practice*. New York: Random House.

Salovey, Hsee and Mayer (2001:185) and Goleman (1996) propose that moods have an influence on perceptions, problem-solving as well as creative abilities. Forgas and Bower (2001:204) suggest that people in a happy mood would form more favorable impressions and make more positive judgments than people in a sad mood (cf. Frijda, 1993:394, 397). Similarly, Weiss (2002:46) notes that "people in positive moods overestimate the likelihood of positive events and underestimate the likelihood of negative events. The reverse is generally true for negative moods." Bless et al. (2001:217) argue that "good moods may facilitate the use of simple heuristics whereas bad moods may facilitate the use of detail-oriented, analytic processing strategies."

Wilk and Rothbard's (2004) research on employee moods in contact center environment show the importance of negative or positive moods spilling over private and working lives of call center employees (cf. MacDermid, Seery, & Weiss, 2002). Wilk and Rothbard (2004) suggest that workers arriving in a positive mood, are likely to stay positive and vice versa; and "as for the contagion effect of customers, there is spillover, but more for positive interactions than for negative ones."

Confirming the importance of CSR emotions, Pugh (2001:19) suggests that "displayed emotions by employees may have important consequences for organizations, as they were positively related to customer affect and customer evaluations of the quality of service received."

However, CSR emotions also depend on many other issues like emotional culture, emotional climate in the organization, emotional labor, role stress, emotional abilities, and emotional intelligence of the employees. Therefore, the next section will very briefly discuss such issues in order to sketch customer contact environment from different emotional perspectives.

## 3.5 Organization & Emotions

Emotion is relevant to understanding specific topics in organizational psychology, such as job satisfaction, worker motivation, and understanding how job characteristics contribute to important outcomes, such as productivity.[41] Lord and Kanfer (2002:11), generalizing Fredericson's (1998) perspectives, suggest that positive emotions promote a number of organizational processes such as creativity, effective social relations, and organizational commitment. According to a North American study,[42] strong positive emotions correlate with better financial results for an organization; whereas, negative emotions about work not only relates to higher employee turnover rates, but can also diminish productivity and performance of the employees. In a team environment, when

[41] As cited in Larsen, Diener, and Lucas (2002): Warr, P. (1999). Well-Being in the work place. In: D. Kahneman, E. Diener, & N. Schwarz (Eds.), *Well-being: The foundations of hedonic psychology* (pp. 392-412). New York: Russel Sage Foundation.

[42] Working Today: Exploring Employees' Emotional Connection to Their Jobs. Retrieved from www.towers.com accessed on 4/10/2003.

members experience negative moods, they may be more critical and discerning; whereas they may be more helpful to each other as well as to people outside the group when they experience positive moods (George (2002:189).

*Emotional culture* of the organization refers to the dominant values, beliefs, assumptions, and norms regarding affective issues. It can be, in an organizational context or in a society, a *tight culture* in which rules and norms are present and enforced, or a *loose culture* in which norms are described in a wide range and deviant behavior is widely tolerated (Earley & Francis, 2002:378).

*Emotional climate* refers to the dominant affective tones, pleasantness and arousal levels in the organization; and emotional culture and climate reinforce each other (Ashforth & Saks, 2002:353-354). For example, in a macho culture yelling at each other may be acceptable, or the organization may encourage the use of fear or guilt to motivate employees (ibid., p.355) creating an unpleasant and agitated emotional climate.

*Emotional labor* is the regulation of feelings and their expression at work (Hochschild, 1983; Zeithaml & Bitner, 2003:322; Grandey & Brauburger, 2002:260; George, 2002). For example, customer service employees constantly regulate their emotions and emotional expressions while interacting with customers. They apply more effort when they have feelings that are contrasting with friendly displays or "service with a smile" which is required of them.

According to Grandey and Brauburger (2002:260) emotional labor jobs have three characteristics: frequency of customer contacts, display rules, and autonomy. Frequency of customer contacts, together with its duration and intensity, determines the 'tone' of emotions. 'Display Rules'[43] describe the constraints that govern socially acceptable expression of emotion, and they are different in different jobs: *CSRs* should display friendliness, *bill collectors* display perhaps anger, where as *judges* or therapists should display neutral emotions (ibid., p.264). Display rules, required by the companies, decrease the emotional autonomy of the workers and "organizational control over emotional displays may create less intrinsic motivation and less authentic displays to customers, with detrimental results."[44] According to Zapf and colleagues (1999:375) "emotional dissonance occurs when an employee is required to express emotions that are not genuinely felt in the particular situation." This might occur when, for example, service employees have contradictory or ambiguous requirements like being friendly to customers on the phone but also limiting the service calls to three minutes (cf. Zapf et al., 1999:381).[45]

[43] As cited in Cowie (2000): Ekman , P. & Friesen, W. (1969). The Repertoire of non verbal behavior: categories, origins, usage and coding. *Semiotica,* 1, 49-98.

[44] As cited in Grandey & Brauburger (2002:266): Grandey, A. (2000). Emotion regulation in the workplace: A new way to conceptualize emotional labor. *Journal of Occupational Health Psychology*, 5, 95-110.

[45] See also: Zapf, D. & Holz, M. (2006). On the positive and negative effects of emotion work in organizations. *European Journal of Work and Organizational Psychology*, 15, 1-28.

Lovelock and Wirtz (2004:311-2) identify three main causes of *role stress* in frontline positions: CSRs feel conflicts between what their jobs require and their personalities (person/role conflict). CSRs face the dilemma of whether they should follow company rules or satisfy the customer demands (organization/client conflict). Finally, CSRs especially in face-to-face service environments may also face conflicts between customers. As Iacobucci (1999) puts it, '*role conflict*' of front-line employees is that they wish to please customers but they have to follow the bureaucratic rules, or, wishing to do a good job but wanting the customers to go away.

Thompson and colleagues (2001:937) argue that "...workers must be able to consciously and continually manage their emotions." A descriptive study on emotional regulations[46]obtained descriptions from employees about how they coped with difficult customers. "Responses included leaving the work-floor (situation selection), thinking of something funny (attention deployment), realizing some people are never happy no matter what (cognitive change), and trying to stay calm and taking deep breaths (response modulation)" (Grandey & Brauburger, 2002:281). According to George (2002:204), "emotion management includes both emotion work (the regulation of feelings and their expression in one's personal life) and emotional labor (the regulation of feelings and their expression at work)." Managing emotions, however, require some abilities that are studied under the term 'emotional intelligence.'

The concept of *emotional intelligence*[47] investigates how individuals try to control their own and other people's feelings (Dulewics & Higgs, 2004; Salovey, Hsee, & Mayer, 2001; Larsen, Diener, & Lucas 2002:78; Goleman, 1996). Emotional intelligence facilitates emotional stability which is "positively related to job performance in service jobs."[48] Goleman (1996) labels the emotional intelligence as EQ[49] similar to IQ (intelligence quotient) and suggests that IQ is genetic, whereas, EQ is teachable. Similarly, Dulewics and Higgs (2004) suggest that emotional competence can be developed with training for handling the emotions of self and others, and for creating more positive relationships (cf. Barlow & Maul, 2000:61).

Work environment can determine the emotions and moods of employees. "In task-driven companies the aspect of psychology is ignored and results in customer alienation and a perception of service deterioration. Conversely in people-oriented companies much attention is given to motivation and making

---

[46] As cited in Grandey & Brauburger (2002:281): Bailey, J.J. & McCollough, M.A. (2000). Emotional Labor and the difficult customer: Coping strategies of service CSRs and organizational consequences. *Journal of Professional Services Marketing*, 20, 51-72.

[47] Dulewics & Higgs (2004) identified seven separate elements of Emotional Intelligence: Self Awareness (of own feelings), Emotional resilience (under pressure), Motivation, Inter-personal sensitivity (empathy), Influence (persuasion), Intuitiveness (when deciding), Conscientiousness (consistent & ethical).

[48] As cited in Ashforth & Saks (2002:337): Hogan, R., Hogan, J., & Roberts, B.W. (1996). Personality measurement and employment decisions: Questions and answers. *American Psychologist*, 51, 469-477.

[49] Emotional Intelligence at work in Goleman's (1998) definition has five concrete traits and skills: self-awareness, self-regulation, motivation, empathy, and social skills.

people, both customers and employees, really feel good" (Freemantle, 2003). George (2002:195-196) argues that family-friendly policies, flexible work schedules and a pleasant work environment may result in favorable moods; whereas, a punitive leadership style, unpleasant, uncomfortable working conditions or a chronic job insecurity may create unfavorable moods.

## 3.6 Emotion Measurement

Psychology researchers develop many tools that are helpful for detecting, registering or analyzing emotions by different approaches and techniques, varying from pen-and-paper rating scales to high-tech equipment measuring brain waves (Desmet, 2003) or speech synthesis (Scherer, 2003).

Desmet (2002; 2003) analyzes the emotion measurements in two categories: "non-verbal (objective) instruments" and "verbal (subjective) instruments." Non-verbal measurements include facial expressions (e.g., Ekman, 1987), vocal expressions (e.g., Scherer, 2003), and other physiological changes like heartbeat rates. Advantages of these methods are that they are language-independent and they do not disturb participants during measurements; their disadvantages, however, are that they can only reliably assess basic emotions like anger, and cannot assess mixed emotions (Desmet, 2003). Verbal (self-report) measurements, on the other hand, can be used to measure mixed emotions with culture and language difficulties (ibid.).

Larsen, Diener and Lucas (2002:98) distinguish five relatively different aspects of emotion measurements: experience, expression, behavior, cognition, and physiology. They suggest that "no single emotion measure can serve as the gold standard. Each measure reflects one specific facet of emotion, has its strengths and weaknesses, and, when used in isolation, provides an incomplete picture of emotion" (ibid.). They also categorize emotion measurements in four areas as follows:

1. Self-report measures for experience
2. Observation for expression
3. Performance tasks for behavior and cognition
4. Physiological measurements for the physiological aspects

One of the well-known models in measuring emotions is the 'affect circumplex' model (Russel, 1980). This model uses a two-dimensional space defined by pleasantness (x-axis) and activation (y-axis), and the points corresponding to various emotions form a circle (ibid.). Although this model "lacks simple structure" (Larsen, Diener, & Lucas, 2002:69), "overall, research seems to indicate that when appropriate measures are created and latent variables examined, pleasantness and activation appear to be most useful for describing momentary affect."[50]

[50] As cited in Weiss (2002:33): Russel, J.A. & Carroll, J.M. (1999). On the Bipolarity of positive and Negative Affect. *Psychological Bulletin*, 125, 3-30.

Satisfaction and dissatisfaction are also analyzed on circumplex settings (Oliver, 1992),[51] and appeared to be between activated positive affect and inactivated negative affect inline with the findings of Plutchik (1980).[52]

Figure 3-1: Affect Circumplex Model

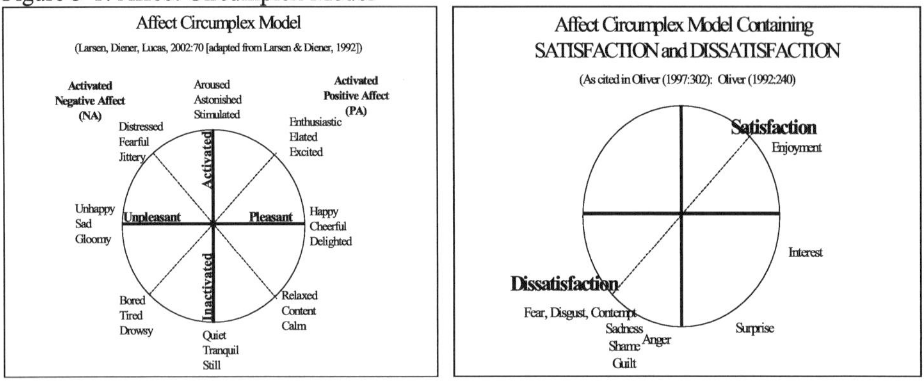


Similar to the principles of the Affect Circumplex model, Cowie (2000b) and his colleagues have tested a system, called *feeltrace*,[53] which uses an activation/evaluation space to let observers record their impression of a person's emotional state. In the test process, selected persons were watching 16 different video clips from TV programs, and observers were registering their impressions in real time on a computer screen using a mouse and with the help of colors.

Figure 3-2: Feeltrace model with selected emotions. Adapted from Cowie et al. (2000b)

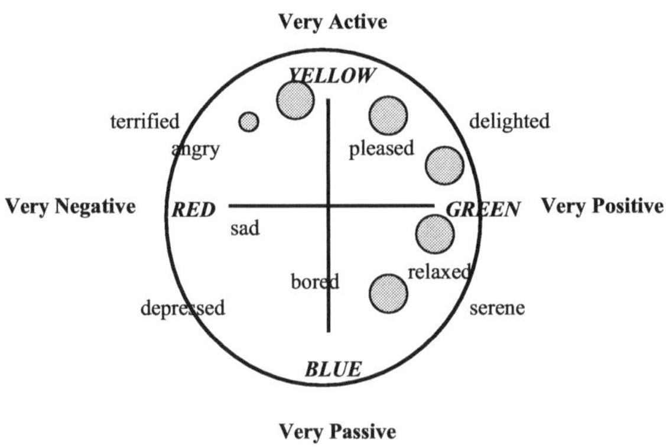


---

[51] As cited in Oliver (1997:302): Oliver, R.L. (1992). An Investigation of the Attribute Basis of Emotion and Related Affects in Consumption: Suggestions for a Stage-Specific Satisfaction Framework. In: Sherry, J.F. Jr. & Sternthal, B. (eds.), *Advances in Consumer Research*, (pp. 237-244), vol. 19. Provo, UT: Association for Consumer Research.

[52] As shown in Oliver (1997:302).

[53] Feeltrace is an instrument developed to let observers track the emotional content of a stimulus as they perceive it over time, allowing the emotional dynamics of speech episodes to be examined. The cursor was color coded using a scheme derived from Plutchik (1994), which subjects find reasonably intuitive. The pointer took the form of a disc" (Cowie, 2000b).

Desmet (2002) used cartoon animations in measuring emotions (Figure 3-3). His model, called PrEmo (the product emotion measurement instrument), is a non-verbal, self-report instrument, measuring 14 emotions that are often elicited by product design. Instead of relying on the use of words, respondents in PrEmo reported their emotions with the use of a set of 'cartoon' animations.

Figure 3-3: PrEmo

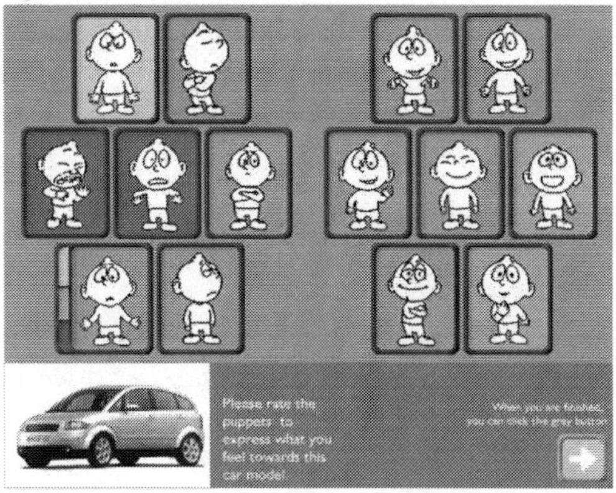


During their experimental settings, Ouwersloot and Lemmink (1999) showed respondents different video scenes of hotel service encounters and measured their continuous *feelings of warmth*. They measured the warmth construct following the definition of Aeker et al. (1986).[54] Respondents watched the recorded videos of service encounters performed by actors, and with the help of a coding keyboard they rated the scenes on a 1 to 8 scale, ranging from "absence of warmth" to "very strong feeling of warmth" (ibid.). Researchers explained respondents the definition of warmth, and explicitly mentioned that they wanted to know how warm respondents' feelings were with regard to the service employee in the service situation, as if they were the customer taking part.

Another approach in emotion measurement is using *Visual Analog Scales* (VAS). VAS might present the participant with a horizontal line separating two opposing adjectives, and the participant is asked to place a mark on the line describing how he or she is feeling. Other VAS models can be devised for unipolar response options, with the line anchored with "none at all" to "extremely much" for a specific emotion. Alternatively, an analogue of emotion can be presented to the participant, such as a series of cartoon faces, going from a frown expression on the face at one end to an extreme smile face on the other end [**...☹... ...😐... ...☺...**]. The participants in this measurement are asked to circle the face that represents how they are feeling (Larsen, Diener, & Lucas, 2002:85).

---

[54] As cited in Oueweslot & Lemmink (1999): Aeker, D.A., Stayman, D.M., & Hagerty, M.R. (1986). Warmth in Advertising: Measurement, Impact, and Sequence Effects. *Journal of Consumer Research*, 12, 365-81.

## 3.7 The ESCC Measurement Model

There were several considerations in designing the ESCC measurement model. Firstly, the model should be easy to understand, as well as, easy to use in a customer service environment. Secondly, it should be as simple and as clear as possible so that it could be interpreted similarly by CSRs, customers, as well as, the others who would listen and evaluate the calls such as contact center supervisors. Therefore, specific emotions or adjectives that are open for discussion were avoided (e.g., *was the customer pleased or delighted?*). Thirdly, the model should be easy to communicate to others for verification purposes, for example, when surveying customers on the phone with no visual aid. Fourthly, the measurement scale should be easy to interpret and similarly by CSRs, customers, and others when necessary. Therefore, a 5-point scale would be more suitable than for example a 10-point scale where even little differences can be disputable (e.g., *was the call 7 or 8?*).

Hence, emotion measurement models, like affect circumplex, feeltrace, or PrEmo would be too complicated for organizations and employees who would use it frequently in a customer service environment where many CSRs continuously deal with many customers. Therefore, a simple model with five colors representing a range of affective states or feelings or emotions is proposed for this research (Figure 3-4).

Figure 3-4: The ESCC Color Scales

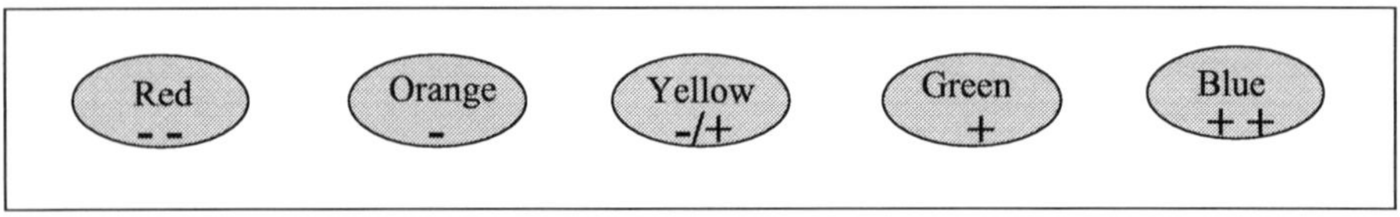


This model actually resembles 'the feelings of warmth' and 'visual analog scales.' The colors in this model represent the observed or perceived satisfaction during customer contacts as follows: very negative (red), negative (orange), neutral (yellow), positive (green) and very positive (blue). CSRs would thus assign a color representing the observed or perceived customer satisfaction after each customer contact. This color would then reflect a general affective state or feeling or a range of emotions rather than a specific emotion about the customer contact.

Selected colors and their orders are similar in the color spectrum where red is on one side, yellow in the middle, and the blue is on the other side. This spectrum is similarly used in the feeltrace, albeit their corresponding emotions were somewhat different due to the combination of two axes and related circular shape in that model (see, Figure 3-2). There are various interpretations on colors and their associations. In traffic lights, for instance, the color 'red' stops, 'orange' warns, and 'green' sets free! Kaya and Epps (2004) suggest that colors can be described in temperature terms such as "warm" (e.g., red, yellow, orange) or "cool" (e.g., blue, green, purple) as related to the dominant wavelength of the color. The cool colors are generally associated with restful and quiet states, while the warm colors are seen as active and stimulating. Furthermore, the color 'red' is associated with excitement, 'orange' is perceived as distressing and upsetting, 'yellow' as cheerful, and 'blue' is associated with comfort and security (ibid., Ballast, 2002[55]; Wexner, 1982[56]). Similarly, as cited in Lovelock and Wirtz (2004:297),[57] 'red' associates with high energy and passion, 'orange' with emotions and expression, 'yellow' with optimism and clarity, 'green' with nurturing, healing and unconditional love, and finally 'blue' with relaxation, serenity, and *loyalty*. However, Terwogt and Hoeksma's (1995) research suggests that color preferences and associations with emotions are not static and thus may change, for instance, with age.

Another aspect in using colors for describing customer contacts is that colors may help to neutralize the effects of specific adjectives and emotions. For instance, a "red customer" sounds more neutral than a "very negative or angry customer;" or a "blue customer" is more appropriate for marketing purposes than a "cheerful customer." Also, "turning orange" would sound more neutral than "getting irritated" among CSRs.[58]

As discussed in previous chapters (e.g., in the introduction) using frontline personnel for observing and registering customer behavior is already practiced in various industries. For example, United Airlines use "note fields," Ritz-Carlton Hotels use guest preference database, and USAA uses internal reporting structures.

Using colors to indicate specific conditions is also practiced in different ways in different industries. For example, at First Union bank in the USA the customer service center handles 45 million calls per year with hundreds of CSRs. When a customer calls, the bank's computer system calculates several customer variables like minimum balances or branch visits, and ranks the customers in three categories: profitable "green," at the border "yellow," and not-profitable "red." Based on this calculation, a small colored square pops-up on the customer information screens next to the customer's name, and CSRs serve customers accordingly (Rust, Zeithaml, & Lemon, 2000:187; Griffin & Lowenstein, 2001:20). In one of the 'unusual workplaces' of Semler (1994), where everyone can see, there is a board on which the names of workers are written. Everyday

---

[55] As cited in Kaya & Epps (2004): Ballast, D. K. (2002). *Interior design reference manual.* Belmont, CA: Professional Publ. Inc.

[56] As cited in Kaya & Epps (2004): Wexner, L. B. (1982). The degree to which colors are associated with mood-tones. *Journal of Applied Psychology*, 6, 432-435.

[57] As cited in Lovelock & Wirtz (2004:297): Sara O.Marberry & Laurie Zagon (1995). *The Power of Color – Creating Healthy Interior Spaces.* New York: John Wiley; Sarah Lynch (2001). *Bold Colors for Modern Rooms: Bright Ideas for People Who Love Color* Gloucester, MA: Rockport Publishers.

[58] Since the effects of using this specific "jargon" cannot be evaluated in single test days, extensive attention is not paid to this aspect. However, it was interesting to observe that the color jargon was easily grasped and used in work floors. For example:

*"I was a very bright blue when I managed to turn an orange customer to a green one."*

*"I started green, then became yellow, and I now feel that I am turning orange! So, it is better that I take a break now."*

workers hang a color label reflecting their moods next to their names: Green means "I'm fine!" yellow means "be careful!", and red means "not today, please!" Therefore, using colors for describing the observed satisfaction of customer contacts is actually a unique way of combining some existing methodologies and practices.

## 3.8 Assessing the ESCC Colors

To make the model simple but also structured, the following criteria (Figure 3-5) are defined for selecting the colors in a customer contact service environment. Here, problematic and unpleasant conversations are classified as orange, and red if customers still articulate their dissatisfaction. Neutral conversations are represented with yellow. Easy and pleasant conversations are on the other hand classified as green, and blue if customers enthusiastically show their appreciation.

Figure 3-5: Color criteria for CSR evaluations of the ESCC

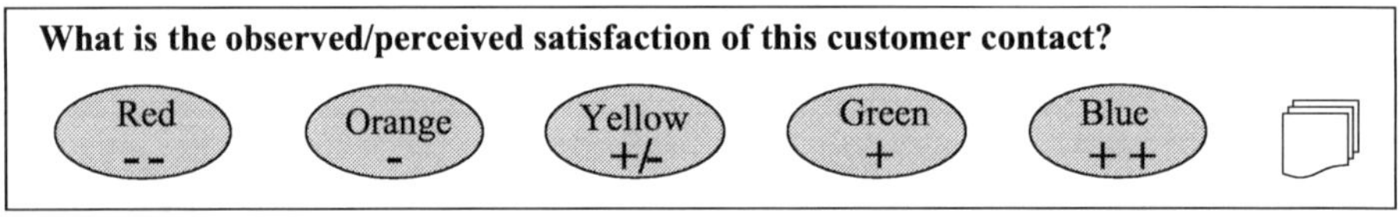


| **Red Contact** | **Orange Contact** | **Yellow Contact** | **Green Contact** | **Blue Contact** | *Select the REASON: Company specific dissatisfaction categories..* |
|---|---|---|---|---|---|
| Encounter or transaction was **very PROBLEMATIC and/or UNPLEASANT.** customer (still) **COMPLAINS** | Encounter or transaction was **somewhat PROBLEMATIC or UNPLEASANT.** customer seems to be **DISSATISFIED** | Encounter or transaction was **NEUTRAL.** customer seems to be **SATISFIED** | Encounter or transaction was **EASY & PLEASANT** customer seems to be **SATISFIED** | Encounter or transaction was **very EASY & veryPLEASANT.** customer **COMPLIMENTS** | |

Reasons of dis/satisfactions are outside of the main focus of this research; nevertheless, when categories are defined specifically for companies, this information can highlight dis/satisfactory areas.[59] Van Dolen and colleagues (2001:366), for instance, use three categories in evaluating critical incidents: emotions towards organization, towards product, or towards employee. Also the satisfaction elements or dimensions of this research can be used to categorize the reasons of dis/satisfaction.

The following model is also identified as a general guideline, rather than a specific tool, in assessing the ESCC (Figure 3-6). Barsade (2001:59) classified customer emotions in pleasantness and energy criteria with high and low levels, similar to the affect circumplex of Russel (1980). In this classification, high energy and high pleasantness is summarized as cheerful enthusiasm (similar to blue contacts), low energy and high pleasantness is summarized as 'serene

[59] Highlighting dis/satisfactory areas will further be evaluated in section 7.2: The ESCC and Organizational Learning Process

warmth' (similar to green contacts), high energy and low pleasantness is summarized as 'hostile irritability' (similar to red contacts), low energy and low pleasantness is summarized as 'depressed sluggishness' (similar to orange contacts). Yellow contacts then are placed in the middle representing neutral conversations.

Figure 3-6: Determining the ESCC Color with Affect Circumplex

| | | PLEASANTNESS | |
|---|---|---|---|
| | | High | Low |
| ENERGY | High | **Cheerful Enthusiasm**<br>•Pleasant<br>•Happy<br>•Optimistic<br>Blue | **Hostile Irritability**<br>•Unpleasant<br>•Frustrated<br>•Pessimistic<br>•Impatience<br>Red |
| | | Yellow | |
| | Low | **Serene Warmth**<br>•Happy<br>•Calm<br>•Serene<br>Green | **Depressed Sluggishness**<br>•Unhappy<br>•Depressed<br>•Dull<br>Orange |

Adapted from Barsade (2001:59). Colors are added.

## 3.9 The ESCC and Other Key Customer Feedback Collection Tools

Wirtz and Tomlin (1997)[60] identify *eight key tools* for collecting customer feedback: Total market survey (including competitors), annual survey on overall satisfaction, transactional survey, service feedback cards, mystery shopping, unsolicited feedback (e.g., complaints), focus group discussions, and service reviews. Garver (2001) divides customer listening or satisfaction research methods in two categories. First category includes *seven quantitative methods*: Critical incident survey, relationship survey, customer complaints, life cycle survey, benchmarking, won-lost and why, and problem resolution. The second category includes *five qualitative methods*: Focus groups, in-depth interviews, customer visits and observations, verbatim comments from surveys, feedback from sales people and CSRs in *ad hoc* or periodic basis.

The ESCC model thus resembles the qualitative method of 'feedback from sales people and CSRs in *ad hoc* or periodic basis.' However, the ESCC model collects this feedback for each customer contact, and will be able to create a full transactional satisfaction picture in the customer contact environment.

[60] As cited in Lovelock & Wirtz (2004:397): Wirtz, J. & Tomlin, M. (2000). Institutionalizing Customer Driven Learning through Fully Integrated Customer Feedback Systems. *Managing Service Quality,* 10, 4, 205-215.

## 3.10 The Relationship between the ESCC Model, Satisfaction Dimensions, and Loyalty

Figure 3-7 illustrates the relations among the colors, emotional, cognitive, transactional, and cumulative satisfaction dimensions used in this research. Here, emotional and cognitive dis/satisfaction are plotted as horizontal and vertical axis, and a diagonal line represents combined dis/satisfaction. When both dimensions are very negative, then it is full dissatisfaction (red), and when both dimensions are very positive then it is full satisfaction (blue). The diagonal line also represents the ESCC color scales, and thus, satisfaction with last customer contacts (transactional satisfaction). There are, however, no clear borders but some indicative lines for describing possible satisfaction areas and related colors. In this illustration, (cumulative effect of) transactional satisfaction improves loyalty, and conversely (cumulative effect of) dissatisfaction increases customer defection or churn.

Figure 3-7: Dimensions of Satisfaction and the ESCC Colors

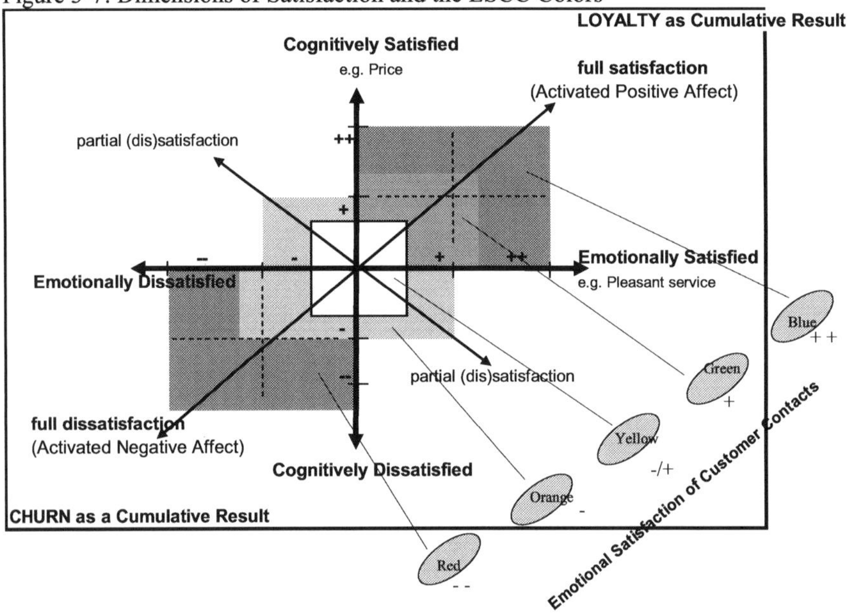

## 3.11 Summary & Research Questions

In this chapter, the definition and the role of emotions in customer satisfaction and in customer contact environment are examined. On the one hand, customer emotions in a contact center are linked to CSR emotions due to the fact that emotions are contagious and thus may spread from one person to another. On the other hand, CSR emotions are linked to many organizational issues like emotional climate in the organization, emotional labor or role stress, emotional abilities or emotional intelligence of the employees. These links suggested that organizational settings influence employee emotions and moods, and consequently influence customer emotions.

After examining various emotions measurement techniques, a simple methodology for observing customer satisfaction during customer contacts by customer service representatives (CSR) is drafted. Rather than a complicated measurement model for assessing specific emotions the ESCC model is based on more simple and generic emotional states ranging from very negative to very positive, represented by a color range of 'red-orange-yellow-green-blue'.

For evaluating the ESCC by CSRs, a very general guideline is drafted for each color by taking easy-going versus problematic situations, and complaining versus complimenting customers. Next to this guideline, some specific emotions are plotted according to high and low levels in energy and pleasantness axis; and the ESCC colors are assigned to these group of emotions as a rough guideline. It is, however, not aimed to restrict the judgments of CSRs with any guidelines. After all, ESCC observations are emotion based judgments and, therefore, should not be squeezed in the boundaries of cognition based evaluation guidelines.

When compared with key tools for assessing customer feedback and satisfaction, the ESCC model resembled the method of 'feedback from sales people and CSRs on an *ad hoc* or periodic basis.' However, rather than acquiring this feedback on an *ad hoc* or periodic basis, the ESCC model is designed to collect information for each customer contact, and thereby sketch a full transactional satisfaction picture of customer contact environment.

These colors, representing transactional satisfaction, are also linked to emotional and cognitive dimensions as well as to churn and to loyalty as a cumulative effect.

To assess the reliability of this observation methodology and to reveal the relationships between the ESCC observations, customer satisfaction dimensions and loyalty intentions, the following research questions are formulated:

6) What are the (emotional) satisfaction levels with customer contacts?

7) Can CSRs accurately observe and evaluate (emotional) satisfaction during customer contacts?

8) What is the relationship between the observed ESCC and emotions of CSRs?

9) What is the relationship between the observed ESCC and

- 9a) Emotional and cognitive dimensions?
- 9b) Transactional satisfaction?
- 9c) General satisfaction?
- 9d) Customer loyalty (intentions)?

Answers to these questions will be presented in chapter 6.

# 4 FROM THE ESCC OBSERVATIONS TO CUSTOMER LOYALTY

Information is valuable when it is actionable! Therefore, the following research question is formulated: 10) 'What can be done with the ESCC information?'

Hence this chapter will attempt to describe the next steps in the ESCC model. These steps, utilizing the ESCC information, will be the follow-up process of negative or positive observations, organizational learning opportunities, especially from the observed failures, and finally the links between these steps and customer satisfaction and loyalty. While this chapter will review the related literature and present some examples, chapter 7 will describe these steps within the ESCC framework and provide some empirical evidence.

## 4.1 Following up Service Experiences

Service interactions in contact centers are an important part of customer experiences. Although the majority of customer contacts are expected to be 'neutral' with no positive or negative tendencies, some of the interactions and consequent customer experiences can be (very) positive or negative. Therefore, the following sections will review the literature on these intense experiences and their likely consequences.

### *4.1.1 Following Up Positive Service Experiences: Sales Actions*

The relationship between customers' repurchase intentions and how they perceive their sales and service interactions are analyzed in the Toyota study.[61] Results indicate that when both interactions are positive then repurchase intentions are as high as 93%, and conversely when both are negative then repurchase intentions are as low as 2%. When positive sales experiences are followed by negative service experiences, then repurchase intentions decrease to 18%. However, when negative sales experiences are followed by positive service experiences, then repurchase intentions decrease to 46%. These figures indicate that service experiences have a stronger impact on repurchase intentions than the initial sales experiences (Figure 4-1).

[61] As cited in Oliver (1997:368): Reported in "Make Sure the Customer Voice Is Heard across the Company", *Executive Report on Consumer Satisfaction,* 7, 1-3 (June 30, 1994).

Figure 4-1: Sales vs. Service Experience in Repurchase Intentions

| Sales Versus Service Experience in repurchase intentions: Results From The Toyota Study | | | |
|---|---|---|---|
| | | Intention to repurchase (%) | |
| SALES EXPERIENCE | *Positive* | 18% | 93% |
| | *Negative* | 2% | 46% |
| | | *Negative* | *Positive* |
| | | SERVICE EXPERIENCE | |

A recent research among Belgian, German and Italian retail-bank customers (N=2229) confirms the importance of service experiences[62] (Beaujean, Davidson, & Madge, 2006). Its results indicate that after a positive experience more than 85% of customers increased their value to the bank by purchasing more products or investing more of their assets. Conversely, after a negative experience more than 70% of the customers reduced their commitment to their banks.[63] Examples of positive experiences (N=1528) varied from 'a caring service from frontline' to 'a good financial advice.' Examples of negative experiences (N=701) varied from 'accessibility of the bank' to 'unfriendly frontline staff.'

### *4.1.2 Following up Negative Service Experiences: Recovery Actions*

Service recoveries are the follow-up actions to dissatisfactory service events in order to regain customer satisfaction and loyalty. Service recoveries will always be needed due to the fact that organizations cannot escape variation in their service quality levels, and thus will hardly be able to establish a 'zero defects' service environment (cf. Hart, Heskett, & Sasser, 1990:150; Reichheld & Sasser, 1990). Tax and Brown (1998) and Hart, Heskett and Sasser (1990:156) argue that recovery is fundamental to service excellence and should, therefore, be regarded as an integral part of company strategies.

It is suggested that negative service experiences play a central role in customer satisfaction and loyalty due to the fact that negative experiences are more "meaningful" to customers and have a stronger impact than positive experiences (e.g., Barlow & Maul, 2000:258). As a recent research reveals, bad customer service experience can translate to lower balances in bank accounts, and

[62] Customers were asked if they have had a positive or negative experience within 24 months with their banks.

[63] 15% switched their main bank, 20% stopped product, 14% decreased value of products, and 23% bought new products elsewhere.

therefore, banks are advised to reexamine their service-recovery processes to keep their funds (Nunez & Yulinsky, 2005; see also Beaujean, Davidson, & Madge, 2006).

Responding reactively to complaints is an important part of recovery processes, and much can be achieved with an effective complaint handling structure in customer satisfaction and loyalty (e.g., Figure 4-2). However, it is argued that complaints are not the ideal predictor of dissatisfaction, since only 5-10% of unsatisfied customers complain (e.g., Kotler, 1996:442; Tax & Brown, 1998; Griffin, 2002:176). Studies of Tax and Brown (1998) and Hart, Heskett and Sasser (1990:150) show that "more than half of all efforts to respond to customer complaints actually reinforce negative reactions to a service." According to Freemantle (1999:130) "when something goes wrong, what influences the customer is not necessarily the problem itself but the way it is handled." He also argues (ibid., p.83) that standardized responses to complaints are ineffective due to the fact that they carry little emotional value.

There are some suggestions on service recoveries. Robinette et al. (2001:93) argue that "a sincere, timely apology showing genuine concern, followed by prompt action to fix the problem, leads to a market increase in overall loyalty and feelings of trust." In the case of service failure, recovery efforts might include any approach from an apology to a gift to full compensation" (ibid., p.123). But these efforts, according to the authors, should not look like a "bribe." Iacobucci (1999) suggests that the collective wisdom regarding service recovery should be empathy plus one: a caring and understanding attitude towards the complaint, fixing the problem, and (over)compensating for the mistake by doing something beyond what the customer paid for. It is, however, important not to exaggerate it, as overly generous compensations may raise questions about the soundness of the business and may encourage dishonest customers to seek service failures (Lovelock & Wirtz, 2004:402).[64]

Hart, Heskett and Sasser (1990:150) suggest that "companies that want to build the capacity of recovering from service problems should do these things: measure the costs of effective service recovery, break customer silence and listen closely for complaints, anticipate needs for recovery, act fast, train employees, empower the front line, and close the customer feedback loop."

Tax and Brown (1998) describe four stages in dealing with service failures (Figure 4-2): 1) Identify by encouraging it; 2) Resolve with fair outcomes, fair processes, and fair interactions; 3) Communicate & Classify; 4) Integrate data and improve overall service. According to the authors, doing the job right the first time together with effective complaint handling leads to an increase in customer satisfaction and loyalty (ibid). These stages are comparable with the

[64] Lovelock & Wirtz (2004:402) refers to: H.Estelami & P. de Maeyer (2002). Customer Reactions to Service Provider Overgenerosity. *Journal of Service Research,* 4, no. 3, 202-217.

Deming cycle "*Plan-Do-Check-Act*"[65] and the Six Sigma's "*Define-Measure-Analyze-Improve-Control*"[66] steps.

Figure 4-2: Components of an Effective Service Recovery System

| Components of an Effective Service Recovery System[67] | | | | |
|---|---|---|---|---|
| Do the Job Right the First Time | + | Effective Complaint Handling | = | Increase Satisfaction and Loyalty |
| ↑ | | ↓ Identify Service Complaints | | -Conduct Research<br>-Monitor Complaints<br>-Develop "Complaints as Opportunity" Culture |
| | | ↓ Resolve Complaints Effectively | | -Develop Effective System and Training in Complaints Handling |
| Close the Loop via Feedback | ← | ↓ Learn from the Recovery Experience | | -Conduct Root-Cause Analysis |

There are some examples of structural customer recovery approaches in business. The Dutch utility firm Essent sends free gift vouchers if they are too late in sending documents to customers (de Volkskrant, 11-3-2005). Ford authorizes its dealers to spend up to $250 of goodwill money per customer to correct, without charge, problems the customer sees as the fault of either the dealer or the company (Griffin, 2002:125). Ritz-Carlton hotel employees at all levels are empowered to redress customer dissatisfactions; they also observe and report customer likes and dislikes for a 'guest preference database,' and 'guest historians' in each hotel review the database and suggest 'extra touches' that might delight each guest (Armstrong & Kotler, 2003:239).

Indeed many companies practice some recovery actions reactively when customers ring the complaint-bell, or, when the failure is very obvious to everyone. Airlines, for example, arrange free-tickets for next flights and free accommodation when customers cannot be flown due to firm's fault. It is very easy to notice that a flight is cancelled; passengers and the management recognize it immediately. However, in other service settings like large contact centers one cannot see such failures or shortcomings as easy as a cancelled-flight. Maybe this is the reason why many authors advocate that service recovery should be proactive, and should involve frontline employees.

---

[65] (Edward) Deming Cycle is a modified version of (Walter) Shewart Cycle, which is Plan-Do-Study-Act. It is widely used in continuous improvement of processes, services and systems.

[66] As cited in Lovelock & Wirtz (2004:433): Pande, P., Neuman, R.P., & Cavanagh, R.R. (2000). *The Six Sigma Way*. McGraw- Hill.

[67] As cited in Lovelock & Wirtz (2004:387): Adapted from C.H. Lovelock, P.G.Patterson, & R.Walker (1998). *Services Marketing: Australia and New Zealand.* Sydney: Prentice-Hall Australia. p.455.

Lovelock and Wirtz (2004:388) propose that companies need to be proactive in their customer approaches and should find the ways to observe or detect the issues before they become a complaint. Hart, Heskett and Sasser (1990:150, 154, 155) suggest that the surest way to recover from service mishaps is for workers on the front line to identify and solve the customer's problem with authority, responsibility, and incentives to follow through with customers. Rust, Zeithaml, and Lemon (2000:69) also underline the importance of customer disappointment and recovery cycle and recommend establishing a proactive service recovery system that catches all possible service errors and corrects them promptly (ibid., p.227). Nevertheless, all the above authors do not exactly describe the ways their suggestions can be achieved. Therefore, the ESCC methodologies, as described in 7.1.2, will attempt to fill the gap of "how to make proactive service recoveries operational."

## 4.2 Organizational Learning

In order to survive in business firms must adapt their products and processes to constantly changing economic conditions and increasing customer expectations. De Geus (1988:71) notes that "the ability to learn faster than your competitors may be the only sustainable competitive advantage." Similarly, Senge (1990) suggests that "organizations that truly excel in the future will be the organizations that discover how ... to learn at all levels in an organization."

Argyris (1977) defines organizational learning as a process of detecting and correcting error, and also identifies single- and double-loop learning. Single-loop learning involves learning from consequences of previous behaviors and neglects issues of why the problems arose, just like a "thermostat" that turns the heat on or off. Double-loop learning, in contrast, involves systems that monitor and correct behavior and determine what appropriate behavior is (Ibid; Hatch, 1997:372).

Visser (2004) argues that most scholars conceptualize organizational learning in dichotomous terms which are expressed in a number of different but comparable terms such as: single-loop and double-loop learning (e.g., Argyris, 1977); lower-level and higher-level learning (Fiol & Lyles, 1985);[68] first-order and second-order learning (e.g., Arthur Aiman-Smith, 2001);[69] exploitation and exploration in learning (March, 1991);[70] incremental and radical learning (e.g., Miner &

[68] As cited in Polito & Watson (2002). Fiol, C. M. & Lyles, M. A. (1985). Organizational learning. *Academy of Management Review*, 10(4): 803-813.
[69] As cited in Visser (2004): Arthur, J.B. & Aiman-Smith, L. (2001). Gainsharing and organizational learning; An analysis of employee suggestions over time. *Academy of Management Journal,* 44, 737-754.
[70] As cited in Visser (2004): March, J.G. (1991). Exploration and Exploitation in Organizational Learning. *Organizational Science,* 2, 71-87.

Mezias, 1996);[71] and passive and active learning orientation (Sadler-Smith, Spicer, & Chaston, 2001).[72]

Senge (1990:22, 65, 104) notes that for finding high-leverage changes, organizations need to realize underlying "structures' rather than "events." Because, "solutions that address only the symptoms of a problem, not fundamental causes tend to have short term benefits at best." According to Senge, primary threats to organizations came from slow and gradual processes such as decline in product quality. Learning organizations became aware of such trends and act creatively, whereas other organizations only react to strong events that occur suddenly, and tend to ignore gradual processes. He relates this process to the parable of the frog that jumps out of boiled water, but stays in lukewarm water that is gradually heated until boiling.

As shown in Figure 4-3, Reichheld (1996:68-69) suggests that organizations should grasp value from their failures, learn from those failures, and translate it to improvements and value creation, which in turn will result in more customer loyalty. In his words, "the key to customer loyalty is the creation of value. The key to value creation is organizational learning. And the key to organizational learning is grasping the value of failure" (ibid).

Figure 4-3: From Failures to Loyalty
(adapted from Reicheld, 1996:69)

Argyris and Shön (1978)[73] introduce "deuteron-learning" as a higher level of learning, relative to single- and double-loop learning. In deuteron-learning, organizations learn "how to carry out single- and double-loop learning" (ibid., p.27). Deutero learning influences the ways of thinking about error detection and correction, and improves learning capabilities. This level is similarly examined under the term "triple loop learning" where organizations produce new structures and strategies for learning, and they learn how to learn (Romme & Witteloostuijn, 1999). The third-loop learning thus fully employs the single- and double-loop learning, and accordingly influences the fundamental principles and values in the organization

In the following illustration (Figure 4-4), the learning loops are linked to values, norms, measures, and results in organizations. For example, if initial values for customer services are 'in favor of the organization' such as *"we reply to*

[71] As cited in Visser (2004): Miner, A.S. & Mezias, S.J. (1996). Ugly ducklings no more: Past and futures of organizational learning research. *Organizational Science,* 7, 88-100.

[72] As cited in Visser (2004): Sadler-Smith, E., Spicer, D.P. & Chaston, I. (2001). Learning orientations and growth in smaller firms. *Longe Range Planning*, 34, 129-158.

[73] As cited in Visser (2004): Argyris, C., & Schön, D. A. (1978). *Organizational learning: A theory of action perspective.* Reading, Massachusetts: Addison-Wesley.

*customer e-mails when other daily tasks are completed,*" then this initial value leads to a norm of "*replying to e-mails after 4 p.m.*" If, however, customers start complaining about "late responses" to their e-mails, organizations can do several things. They can make exceptions, fix the specific problems, and send an immediate reply every time a customer complains (single-loop). They can restructure the daily tasks so that some of the e-mails can be replied earlier (double-loop). But, they can also start reevaluating their perceptions, principles, or values on customer services, and they may adapt their norms 'in favor of customers' such as, "*we reply to customer e-mails within an hour*" (triple-loop).

Figure 4-4: Three Loops in Organizational Learning

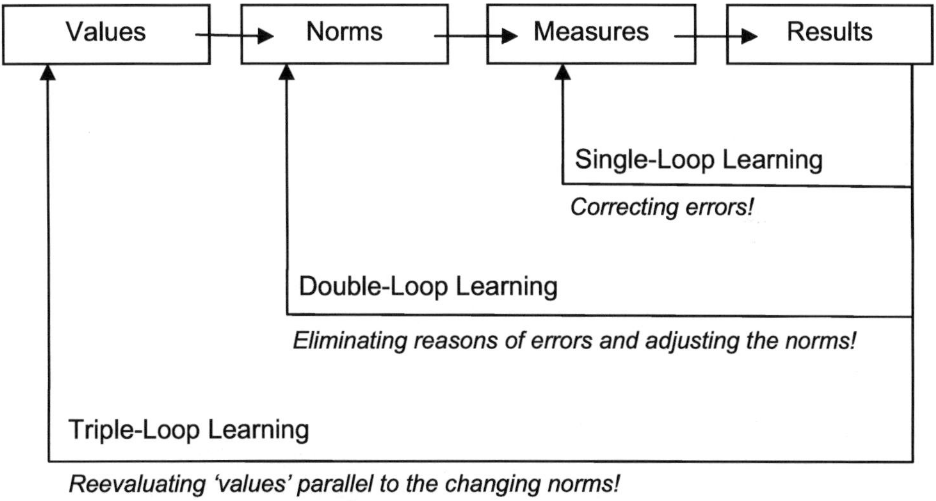


In this illustration, customer complaints *reactively* trigger the learning loops. The ESCC information and methodologies, as described in 7.2, however, will aim at *proactively* triggering the learning loops in organizations with continuous CSR evaluations on customer satisfaction.

## 4.3 Increasing Customer Satisfaction and Loyalty

Previous sections described the follow-up actions and organizational learning possibilities for increasing customer satisfaction and loyalty. This section will attempt to examine the links between improved services, customer satisfaction, and customer loyalty as the final steps in the ESCC model.

In marketing literature there are many studies suggesting and confirming the links between (improved) service quality and customer satisfaction (e.g., Parasuraman, Zeithaml, & Berry, 1988; Zeithaml & Bitner, 2003; Oliver, 1997; Tax and Brown, 1998; Jones & Sasser, 1995; Rust, Zahorik, & Keiningham, 1995). The Service-Profit Chain (Heskett, Sasser, & Schlesinger, 1997; also Wetzels, 1999) even widens these links (Figure 4-5) towards revenue growth and profitability. In this chain, profits and growth are stirred mainly by customer loyalty; loyalty is a consequence of customer satisfaction; satisfaction is primarily influenced by the value of services provided to customers; value is created by satisfied, loyal and productive employees; employee satisfaction, loyalty and productivity, in turn, result largely from high-quality support services and structures that enable employees to deliver successful results to customers (See also Rust, Zeithaml & Lemon, 2000:189; Rust, Zahorik, & Keiningham, 1995; Parasuraman & Grewal, 2000; Luarn & Lin, 2003).

Figure 4-5: The Links in the Service-Profit Chain

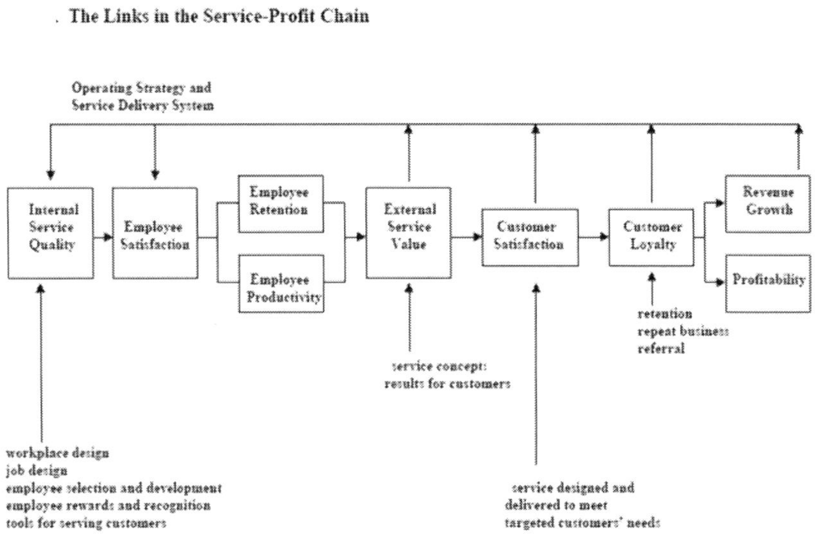


NOTE: From Putting the Service-Profit Chain to Work (p. 112) by J. Heskett, T. Jones, G. Loveman, W. Sasser, Jr., and L. Schlesinger (1996). Business Classics: Fifteen Key Concepts for Managerial Success. Harvard Business School Publishing Corporation.

It is, however, also suggested that satisfaction may signal the beginning of loyalty, but cannot guarantee it, especially in the short run (e.g., Anderson, Fornell, & Lehman, 1994:64; Jones & Sasser, 1995:98; Liu, Bernhardt, & Leach, 1999; Reicheld, 1993, 1996; Oliver, 1997:403-8). Similarly, it is argued that customer loyalty may signal the beginning of profitability, but according to Reinartz and Kumar (2002) the relationship between loyalty and profits is by no means assured.

It seems thus certain that (improved) service quality increases customer satisfaction, but it does not seem very certain that customer satisfaction increases loyalty or profitability *per se*.

## 4.4 Summary & Concluding Remarks

This chapter described the next steps in the ESCC model primarily with literature review.

To start with, different studies showed that positive customer experiences lead to more sales; and negative customer experiences lead to a decrease in customer commitment and consequently a decrease in sales. Therefore, it is suggested that the positive ESCC information, indicating positive customer experience levels, can be utilized for increasing sales.

Various studies confirmed the effectiveness of proactive recovery actions for regaining customer satisfaction and loyalty intentions after a dissatisfactory service episode. Therefore, it is suggested that the ESCC information, indicating negative customer experience levels, can be utilized for initiating proactive recovery actions.

The process of detecting and correcting error is examined under organizational learning. Studies suggested to grasp value from failures by learning from them, to translate them into improvements, and thereby create customer satisfaction and loyalty. Also three learning loops are identified: Single-loop learning, where errors are detected and corrected; double-loop learning where processes and products are improved; and triple-loop learning, where systems learn how to learn, and norms, principles and associated values are adjusted. It is suggested that the ESCC information, indicating negative and positive customer experience levels, can be utilized for initiating organizational learning actions.

Finally, studies showed that there are no disagreements with the links between improvements in services and increases in customer satisfaction; there are, however, some disagreements with what comes after satisfaction. Loyalty and profitability appeared to be reasonable extensions of customer satisfaction but with no guarantees.

Chapter 7 will describe these steps within the ESCC framework and with some empirical evidence.

## 4.5 Summary of the ESCC Model & Research Questions

As already shown in Figure 1-1, the ESCC model starts at the bottom with the elements of customer satisfaction. The selected six items (price, product, convenience, service quality, service treatment, and positive feelings for the firm) form the cognitive and emotional dimensions.

1) What are the elements of emotional and cognitive satisfaction?
2) What is the role of emotional and cognitive satisfaction in:
    - 2a) Customer contacts (transactional satisfaction)?
    - 2b) General satisfaction?
    - 2c) Customer loyalty (intentions)?

Next dimensions are formed by transactional and general satisfaction. Transactional satisfaction represents in this research the satisfaction level of 'last contact' with the related contact center. General satisfaction, on the other hand, represents the overall satisfaction level of the customer with the firm they have contacted.

3) What is the role of transactional and general satisfaction in customer loyalty (intentions)?
4) What is the role of transactional satisfaction in:
    - 4a) General satisfaction?
    - 4b) Customer loyalty (intentions)?
5) What is the role of time in evaluating transactional satisfaction?

Loyalty is analyzed with the intention to stay as a customer. In positive cases it indicates loyalty, whereas, in negative cases it is an indicator of customer defection (churn).

Observed dis/satisfaction by CSRs forms the central theme of this research. It is expected that customer loyalty intentions, at least in their extreme cases, can be detected by CSRs by observing customer satisfaction. It is also expected that emotional satisfaction would play a stronger role in customer loyalty, and its observation would form a reasonably accurate indication of customer loyalty intentions. The ESCC is registered in a five-point scale format ranging from very negative (red) to very positive (blue). These observations would form transactional satisfaction, and accumulated transactional satisfactions would form the expected general satisfaction which in turn would indicate loyalty intentions.

6) What are the (emotional) satisfaction levels with customer contacts?
7) Can CSRs accurately observe and evaluate (emotional) satisfaction during customer contacts?
8) What is the relationship between the ESCC and CSR's emotions?
9) What is the relationship between the ESCC and:
    - 9a) Emotional and cognitive dimensions?

9b) Transactional satisfaction?
9c) General satisfaction?
9d) Customer loyalty (intentions)?

These observed (emotional) satisfaction (of customer contact) levels, indicating loyalty intentions, can be used to recover customer dissatisfactions proactively, and can also be used to segment the customers, who seem to be very satisfied during their last contact with the firm, for cross/up sales actions.

The registry process of the ESCC can be extended and the reasons behind satisfaction and dissatisfaction can also be captured in a simple database. This data would then provide 'organizational learning' opportunities in which processes and products are continuously improved.

Similar to the service profit chain (Heskett et al., 1997), these improvements are then expected to increase internal service quality, external satisfaction, and finally customer loyalty.

10) 'What can be done with the ESCC information?'

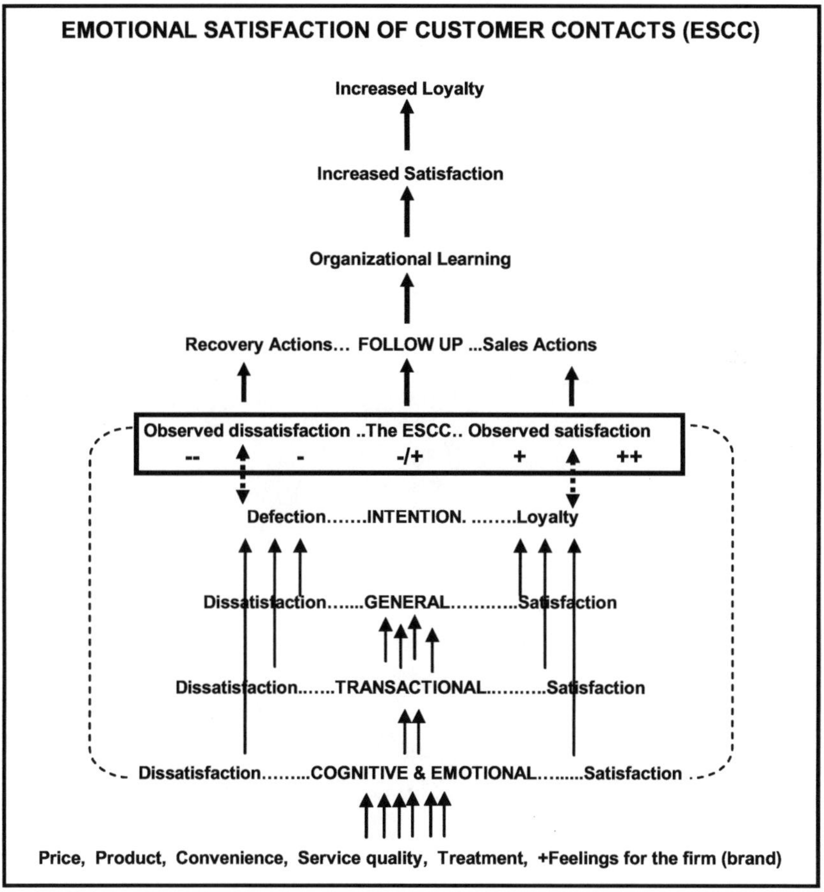

## PART II: The ESCC Surveys & Results

# 5 THE ESCC SURVEYS

## 5.1 Survey Settings

The objectives of the ESCC surveys are, on the one hand, to explore the emotional, cognitive, transactional, and general dimensions of customer satisfaction and loyalty, and to describe the relationships among them, as analyzed in this chapter. On the other hand, it aims to explore the accuracy of the CSRs observations on the ESCC, and its relationships with customer satisfaction and customer loyalty, as analyzed in the following chapter.

For investigating the research questions, firms with a high customer contact volume have been contacted and the ESCC survey has been implemented in four different Dutch firms from different industries, namely book & music firm, insurance, pension fund, and banking. The research is designed as a 'cross sectional' analysis, measuring units from a sample of the population at only one point of time (Burns & Bush, 2003), and are completed in one or two consecutive business days.[74]

Sample size is determined by several factors. First of all the aim was to make the test in five different firms and industries. It is also aimed that total completed surveys should be around 1000 as this would keep the sampling error under 5%[75] (Burns & Bush, 2003:381). Furthermore, 200 completed surveys (100 from test group and 100 from control group) per company in two business days was also a reasonable target. As CSRs are generally able to complete 5-10 calls per hour, companies would engage four full-time (or equivalent) outbound CSRs for test days. However, among the firms contacted, only four of them were willing to employ their resources and expose their customer satisfaction and loyalty figures for this research.

The '*test group*' customers are selected by a random and convenience sampling methodology. Selected inbound CSRs[76] evaluated/rated all inbound calls they received in the test day with the basic ESCC methodology while they were doing their routine work. CSRs received a very brief introduction about the ESCC concepts, and they did not receive an extensive training. For the targeted 100 completed surveys per company, at least 300 ratings were aimed at.

As the CSRs were aware of the fact that customers would be surveyed, their behaviour might have been different than other days (cf. the Hawthorne effect).[77] In order to see the differences between the test day and other days, as

---

[74] Telephone surveys were performed between September 2004 and January 2005.

[75] Considering an estimated standard deviation around 0.75 at the 0.05 level.

[76] CSRs are selected during the test day by the test firm's management. It is requested that the selected CSRs should represent the averages of their contact center in terms of age, education, and experience.

[77] The "Hawthorne effect" refers to the factory where the effect was first observed: the Hawthorne works of the Western Electric Company in Chicago. A series of studies in the factory measured the productivity

well as, to analyze the time factor in customer satisfaction and loyalty process, '*control group*' customers were selected from the firm's databases. These customers were selected by either systematic probability methodology per length of relationship, or randomly. For the targeted 100 completed surveys per test firm, about 300 customers were selected from databases.

Different CSRs surveyed the test group customers afterwards with no particular selection criteria. Therefore, everyone in the test group had equal chance to be selected for the survey. These customers were surveyed with the same questionnaire as the control group. Survey question 9 (How would you evaluate your last telephone contact with the firm?) is used to verify the inbound CSRs' initial ratings on customer satisfaction (the ESCC).

Due to telephone interview method and time constraints the number of questions (items) was restricted to 10 (The survey script and questionnaire can be found in the appendix). Response format was 5-point scale and mainly Likert type between "strongly disagree and strongly agree." In the Likert scale, respondents are asked to choose between five degrees of relative agreement (Riley et al., 2000:121) and these type of questions are considered as the "workhorse" of marketing research as they do the bulk of the measurement work (Burns & Bush, 2003:381). Responses for the evaluation of last calls were between "very negative and very positive," and for the loyalty (intention to stay as customer) between "very unlikely and very likely."

Survey questions were about price, product, convenience, service quality, service treatment, positive feelings for the firm (brand), transactional satisfaction, general satisfaction, and intention to stay as customer. These items were selected parallel to satisfaction dimensions; and to ensure content validity, commonly used satisfaction survey questions were used.

During the test days CSRs also observed their own emotional states and self-rated it in a 5-point scale, from very negative to very positive, with 30 minutes intervals.

Results were analyzed with SPSS (version 12) software.

---

of workers by manipulating various conditions such as light levels, rest breaks, etc., but each change resulted in productivity increase, including eventually a return to the original conditions. Mayo's (1933) interpretation was that the important effect here was 'the feeling of being studied.'

## 5.2 Descriptive Statistics

During the test days 735 surveys have been completed (Figure 5-1). 210 (29%) respondents were from the book & music firm, 148 (20%) from the insurance firm, 177 (24%) from the pension fund, and 200 (27%) from the bank.

Figure 5-1: ESCC Survey Firms

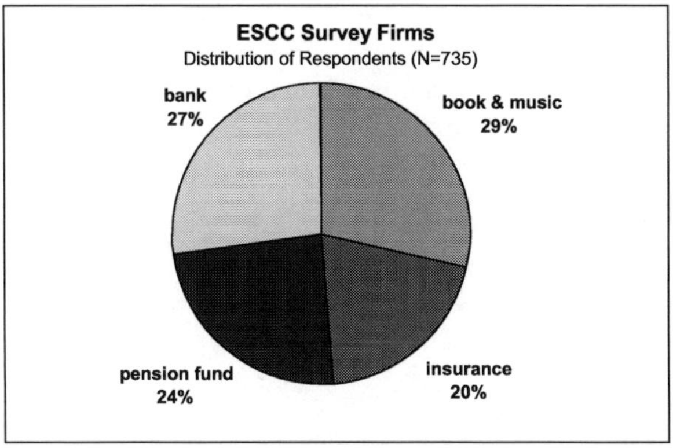


As shown in Table 5-1, approximately among 1200 customers from the control group, 406 surveys have been completed with customers who answered the phone and agreed to participate in the survey. Inbound CSRs have evaluated/rated all inbound calls they received in the test day with the basic ESCC methodology. A total of 842 calls have been rated by 38 CSRs in 4 different firms during test days between 8:30 a.m. and 10:45 p.m. Within a day, all customers with an ESCC rating have been called back, at least once, for the survey. Therefore, everyone in the inbound list had equal chance to be surveyed, and 329 surveys have been performed with the customers who answered the phone and agreed to participate in the survey.[78]

[78] There were few unanswered or missing data in general, and some eliminated data in the bank test group. In the bank test group, 28 surveys were eliminated due to the fact that customers were referring to another contact date (survey question 1) than the test day. It seems that inbound calls have been made with one of the account holders in the test day, and verification surveys have been made, by mistake, with another account holder living at the same address. This was also apparent in customer gender fields in the survey database which were registered during inbound-call and outbound-surveys. Many of the 28 eliminated calls had no identical genders proving that inbound calls have been made with one person, and verification surveys have been made with another.

Table 5-1: The ESCC Survey Sample Population

| | Selected customers* | Completed surveys** |
|---|---|---|
| Control group | 1200 | 406 |
| Test group | 842 | 329 |
| TOTAL | 2042 | 735 |
| *Control group is from test firm databases; test group is all the ESCC evaluations in test days<br>** Numbers may vary per survey item due to unanswered, missing, or eliminated data | | |

Roughly 45% of the respondents were from the test group customers and 55% from the control group. As shown in Figure 5-2 they were not homogenous among the firms, as well as, among the time segments due to random sampling as well as casual response rates during the test days.

Figure 5-2: Last Contact Day Categories (today = test group)

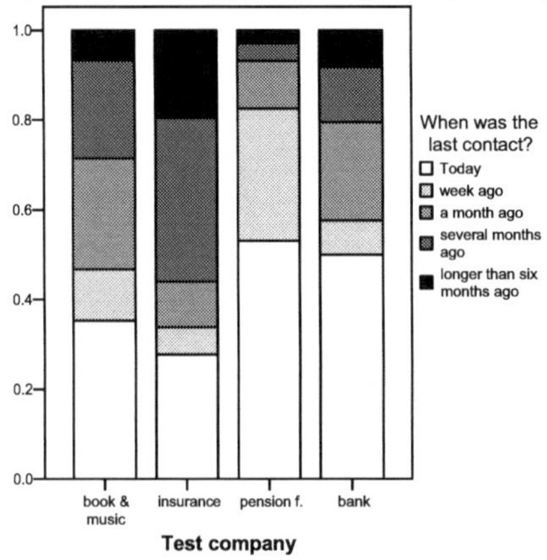


Respondents were mainly female, namely 60%. Percentage of female respondents was around 70% in book & music firm and in pension fund, 50% in bank, and 40% in insurance. Median[79] age of respondents was 45 years, ranging from 31 years in insurance to 59 years in pension fund. Customers' length of relationship with test firms, with a median length of 10 years, ranged from 1 year in insurance to 20 years in bank.

Customer service representatives (CSRs) who have handled and evaluated the incoming (inbound) calls with the ESCC model were mainly female with 70%. CSR ages ranged between 20 and 55 years with a median age of 32 years. Their education levels were 55% at lower secondary (MAVO, MBO) level, 10% at higher secondary (HAVO, VWO) level, 29% at higher vocational (HBO) level, and 6% at university or master's level. CSRs contact center experiences ranged from 0.5 to 8 years with median experience of 3 years. CSRs self ratings on their

[79] Median, the mid-point in a distribution of values, emphasizes the middle of the distribution and ignores the ends that may create distortion in results as a consequence of extreme values (Bryman & Cramer, 2005:102).

emotions were mainly positive (50%), very positive (16%) and neutral (30%); only 4% of the self-ratings were negative, and there was no self-rating with a 'very negative' emotional state.

## 5.3 Frequency Distribution, Measures of Central Tendency, Measures of Dispersion

In this section survey results will be explained by using the frequency distribution of responses summarized in Table 5-2 and in Figure 5-3. Arithmetic mean, which will be used as the measures of central tendency, is the most commonly used average (Riley et al., 2000:177) and is computed by adding together the values for all observations[80] in the data set and dividing by the number of items. Measures of dispersion, known also as measures of variation, describe how scattered or dispersed the data values are (Bryman & Cramer, 2005:102, Riley et al., 2000:186). This measure will be explained by standard deviation indicating an average amount by which all the values deviate from the arithmetic mean. The bigger the dispersion is the bigger the standard deviation.

Chi-square ($\chi^2$) test is used to determine whether or not the frequency distribution is similar to or significantly different from that expected by chance (Riley et al., 2000:217), also referred to as a "goodness-of-fit" test (Burns & Bush, 2003:527). $\chi^2$ test statistics for the survey results presented in Table 5-2 were significant ($p< 0.01$)[81] for all items (see appendix 11.9 for full table).

Table 5-2: Frequency Distribution (in %)

| ESCC Survey Items for 4 test firms | Strongly disagree | Disagree | Neither disagree Nor agree | Agree | Strongly Agree | *Mean* | *Standard Deviation* |
|---|---|---|---|---|---|---|---|
| Generally satisfied | 1.7 | 6.2 | 9.3 | 67.1 | 15.7 | *3.89* | *0.80* |
| Prices are satisfactory | 2.5 | 13.2 | 24.3 | 52.7 | 7.4 | *3.49* | *0.90* |
| Products are satisfactory | 1.0 | 5.0 | 14.5 | 68.3 | 11.2 | *3.84* | *0.72* |
| It is convenient to be firm's customer | 1.8 | 8.9 | 16.8 | 59.9 | 12.5 | *3.72* | *0.87* |
| Satisfied the way the firm treats | 2.5 | 6.9 | 9.6 | 62.3 | 18.6 | *3.88* | *0.88* |
| Reliable, accurate & timely services | 1.3 | 9.1 | 12.3 | 60.7 | 16.6 | *3.82* | *0.86* |
| Positive feelings for the firm | 0.7 | 5.8 | 13.2 | 67.0 | 13.2 | *3.86* | *0.74* |
| Last contact was satisfactory | 2.3 | 5.4 | 12.5 | 57.7 | 23.2 | *3.93* | *0.88* |
| Loyalty Intention | 5.5 | 4.0 | 13.6 | 31.5 | 45.4 | *4.07* | *1.12* |

[80] As the differences between test and control group customers, as well as among specific test firms are not the focal aim of this research, detailed tables and charts highlighting these differences are not displayed in the main text but can be found in the appendix.
[81] The significance levels presented here are the probability (p) values in decimal terms representing the probability of obtaining this result by chance (Bryman & Cramer, 2005:153). Values lower than 0.05 are commonly considered as significant.

Figure 5-3: Frequency Distribution Graph

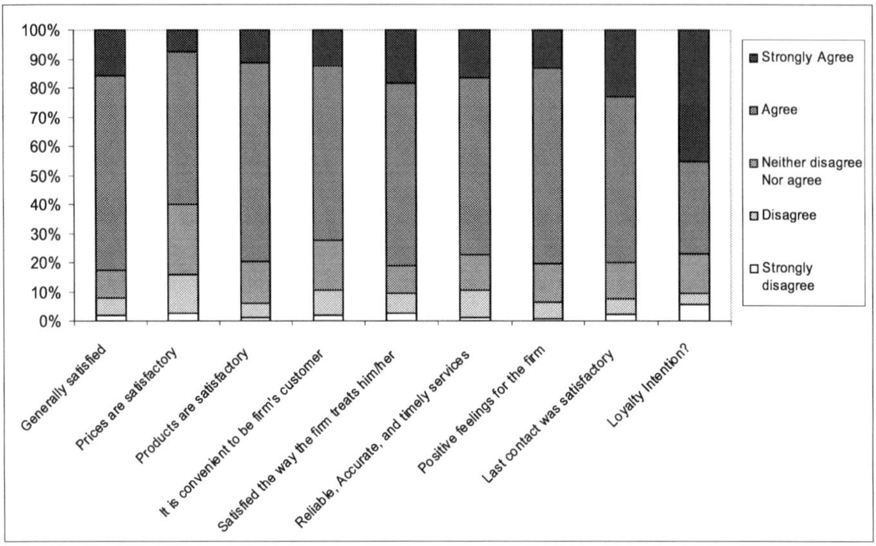


Basic descriptions of the results are as follows:

- Majority of the customers seem to be satisfied in *general satisfaction*. Only less than 7.9% of the customers stated that they were either dissatisfied or very dissatisfied.
- *Pricing* has the lowest mean score of 3.49 in this survey. Customers seem to be least satisfied with prices in comparison with the other satisfaction items. Around 15.7% of the customers were already (very) dissatisfied and 24.3% of them were neither dissatisfied nor satisfied.
- Customers seem to be fairly satisfied with *products* in comparison with the other satisfaction items. About 79.5% of the customers were already (very) satisfied and only 6% of them were (very) dissatisfied with products. This is the lowest dissatisfaction percentage in this survey.
- Customers showed a little disagreement on their satisfaction levels about the *convenience* when they deal with their firms. Over 10% of them were already (very) dissatisfied and 16.8% were hesitating. Nonetheless, over 72% of the customers still showed some appreciation with their firm's convenience.
- It appears that most of the customers, 80.9%, appreciate *the way the firms treat* them. Only 9.4% of them were not satisfied and 9.6% were hesitating.
- 77.3% of the customers were satisfied with the *quality of service* they receive. Over 10% were not happy with it and 12.3% were hesitating.

- Over 80% of customers had *positive feelings* towards their firms. This is one of the highest satisfaction levels among the satisfaction items. Customers who disagreed here were only 6.5% and 13.2% were hesitating.
- Again over 80% of all customers perceived their *last contact*[82] (very) positive. 2.3% of customers experienced their last contact as very negative and 5.4% as negative. 12.5% of customers stated that their last contact with the firm was neutral.
- 76.9% of all customers had positive *intentions to stay* as customer with their firms. 45.4% of all customers even have chosen 'very likely', which was the most extreme positive answer. 9.5% customers had negative intentions where 5.5% of all customers have chosen the most negative answer. Finally, 13.65% of all customers had neutral intentions.

Although a 50/50 situation is aimed in terms of respondents from test and control group customers, about 40% of respondents were from the test group who had their contact in the same day or a day earlier, and about 60% of respondents were from the control group (Figure 5-4). Pension fund customers had most recent contacts and insurance firm customers had the least recent contacts.

Figure 5-4: When Was the Last Contact?

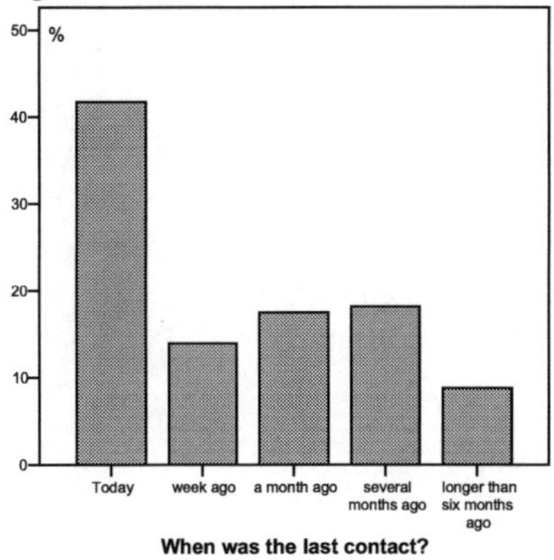


## 5.4 Discussions on Frequency Distribution

The summary table of frequency distribution and the arithmetic mean of all survey questions indicate that, on average, about 18% of all customers are very satisfied, 59% satisfied, 14% neutral, 7% dissatisfied and 2% very dissatisfied with their firms. These averages are in line with the description of Heskett et al.

[82] Last contact refers to the contact in the test day for the test group customers, and to the most recent contact in the past for the control group.

(1997:88) on typical data regarding customer satisfaction (Figure 5-5). According to them, it is typical to see the following percentages: 5% for the lowest rating followed by 10% for negative, 25% for neutral, 50% for positive, and 10% for the highest rating.

Figure 5-5: Mean Frequency Distribution in the ESCC Survey

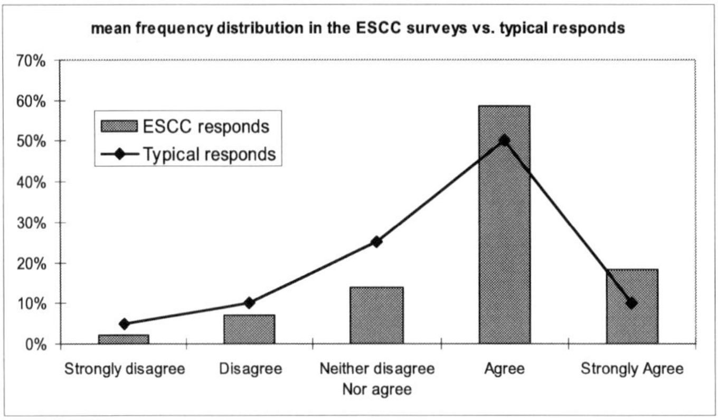


When compared with all satisfaction items, price appears to be the most dissatisfying item. The other most dissatisfying items appear to be the convenience and the service quality as their averages on negative areas are higher than the other items. This is in line with the initial observations of this research suggesting that customers are frequently frustrated with the services they receive.

Another remarkable result emerges in loyalty intentions. Customer loyalty intentions are more positive than how customers perceive the satisfaction items. In other words, customers seem to be more loyal than they are satisfied. Furthermore, loyalty intentions receive the most extreme positive answers as well as the most extreme negative answers. Thus, it appears (Figure 5-6) that customer satisfaction cannot be translated directly to customer loyalty.

Figure 5-6: Average Satisfaction vs. Loyalty Intentions

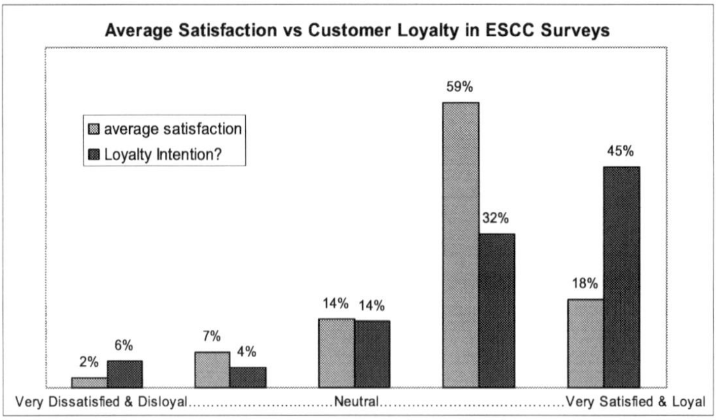

There are several alternatives that might explain why customers are more loyal than they are satisfied. Firstly, customers stay with their firm but might actually use another firm's services, resembling the term *polygamous loyalty.*[83] Secondly, it can be *false loyalty* in which customers seem to be loyal until certain benefits are exhausted (Jones & Sasser, 1995:90). Thirdly, customers do not change their firms because they might expect that other firms will also give similar (low) service levels, akin to the *trance of mediocrity* in which firms set their standards by looking at each other and create industry-wide quality erosions (Senge, 1990:333). Fourthly, customers might find it difficult to change their firms due to many administrative burdens, resembling *inertia loyalty* (Jones & Farquhar, 2003:71; Griffin, 2002:22).

Confirming the conclusion that customer satisfaction cannot be translated directly to customer loyalty, Reichheld (1993:71; 1996:58) *reversely* suggests that customers can also be less loyal than they are satisfied. According to Reichheld (ibid.) satisfaction scores average 85% to 95% in the automobile industry while repurchase rates average only 40%; and that telephone companies are likely to suffer the carmakers' fate.

It appears thus that "current satisfaction measurement systems are simply not designed to provide insight into how many customers stay loyal to the company and for how long" (ibid; see also Edwardson, 1998[84]; Jones & Sasser, 1995; Liu, Bernhardt, & Leach, 1999).

As shown in Figure 5-7 there is indeed no straight line relationship between satisfaction and loyalty. It also seems that only very satisfied customers can be considered as loyal. This relationship has already been investigated among others by Jones & Sasser (1995) and by Heskett et al. (1997:83), and the ESCC survey findings are, although less sharp, similar to their description.

Figure 5-7: Satisfaction and Loyalty

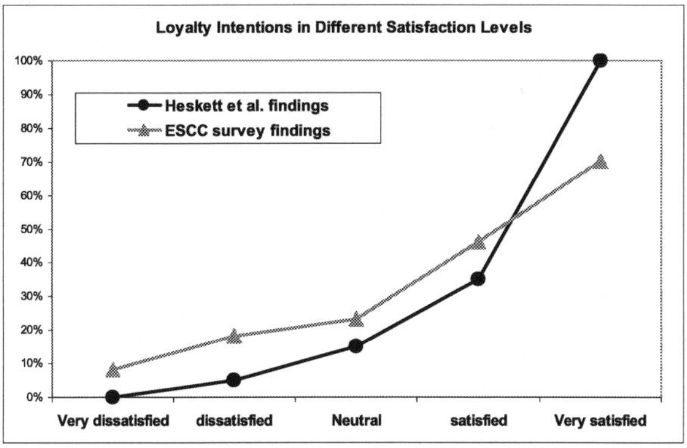


[83] As cited in Rust, Zeithaml, and Lemon (2000:37): G.R.Dowling & M.Uncles (1997). Do Customer Loyalty Programs Really Work? *Sloan Management Review*, 38/4, 71-82.
[84] As cited in Edwardson (1998:4): Hennig-Thurau, T. & Klee, A. (1997). The Impact of Satisfaction and Relationship Quality on Customer Retention: A Critical Reassessment and Model Development. *Psychology & Marketing*, 14, 8, 737-764.

## 5.5 Discussions on the Differences among Sample Groups

Differences in survey results were investigated in two areas. First, it was investigated whether or not differences exist between test group customers, who called the firms during test days, and the control group customers who were randomly selected from the firm's databases. Secondly, it was investigated whether or not there significant differences exist among the responses from different test firms.

Since the response scales used in this research[85] are considered as "ordinal" (Bethlehem & De Gooijer, 1999:8) in order to test the statistical significance of the differences between test and control customers the 'Mann-Whitney U test' was used; and in order to test the statistical significance of the differences among four test firms the 'Kruskal-Wallis H test' was used (Bryman & Cramer, 2005:146; Hill & Lewicki, 2006).

As the differences between test and control group customers, as well as among specific test firms, are outside of the focal aim of this research, detailed tables and charts highlighting these differences are not displayed in the main text but can be found in the appendix (between 11.4 and 11.9).

Table 5-3: Differences between Test and Control Group, and among Test Firms

| Survey Item | Differences between Test and Control group customers (Mann-Whitney U test) p< | Differences among 4 Test Firms (Kruskal-Wallis H test) p< |
|---:|:---:|:---:|
| Generally satisfied | 0.58 | 0.12 |
| Prices are satisfactory | 0.19 | 0.27 |
| Products are satisfactory | 0.42 | 0.01* |
| It is convenient to be firm's customer | 0.44 | 0.31 |
| Satisfied the way the firm treats him/her | 0.06 | 0.01* |
| Reliable, accurate, and timely services | 0.50 | 0.08 |
| Positive feelings for the firm | 0.43 | 0.01* |
| Last contact was satisfactory | 0.01* | 0.12 |
| Loyalty Intention? | 0.98 | 0.01* |

* Significant at the 0.01 level; Detailed tables can be found in appendix (11.9).

[85] Strongly disagree – disagree - neither disagree nor agree – agree - strongly agree.

### *5.5.1 Test and Control Group Customers*

Extreme negative answer proportions among test group customers were higher in all questions than the control group customers. Also extreme positive answer proportions among test group customers were higher in 2/3 of the survey questions (see appendix 11.7). Nevertheless, the differences were not significant (Table 5-3) except for the satisfaction with the last contact (transactional satisfaction) (Figure 5-8).

Figure 5-8: Differences between Test and Control Group in Evaluation of Transactional Satisfaction

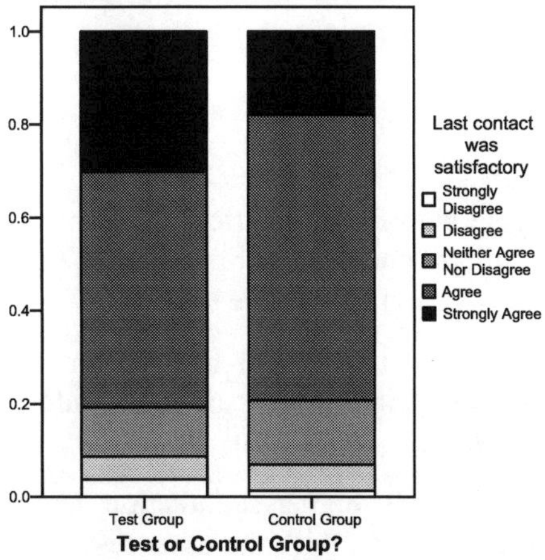


On the one hand, insignificant differences between the responses of test and control group customers indicated that they gave comparable answers to almost all survey questions, and thus they represent same values and attitudes in general. On the other hand, the only significant difference in 'transactional satisfaction' indicated that the test group customers perceived their last contact significantly more positive than the control group customers.

The percentage of customers who were very satisfied with their last contact, for example, was 18% in the control group, and 30.2% in the test group. More positive responses among the test group customers, on the one hand, resemble the Hawthorne effect (Mayo, 1933) which assumes that CSRs might have made extra efforts to create more positive service experiences. On the other hand, it indicates that firms can increase customer satisfaction if they create an environment similar to the ESCC test days, in which customer satisfaction is continuously observed and surveyed. However, as the extreme dissatisfactions among test group customers (3.7%) were also higher vis-à-vis control group customers (1.2%), it also appears that with only 'extra smile and attention' firms cannot fully compensate their other shortcomings.

High proportion of positive as well as negative responses in the test group indicates that extreme good or extreme bad perceptions about the firms are more visible around customer contact moments. Therefore, it can be concluded that customer contacts create a strong momentum for building intense opinions about the contacted firms. This fact, however, seems not to be fully recognized in many organizations that regularly frustrate their customers through their contact centers, as already discussed in chapter 1.

As already shown in Figure 5-7, a higher proportion of very satisfied customers is very critical for firms due to the fact that their loyalty tendencies are much stronger than the rest of the customers. It is, however, interesting to see that the difference between test and control group customers was not significant in loyalty intentions. In other words, despite the differences in various satisfaction levels, on average, there is no difference found between the test and control group customers in terms of loyalty intentions.

### *5.5.2 Test Firms*

Among the survey questions, four items were significantly different among the test firms: product, treatment, positive feelings, and loyalty intentions (Table 5-3, see also appendix 11.6). These items thus varied among the test firms.

General satisfaction, prices, convenience, service quality, and satisfaction with last contact did not significantly differ among the firms, thus can be considered as common denominators among the test firms.

Although the *book & music* firm showed relatively higher satisfaction scores, customer loyalty intentions were lowest in comparison with the other test firms. Because book & music firm customers renew their subscriptions every year, and book and music articles are found at many other suppliers, customers seem to choose the 'churn' option relatively easier than the other test firms.

The *insurance* firm had the highest ratio of very negative contacts (12.7% of the test group customers and 6.1% of all responses in insurance firm[86]), as well as, relatively high loyalty intentions. It is, however, important to mention that in the test firm the control group is selected among newly acquired internet customers, but the majority of calls received during the test day were health insurance related calls from all customer segments. This fact thus dilutes test group and control group comparisons.

The *pension fund* customers, according to survey results, were highly satisfied and highly loyal to their firms. Although a casual relationship cannot be sketched with the available information, it seems that the long term orientation in the pension business, unlike the insurance business which yearly renews customer contracts, availability of few pension fund firms in the market, and the compulsory membership due to employer's collective agreements, might have created this 'rush-free' atmosphere around customer contacts where loyalty seems to be taken for granted.

[86] The percentage of 'very negative' responses of the insurance company customers to the survey question 9 (how would you evaluate your last telephone contact with the firm?).

The *bank* customers demonstrated a high dissatisfaction, but also high loyalty intentions. Customers apparently experience some difficulties especially when contacting the bank; nevertheless, these difficulties seem not to be a reason for changing their banks. For example, only 2% of 40 million British bank customers have changed their banks; and an average Dutch bank-customer is for the same reasons described as "loyal as a dog" in 2002.[87] As banking relationship has many other aspects like automatic payments, mortgage, salary accounts, changing a bank is generally perceived as a matter of avoidance; at least until bank account number portability is fully liberalized just like in the mobile phone business.

Loyalty intentions among the test firms indicate that the least loyal customers were from the book & music and insurance firm. These are actually the firms that need to renew their contracts almost every year with their customers. Most loyal customers, on the other hand, were from the bank and from the pension fund firms in which products are sold for a much longer time frame, and changing the provider is much more complicated than the other two test firms (e.g., de Volkskrant, 30-9-2005). It therefore seems that the loyalty can also be explained by the threshold levels for switching a product. Nevertheless, to verify this assumption further research is needed.

## 5.6 Associative Analyses

Associative analysis investigates if, and how, two or more variables are related, and determine the strength and direction of the relationship. A relationship is a consistent and systematic linkage between the levels or labels for two variables. Correlations and Chi-square ($\chi^2$) analysis are the basic associative analysis methods used in marketing research (Burns & Bush, 2003:435). Chi-square ($\chi^2$) analysis describes a non-monotonic relationship and a rank correlation describes a monotonic relationship between two variables.[88]

*Pearson Chi-square ($\chi^2$) analysis* is the examination of frequencies for two variables in a cross-tabulation table to determine whether the variables have a non-monotonic relationship (ibid., p.525). To assess the strength of the association there are some applications, in the SPSS statistical program, such as Cramér's V. The value of V is always between 0 and 1 and the bigger is the value, the stronger the association. As a rule of thumb, V values up to 0.3 are considered as a weak association; between 0.3 and 0.7 moderate; and above 0.7 as strong associations (Bethlehem & De Gooijer, 1999:66).

*Correlation coefficients* are concerned with the associations between actual values, and not frequency distributions like in cross-tabulations. Spearman's rho is one of the two types of correlation coefficient and is used for calculating

[87] Cohen, E., *Klant wil draagbare bank,* Het Financieele Dagblad, 5-4-2002.

[88] Non-monotonic relationship means that two variables are associated, but only in a general sense. A monotonic relationship means that the association and the general direction (increasing or decreasing) of the relationship between two variables are known.

correlations in respect of ordinal data[89] as assessed in this research. Correlation coefficients vary between -1 and +1, where -1 indicates a perfect negative correlation and +1 is a perfect positive correlation between the assessed variables. The nearer the coefficient is to zero, the weaker the relationship (Bryman & Cramer, 2005:219). As a rule of thumb, correlation coefficients up to 0.19 are considered as very low, between 0.20 and 0.39 is low, 0.40 to 0.69 is modest or moderate, 0.70 to 0.89 is high, and 0.90 and 1.00 is very high.[90] It is also worth to note that correlation coefficient indicates a 'statistical relationship' between two variables, and not a 'cause and effect' relationship which is a condition of one variable bringing about the other variable (Burns & Bush, 2003:540).

The *significance levels* presented here are the probability (p) values in decimal terms representing the probability of obtaining this result by chance (Bryman & Cramer, 2005:153). The value 0.05 indicates the 95 percent confidence limit which is normally taken as the minimum for deciding upon whether or not the null hypothesis should be accepted or rejected (Riley et al., 2000:201). In this particular case, the null hypothesis assumes that there is no significant association or relationship between the assessed variables. Therefore, p-values greater than 0.05 mean that the null hypothesis (no difference between groups) can be accepted; and p-values less than 0.05 mean the null hypothesis can be rejected, and it can be stated that there are significant associations or relationships between the assessed variables.

[89] Pearson's product moment correlation is used when scores or values have at least interval status (Riley et al., 2000:233).

[90] As cited in Bryman & Cramer (2005:219): Cohen, L. & Holliday, M. (1982). *Statistics for Social Scientists.* London: Harper & Row.

### *5.6.1 Correlation Analysis*

Table 5-4: Correlation Table of the ESCC Surveys

| The ESCC Survey Question Correlations Spearman's rho* | Generally satisfied | Prices are satisfactory | Products are satisfactory | It is convenient to be firm's customer | Satisfied the way the firm treats him/her | Reliable, accurate, and timely services | Positive feelings for the firm | Last contact was satisfactory |
|---|---|---|---|---|---|---|---|---|
| Generally satisfied | - | | | | | | | |
| Prices are satisfactory | 0.31 | - | | | | | | |
| Products are satisfactory | 0.40 | 0.25 | - | | | | | |
| It is convenient to be firm's customer | 0.52 | 0.28 | 0.38 | - | | | | |
| Satisfied the way the firm treats him/her | 0.55 | 0.18 | 0.31 | 0.47 | - | | | |
| Reliable, accurate, and timely services | 0.53 | 0.23 | 0.31 | 0.48 | 0.61 | - | | |
| Positive feelings for the firm | 0.53 | 0.28 | 0.41 | 0.46 | 0.46 | 0.52 | - | |
| Last contact was satisfactory | 0.43 | 0.16 | 0.28 | 0.34 | 0.45 | 0.46 | 0.36 | - |
| Loyalty Intention | 0.38 | 0.17 | 0.25 | 0.34 | 0.27 | 0.29 | 0.34 | 0.32 |

* All items are significantly correlated at the 0.01 level; Sample size +/- 680

Spearman's rank order correlations among survey items are all positively associated, and are either moderately correlated (0.40-0.70) or weaker. The survey items and their relationships are summarized below, and the highest correlation coefficient is noted between [brackets] after its related item:

- *General satisfaction* is moderately correlated with products, convenience, treatment [0.55], positive feelings, and satisfaction with the last contact; and weakly correlated with price and loyalty intention.
- *Price* is moderately correlated with products [0.40], weakly with general satisfaction, convenience, treatment, service, and positive feelings; and very weakly with last contact and loyalty.
- *Product quality* is weakly correlated with all items and slightly more moderately with general satisfaction and positive feelings with the firm [0.41].

- *Convenience* is moderately correlated with general satisfaction [0.52], treatment, service quality, and positive feelings; and weakly with prices, products, last contact, and loyalty.
- *Treatment* is moderately correlated with general satisfaction, convenience, service quality [0.61], positive feelings, and last contact; and weakly with prices, products, and loyalty.
- *Service quality* is moderately correlated with general satisfaction, convenience, treatment [0.61], positive feelings, and last contact; and weakly with price, products, and loyalty.
- *Positive feelings* for the firm is moderately correlated with general satisfaction [0.53], products, convenience, treatment, service quality; and weakly with prices, last contact, and loyalty.
- *Satisfaction with last contact* (transactional satisfaction) is moderately correlated with general satisfaction, treatment, and with service quality [0.46]; and weakly with prices, products, convenience, positive feelings, and loyalty.
- *Loyalty intention* is weakly correlated with all items and very weakly with prices. Its highest correlation item was with general satisfaction [0.38].

These results indicate that almost all satisfaction items are moderately associated with general satisfaction; somewhat weaker with transactional satisfaction; and weakly with loyalty intentions.

In order to analyze these items further it is necessary to categorize variables into a small number of groups such as emotional and cognitive dimensions.

### *5.6.2 Principal Component Analysis & Research Question 1: What are the elements of emotional and cognitive satisfaction?*

Principal component analysis is a technique for forming new variables which are linear composites of the original variables and which are not correlated among themselves (Sharma, 1996:58). The general objectives of this analysis are data reduction and interpretation (Johnson & Wichern, 2002:426). In other words, principal component analysis basically aims at grouping interrelated, and thus correlated, variables together so that further analysis can be performed with a less number of new variables.

The SPSS program does the principal component analysis and reports the loadings[91] for each variable on the components. Each number thus represents the correlation between the item and the component. These correlations are then used to formulate an interpretation of the components. This is done by looking

[91] The relationship between each item and a component (i.e. the new variable) is expressed as a correlation or loading.

for a common thread among the variables that have large loadings for a particular component.[92]

How many components will be retained is determined, although not compulsorily (Sharma, 1996:76), by two main criteria. The first is known as Kaiser's criterion and selects those factors which have an eigenvalue[93] of greater than one, and the second is the graphical scree test (Bryman & Cramer, 2005:330) which is a plot of the variance associated with each factor. Scree plot is used to determine how many factors should be kept. Typically the plot shows a distinct break between the steep slope of the large factors and the gradual trailing of the rest (the scree).[94]

As this research investigates the relationships among transactional satisfaction, general satisfaction, loyalty and the six other satisfaction items which would form emotional and cognitive dimensions, the principal component analysis is performed among the six satisfaction items so that they can be grouped according to their interrelations.

As shown in Table 5-5 the first four satisfaction item loadings are negative with component 2, which has positive loadings with price and products. Based on this, we can group the first four variables (positive feelings for the firm, service quality, service treatment, and convenience) under the component 1; and the last two variables (prices and products) under the component 2. As the highest loading of component 1 is 'positive feelings for the firm' and the other items also cannot be measured or compared objectively, these items may be considered as the '*emotional satisfaction*' component or dimension. As the highest loading of component 2 is 'price,' and the other item 'product quality' can also be measured or compared objectively, these items may be considered as the '*cognitive satisfaction*' component or dimension. This distinction is also verified by Varimax rotation and correlation coefficients of the two dimensions.

Eigenvalues and the scree plot of the components are shown in Table 5-6 and in Figure 5-9 respectively. Component 1 (emotional satisfaction) has an eigenvalue of 3.066, which explains 51.09% of the total variance; and the component 2 (cognitive satisfaction) has an eigenvalue of 0.894, which explains 14.89% of the total variance. The eigenvalue of component 2 is slightly under the Kaizer's criterion of 1, but valuable enough to keep for distinguishing the cognitive factors. Consequently, these two components account for the 65.99% of the total variance explained by all six items. This level is in fact acceptable for the purpose of this research which aims at exploring the relationships among the satisfaction dimensions and loyalty in a general sense, rather than aiming at calculating them with a high precision.

---

[92] SPPS tutorial information.

[93] Principal component analysis is primarily concerned with describing the variation or variance which is shared by the scores of people on three or more variables. The *eigenvalue* is the amount of the variance explained by the component, or its proportion in the total variance (Bryman & Cramer, 2005:327-329). In other words, eigenvalues are the variances of the new variables (Sharma, 1996:68).

[94] SPPS tutorial information.

Table 5-5: Principal Component Analysis: Component Matrix (a)

| | Component | |
|---|---|---|
| | 1 | 2 |
| Positive feelings for the firm | .792 | -.014 |
| Reliable, accurate, and timely services | .789 | -.335 |
| Satisfied the way the firms treats him/her | .772 | -.368 |
| It is convenient to be firm's customer | .767 | -.010 |
| Products are satisfactory* | .629 | .338 |
| Prices are satisfactory | .486 | .730 |

Extraction Method: Principal Component Analysis. (a) 2 components extracted.
*Product item loadings were .369 for component 1 and .611 for component 2 with Varimax rotation.

Table 5-6: Principal Component Analysis: Total Variance Explained

| Component | Initial Eigenvalues | | | Extraction Sums of Squared Loadings | | |
|---|---|---|---|---|---|---|
| | Total | % of Variance | Cumulative % | Total | % of Variance | Cumulative % |
| 1 | 3.066 | 51.094 | 51.094 | 3.066 | 51.094 | 51.094 |
| 2 | .894 | 14.899 | 65.993 | .894 | 14.899 | 65.993 |
| 3 | .718 | 11.967 | 77.960 | | | |
| 4 | .507 | 8.449 | 86.410 | | | |
| 5 | .461 | 7.689 | 94.099 | | | |
| 6 | .354 | 5.901 | 100.000 | | | |

Extraction Method: Principal Component Analysis.

Figure 5-9: Principal Component Analysis: The Scree Plot

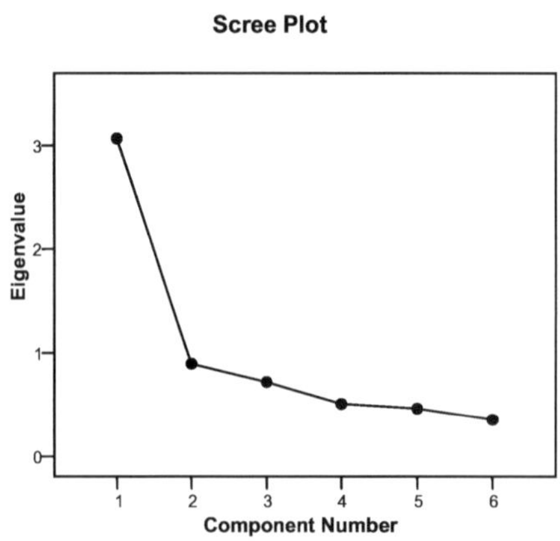

### *5.6.3 Cross-tabulation & Chi-Square Analyses*

Cross-tabulation and the associated chi-square values are used to assess whether a nonmonotonic relationship, in which the presence of one variable coincides with the presence of another variable, exists between two variables. Cross-tabulation consists of rows and columns defined by the categories classifying each variable (Burns & Bush, 2003:522). As mentioned earlier, to assess the strength of the association Cramér's V value is used.[95] The significance levels are again presented with the probability (p) values in decimal terms representing the probability of obtaining this result by chance.[96]

In this section, relationships among transactional satisfaction, general satisfaction, emotional satisfaction, cognitive satisfaction and loyalty intentions will be investigated by using data derived from cross-tabulations.

In order to draw these cross-tabulations, to begin with, emotional and cognitive scores are calculated by taking the arithmetic means of their related items as derived from the principal component analysis. Emotional satisfaction is thus the arithmetic mean of the survey scores of positive feelings for the firm, service quality, service treatment, and convenience. Cognitive satisfaction is the arithmetic mean of the survey scores of price and products. Means up to 0.49 decimals are rounded-down, and from 0.50 onwards are rounded-up in order to create a 5-point scale grouping.

Then all items used are re-grouped into three groups by: (1) combining lowest two scores together, (2) taking the middle score as it is, and (3) combining the highest two scores together. The first reason for grouping items is to create larger samples in each group so that enough respondents fall into each category – a necessity for statistical significance.[97] Secondly, three groups in two dimensions created nine categories ($3^2$) to be interpreted; these categories would be twenty-five ($5^2$), which would further dilute the interpretations, if five scales were analyzed in two dimensions.

---

[95] The value of V is always between 0 and 1 and the bigger the value, the stronger the association. As a rule of thumb, V value up to 0.3 is considered as a weak association; between 0.3 and 0.7 is moderate; and above 0.7 is strong association (Bethlehem & De Gooijer, 1999:66).

[96] The value 0.05 indicates the 95 per cent confidence limit which is normally taken as the minimum for deciding upon whether or not the associations are significant.

[97] Even this grouping did not help to create enough respondents in some (extreme) categories like 'cognitively very satisfied' but 'emotionally very dissatisfied.'

### 5.6.3.1 Research Question 2a: What is the role of emotional & cognitive dimensions in transactional satisfaction?

One of the investigation areas of this research is to find out the relationships between emotional and cognitive dimensions of satisfaction and their effects on transactional satisfaction – more specifically customer contacts. Figure 5-10 reveals these relationships based on the ESCC survey results. As Chi-square analyses indicate, satisfied, maybe-satisfied, and dissatisfied customers are significantly associated with emotional and cognitive dimensions; and as Cramér's V scores indicate, associations of dissatisfied-customers are moderate, and maybe-satisfied and satisfied customers are weak.

Figure 5-10: Emotional and Cognitive Dimensions in Transactional Satisfaction

**EMOTIONAL vs COGNITIVE SATISFACTION in TRANSACTIONAL SATISFACTION**

Crosstabulation in number of respondents, and their percentages within their group.

| COGNITIVE SATISFACTION | Transactional | EMOTIONAL SATISFACTION: (very) Dissatisfied | | Neutral | | (very) Satisfied | |
|---|---|---|---|---|---|---|---|
| (very) Satisfied | Satisfied | 4 | 33% | 22 | 47% | 399 | 88% |
| | Maybe satisfied | 1 | 8% | 14 | 30% | 39 | 9% |
| | Dissatisfied | 7 | 58% | 11 | 23% | 16 | 4% |
| | | 12 | 100% | 47 | 100% | 454 | 100% |
| Neutral | Satisfied | 3 | 30% | 18 | 56% | 91 | 86% |
| | Maybe satisfied | 4 | 40% | 10 | 31% | 11 | 10% |
| | Dissatisfied | 3 | 30% | 4 | 13% | 4 | 4% |
| | | 10 | 100% | 32 | 100% | 106 | 100% |
| (very) Dissatisfied | Satisfied | 1 | 11% | 2 | 33% | 5 | 83% |
| | Maybe satisfied | 1 | 11% | 4 | 67% | 1 | 17% |
| | Dissatisfied | 7 | 78% | 0 | 0% | 0 | 0% |
| | | 9 | 100% | 6 | 100% | 6 | 100% |

| | | |
|---|---|---|
| **Satisfied:** | Agree & strongly agree in transactional satisfaction.............. | $x^2$ p< 0.000, Cramér's V: 0.159 |
| **Maybe Satisfied** | Neither agree nor disagree in transactional satisfaction.......... | p< 0.010, V: 0.279 |
| **Dissatisfied:** | Strongly disagree + disagree in transactional satisfaction...... | p< 0.002. V:0.405 |
| **Cognitive:** | Mean of survey scores about (price, product) * | N= 682 |
| **Emotional:** | Mean of survey scores about (treatment, feelings, service, convenience) * | |

* Mean scores are first rounded; then 1&2 formed dissatisfied, 3 formed maybesatisfied and 4&5 formed satisfied.

Figures may not sum up to 100%, because of rounding.

The percentages of satisfied customers on the diagonal-line between bottom-left and upper-right corners (11% →56% →88%) indicate that transactional satisfaction consistently increases when cognitive and emotional satisfaction increase simultaneously. Dissatisfaction also consistently decreases in the same diagonal line.

The percentages of satisfied customers in the upper-row from right to left indicate that when cognitively satisfied, emotional satisfaction plays a very strong role in transactional satisfaction, as the transactional satisfaction decreases from 88% to 47% and to 33% as a result of a decline in emotional satisfaction. Dissatisfaction also consistently increases when emotional satisfaction decreases in the same line.

The percentages of satisfied customers in the right-hand-side column from top to bottom indicate that when emotionally satisfied, cognitive satisfaction plays hardly any role in transactional satisfaction as the transactional satisfaction decreases from 88% to 86% and to 83% as a result of a decline in cognitive satisfaction. Also the changes in dissatisfaction are very slight in the same line.

It can thus be concluded that transactional satisfaction or satisfaction with customer contacts depends on the emotional dimensions of satisfaction, which are convenience, service quality, service treatment, and positive feelings toward the firm, rather than cognitive dimensions of satisfaction which are price and product quality.

### 5.6.3.2 Research Question 2b: What is the role of emotional & cognitive dimensions in general satisfaction?

Another investigation area of this research is to find out the relationships between emotional and cognitive dimensions of satisfaction and their effects on general satisfaction. Figure 5-11 reveals these relationships based on the ESCC survey results. As Chi-square analyses indicate satisfied customers are significantly associated with emotional and cognitive dimensions, whereas maybe-satisfied and dissatisfied customers' associations are not significant. As the Cramér's V score indicates, the association of satisfied-customers is weak.

Figure 5-11: Emotional and Cognitive Dimensions in General Satisfaction

**EMOTIONAL vs COGNITIVE SATISFACTION in GENERAL SATISFACTION**

Crosstabulation in number of respondents, and their percentages within their group.

| COGNITIVE SATISFACTION | General satisfaction | EMOTIONAL SATISFACTION: (very) Dissatisfied | | Neutral | | (very) Satisfied | |
|---|---|---|---|---|---|---|---|
| (very) Satisfied | Satisfied | 0 | 0% | 21 | 45% | 438 | 96% |
| | Maybe satisfied | 2 | 17% | 16 | 34% | 15 | 3% |
| | Dissatisfied | 10 | 83% | 10 | 21% | 3 | 1% |
| | Total | 12 | 100% | 47 | 100% | 456 | 100% |
| Neutral | Satisfied | 2 | 20% | 16 | 50% | 89 | 84% |
| | Maybe satisfied | 2 | 20% | 9 | 28% | 12 | 11% |
| | Dissatisfied | 6 | 60% | 7 | 22% | 5 | 5% |
| | Total | 10 | 100% | 32 | 100% | 106 | 100% |
| (very) Dissatisfied | Satisfied | 0 | 0% | 1 | 17% | 2 | 33% |
| | Maybe satisfied | 1 | 11% | 3 | 50% | 2 | 33% |
| | Dissatisfied | 8 | 89% | 2 | 33% | 2 | 33% |
| | Total | 9 | 100% | 6 | 100% | 6 | 100% |

| | | |
|---|---|---|
| Satisfied: | Agree & strongly agree in general satisfaction | $x^2$ p< 0.000, Cramér's V: 0.155 |
| maybe satisfied: | Neither agree nor disagree in general satisfaction | p< 0.842 (not significant) |
| Dissatisfied: | Strongly disagree + disagree in general satisfaction | p< 0.325 (not significant) |
| Cognitive: | Mean of survey scores about (price, product) * | N= 684 |
| Emotional: | Mean of survey scores about (treatment, feelings, service, convenience) * | |

* Mean scores are first rounded; then 1&2 formed dissatisfied, 3 formed maybesatisfied and 4&5 formed satisfied.

Figures may not sum to 100%, because of rounding.

The percentages of satisfied customers on the diagonal-line between bottom-left and upper-right corners (0% →50% →96%) indicate that general satisfaction very consistently increases when cognitive and emotional satisfaction increase simultaneously. Dissatisfaction also consistently decreases in the same diagonal line.

The percentages of satisfied customers in the upper-row from right to left indicate that when cognitively satisfied, emotional satisfaction plays a very strong role in general satisfaction as the general satisfaction decreases from 96% to 45% and to 0% as a result of a decline in emotional satisfaction. Dissatisfaction also consistently increases when emotional satisfaction decreases in the same line.

The percentages of satisfied customers in the right-hand-side column from top to bottom indicate that when customers are emotionally satisfied, cognitive satisfaction plays only a modest role in general satisfaction as the general satisfaction decreases from 96% to 84% and to 33% as a result of a decline in cognitive satisfaction. Also the changes in dissatisfaction are similar to the changes in general satisfaction, but in the opposite direction.

It can be concluded from this picture that general satisfaction depends much more on emotional dimensions than on cognitive dimensions; and customers seem to be more tolerant towards a decline in cognitive satisfaction than a decline in emotional satisfaction.

### 5.6.3.3 Research Question 2c: What is the role of emotional and cognitive dimensions in customer loyalty (intentions)?

The relationships between emotional and cognitive dimensions of satisfaction and their effects on customer loyalty (intentions) are also analyzed with the ESCC survey results (Figure 5-12). In this analysis, the loyal and defector customers are significantly associated with emotional and cognitive dimensions, whereas maybe-loyal customers' association is not significant. As the Cramér's V scores indicate, the associations of loyal customers are weak, and defectors are moderate.

Figure 5-12: Emotional and Cognitive Dimensions in Customer Loyalty

**EMOTIONAL vs COGNITIVE SATISFACTION in CUSTOMER LOYALTY**

Crosstabulation in number of respondents, and their percentages within their group.

| COGNITIVE SATISFACTION | | EMOTIONAL SATISFACTION: (very) Dissatisfied | | Neutral | | (very) Satisfied | | |
|---|---|---|---|---|---|---|---|---|
| (very) Satisfied | | 1 | 8% | 28 | 60% | 393 | 86% | Loyal |
| | | 7 | 58% | 9 | 19% | 47 | 10% | Maybe loyal |
| | | 4 | 33% | 10 | 21% | 15 | 3% | Defector |
| | | 12 | 100% | 47 | 100% | 455 | 100% | |
| Neutral | | 4 | 40% | 16 | 50% | 75 | 71% | |
| | | 2 | 20% | 6 | 19% | 17 | 16% | |
| | | 4 | 40% | 10 | 31% | 14 | 13% | |
| | | 10 | 100% | 32 | 100% | 106 | 100% | |
| (very) Dissatisfied | | 1 | 11% | 2 | 33% | 3 | 50% | |
| | | 2 | 22% | 2 | 33% | 2 | 33% | |
| | | 6 | 67% | 2 | 33% | 1 | 17% | |
| | | 9 | 100% | 6 | 100% | 6 | 100% | |

| | | |
|---|---|---|
| **Loyal:** | Somewhat likely & very likely to stay as customer................. | $x^2$ p< 0.000, Cramér's V: 0.194 |
| **Maybe loyal** | Neither unlikely nor likely to stay as customer........................ | p< 0.213 (not significant) |
| **Defector** | Very unlikely & somewhat unlikely to stay as customer.......... | p< 0.010, V: 0.317 |
| **Cognitive:** | Mean of survey scores about (price, product) * | N= 683 |
| **Emotional:** | Mean of survey scores about (treatment, feelings, service, convenience) * | |

* Mean scores are first rounded; then 1&2 formed dissatisfied, 3 formed maybesatisfied and 4&5 formed satisfied.

Figures may not sum to 100%, because of rounding.

The percentages of loyal customers on the diagonal-line between bottom-left and upper-right corners (11% →50% →86%) indicate that loyalty consistently increases when cognitive and emotional satisfaction increase simultaneously. Defection also consistently decreases in the same diagonal line.

The percentages of loyal customers in the upper-row from right to left indicate that when cognitively satisfied, emotional satisfaction plays a modest role between satisfied and neutral customers, and a very strong role between neutral and dissatisfied customers in terms of loyalty. In this line, the loyalty decreases from 86% to 60% between satisfied and neutral customers, and sharply from 60% to 8% between neutral and dissatisfied customers as a result of a decline in emotional satisfaction. Dissatisfaction also consistently increases when emotional satisfaction decreases in the same line.

The percentages of loyal customers in the right-hand-side column from top to bottom indicate that when emotionally satisfied, cognitive satisfaction plays a very modest role in loyalty. In this line, loyalty decreases from 86% to 71% and to 50% as a result of a decline in cognitive dissatisfaction. Also the changes in defection are very modest in the same line.

It can thus be concluded that loyalty depends more on emotional dimension than on cognitive dimension, and therefore, customers seem to be more tolerant towards a decline in cognitive satisfaction than a decline in emotional satisfaction.

This conclusion is in line with the findings of Wetzels (1999), and somewhat more explicit than prior studies (Oliver, 1997:316; Mano & Oliver, 1993:451; Jones & Sassers, 1995:90) that tend to consider the weight of emotion and cognition equally in terms of loyalty (intentions).

#### 5.6.3.4 Research Question 3: What is the role of transactional & general satisfaction in customer loyalty (intentions)?

The ESCC survey results (Figure 5-13) also reveal the relationships between transactional (customer contact) satisfaction and general satisfaction and their effects on customer loyalty (intentions). In this analysis, loyal and maybe-loyal customers are significantly associated with transactional and general satisfaction, whereas defector customers' association is not significant. As the Cramér's V scores, 0.252 and 0.225 respectively indicate, associations of loyal and maybe-loyal customers are weak.

Figure 5-13: Transactional and General Satisfaction in Customer Loyalty

**TRANSACTIONAL vs GENERAL SATISFACTION in CUSTOMER LOYALTY**

Crosstabulation in number of respondents, and their percentages within their group.

| TRANSACTIONAL SATISFACTION | | GENERAL SATISFACTION: (very) Dissatisfied | | Neutral | | (very) Satisfied | |
|---|---|---|---|---|---|---|---|
| (very) Satisfied | Loyal | 7 | 29% | 15 | 42% | 435 | 87% |
| | Maybe loyal | 4 | 17% | 13 | 36% | 43 | 9% |
| | Defector | 13 | 54% | 8 | 22% | 23 | 5% |
| | | 24 | 100% | 36 | 100% | 501 | 100% |
| Neutral | Loyal | 4 | 27% | 12 | 63% | 38 | 70% |
| | Maybe loyal | 4 | 27% | 5 | 26% | 14 | 26% |
| | Defector | 7 | 47% | 2 | 11% | 2 | 4% |
| | | 15 | 100% | 19 | 100% | 54 | 100% |
| (very) Dissatisfied | Loyal | 4 | 24% | 7 | 70% | 18 | 67% |
| | Maybe loyal | 5 | 29% | 2 | 20% | 6 | 22% |
| | Defector | 8 | 47% | 1 | 10% | 3 | 11% |
| | | 17 | 100% | 10 | 100% | 27 | 100% |

| | | |
|---|---|---|
| **Loyal:** | Somewhat likely & very likely to stay as customer................. | $x^2$ p< 0.000, Cramér's V: 0.252 |
| **Maybe loyal:** | Neither unlikely nor likely to stay as customer......................... | p< 0.046, V: 0.225 |
| **Defector:** | Very unlikely & somewhat unlikely to stay as customer.......... | p< 0.071 (not significant) |
| **Transactional:** | Satisfaction level with the last transaction * | N= 703 |
| **General:** | General satisfaction level * | |

* Very Satisfied = strongly agree & agree; Neutral = neither agree nor disagree; Dissatisfied = strongly disagree & disagree

Figures may not sum to 100%, because of rounding.

The percentages of loyal customers on the diagonal-line between bottom-left and upper-right corners (24% →63% →87%) indicate that loyalty consistently increases when transactional and general satisfaction increase simultaneously. Defection also consistently decreases in the same diagonal line.

The percentages of loyal customers on the upper-row from right to left indicate that when satisfied with transaction (last call), general satisfaction plays a very strong role in loyalty as the loyalty intentions decrease from 87% to 42% and to

29% as a result of a decline in general satisfaction. Defection also consistently increases when general satisfaction decreases in the same line.

The percentages of loyal customers on the right-hand-side column from top to bottom indicate that when generally satisfied, transactional satisfaction plays a modest role in loyalty. In this line, the loyalty decreases from 87% to 70% and to 67% as a result of a decline in transactional satisfaction. Also the changes in defector customers are very slight in the same line.

The percentages of loyal customers in the middle column from top to bottom suggests that when general satisfaction is neutral, then transactional satisfaction plays a reverse (!) role in loyalty; i.e. loyalty tendencies increase from 42% to 63% and to 70% when transactional satisfaction decrease from satisfied to neutral and to dissatisfied. This finding is contradictory to the generally accepted marketing theories. As the numbers of customers linked to these specific percentages are 36, 19, and 10 respectively, a few extraordinary answers in the survey may have caused this contradiction. A future research, however, with more respondents might clarify this issue.

The percentages of loyal customers on the left-hand-side column from top to bottom indicate that when generally dissatisfied, the transactional satisfaction level has almost no effect on already low loyalty intentions. In this line, the loyalty decreases from 29% to 27% and to 24% as a result of a decline in transactional satisfaction. Also in this column, where customers are generally dissatisfied, about 50% of the customers have the intention to defect; and transactional satisfaction has again no effect on this tendency. It can be concluded from this picture that loyalty depends more on general satisfaction than on the last transactional satisfaction, and therefore, customers seem to be more tolerant towards a single transactional dissatisfaction than general dissatisfaction.

The added value of a transactional satisfaction, however, is among generally satisfied customers which are the vast majority of customers (82% in this case).[98] In this segment, the difference in loyalty intentions between a satisfactory and a neutral transaction is 17%,[99] and it is, therefore, still very important to uphold the transactional satisfaction levels of customers. After all, transactional and general satisfactions are interrelated and require each other's presence especially to generate stronger effects on both sides.

The findings presented above are complementary to the previous studies of Parasuraman, Zeithaml and Berry (1994:122) who argue that global evaluations are the aggregation of transaction experiences; Anderson, Fornell and Lehman (1994) who advocate 'cumulative satisfaction;' and Rust, Zahorik and Keiningham (1995:64) who suggest that both evaluations are equally useful.

[98] Customers who are generally satisfied, right-hand-side column (501+54+27=582), divided by total sample group (N=703) is 0.82.

[99] The absolute difference between the satisfied customers' loyalty intentions (87%) and the neutral customers' loyalty intentions (70%), at the right-hand-side column, is 17%.

#### 5.6.3.5 Research Question 4a & 4b: What is the role of transactional satisfaction in general satisfaction and in customer loyalty (intentions)?

The effects of transactional satisfaction on the general satisfaction and loyalty are further analyzed in the following two charts (Figure 5-14). These charts indicate significant, however somewhat weak associations between transactional and general satisfaction ($\chi^2$ p< 0.01; Cramér's V: 0.29), as well as, between transactional satisfaction and loyalty intentions ($\chi^2$ p< 0.01; Cramér's V: 0.21). As transactional satisfaction is measured by the last customer contact, it can be concluded that, albeit weakly, customer contacts (statistically) significantly changes customer satisfaction and loyalty intentions in the same direction.[100] In other words, the more positive the last contact, the stronger the general satisfaction and loyalty intention.

Figure 5-14: Relationship between Transactional Satisfaction, General Satisfaction, and Loyalty

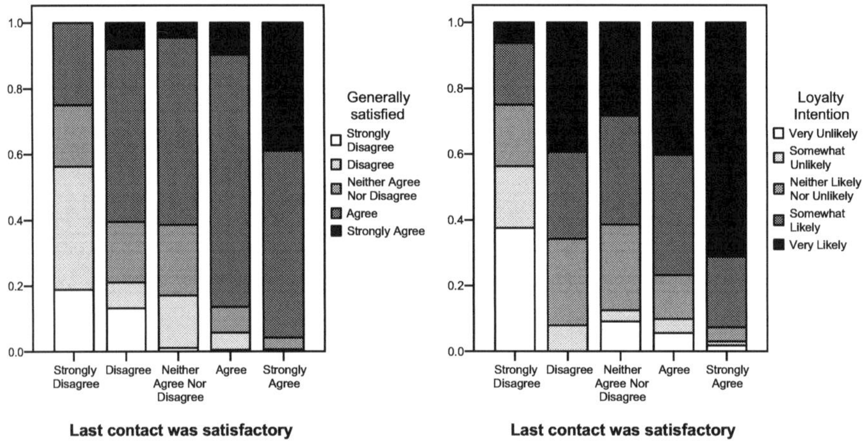


[100] Significant and positive correlations as analyzed in previous sections confirm these relationships. Correlation coefficient between transactional and general satisfaction is 0.43, and between transactional satisfaction and loyalty intention is 0.32 in this research.

## 5.7 Role of the Length of Relationship in Satisfaction and Loyalty

As Figure 5-15[101] shows, the length of relationship with a firm plays no significant ($\chi^2$ p< 0.68) role in customer's general satisfaction, but seems to play a significant role in loyalty intentions ($\chi^2$ p< 0.01). This finding is also confirmed with correlation analysis, which indicates that there is no significant relationship between the length of relationship and general satisfaction, and a significant (p< 0.01) but a weak positive correlation (0.22) between the length of relationship and loyalty intentions. This means that new customers, as well as, old customers expect and perceive the satisfaction with no significant differences. However, when several years pass, then customer's loyalty intentions gradually increase. It appears thus that customer satisfaction is an issue that plays a continuous and stable role during customer lifetime, on the other hand, customer loyalty appears to be strengthened with time.

It is also interesting to see (Figure 5-15) that the loyalty intentions are fairly high in the first two years of relationship, but declines sharply between 2nd and 4th years, and gradually increases together with the length of the relationship. Further research and analysis is necessary to comment in detail on this issue which falls outside the main focus of this research.

Figure 5-15: Length of Relationship vs. Satisfaction and Loyalty

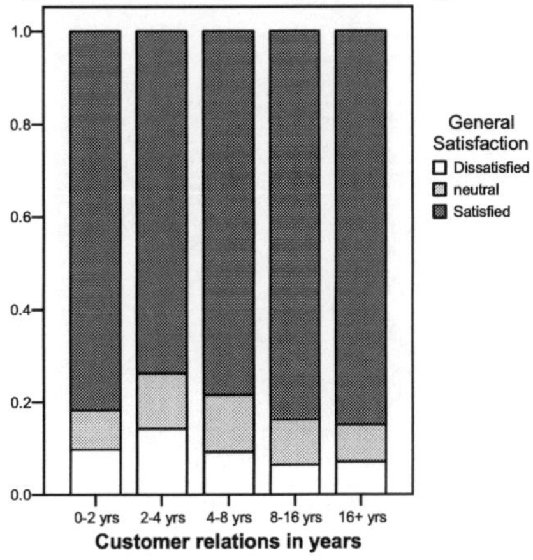


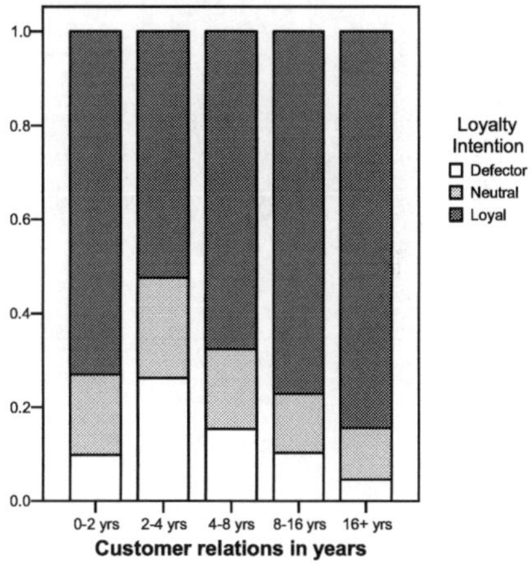


[101] Dissatisfied and Defector represent 1 & 2 in the 5-point scale responses of the related ESCC survey questions; Neutral represents the middle response possibility of 3; and Satisfied and Loyal represent 4 & 5 in the same scale.

## 5.8 Research Question 5: What is the role of time in evaluating transactional satisfaction?

The survey question "when was your last contact?" reveals the time factor in evaluation of last contacts. The association between 'the length of time' and evaluation of last contacts (transactional satisfaction) is significant ($\chi^2$ p< 0.01); however, as Cramér's V (0.11) and Spearman correlations (-0.14, p< 0.01) [102] indicate the strength of this association is weak.

As Figure 5-16 shows, most recent contacts (today) contain higher proportion of extreme answers than the rest of the group (week ago, month ago, etc). This fact was also consistently apparent in the previous comparisons between test and control group of customers, where test group of customers tend to chose more extreme answers. This confirms, thus, that customer contacts create momentum for building strong opinions about firms; and also indicates that strong perceptions about the last contact with firms fade and become more moderate when time passes.

Figure 5-16: Time Factor in Transactional Satisfaction

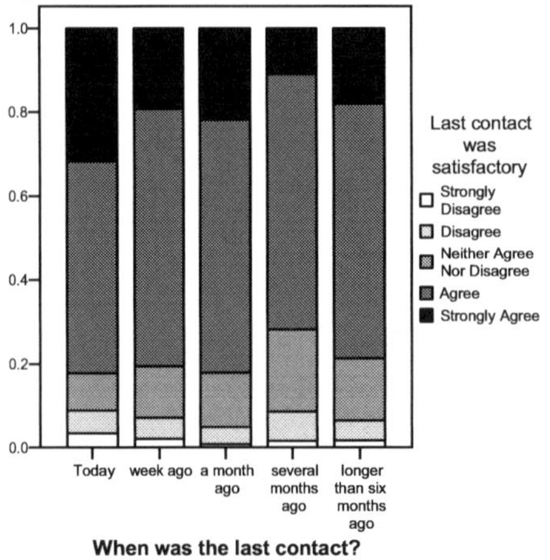


Thus, customer contact satisfaction can be particularly important close to the decision making moments of customers. For instance, when a customer calls a firm a few days before the renewal date of a yearly subscription, then the (emotional) impact of this contact would likely have a strong influence on the decision. The impact would, however, be less strong if the decision moment would be, for example, a few months ahead. According to Norman (1993:128) human memory is flawed: The things available in memory are apt to have one of two characteristics – they happened recently, or they had some unique, emotional impact. "Thus we remember recent events, instances of good fortune, and major calamities" (ibid).

[102] Negative correlation indicates when time increases then satisfaction decreases.

This finding has a strong potential in managerial implications. Since such decision moments can be specified and traced with customer information systems, such customer contacts can be treated differently. For instance, with the help of technology such customers may be connected to expert (sales) employees, and they may even be served quicker than the other customers whose decision moments are more distant. Consequently, a rapid service with expert assistance would increase the chances that the contact is more positively experienced, and this positive contact experience would increase customer satisfaction and loyalty intentions.

## 5.9 Summary & Concluding Remarks

This chapter explored emotional, cognitive, transactional, and general dimensions of customer satisfaction and loyalty, and described the relationships among them based on customer surveys done in four different test firms from different industries in The Netherlands.

Results showed that customers are least satisfied with prices, convenience, and service quality issues with their firms. Customers, however, appeared to be more loyal than they are satisfied, indicating that customer satisfaction cannot be translated directly to customer loyalty.

Almost all satisfaction items were moderately associated with general satisfaction, somewhat weaker with transactional satisfaction, and finally weakly with loyalty intentions. This outcome confirmed the effectiveness as well as the necessity of analyzing customer loyalty with more specific constructs (cf. Reichheld, 1993:71; 1996:58).

Mann-Whitney U test indicated a significant difference between test and control group customers in their 'transactional satisfaction.' Differences were, however, both in the positive as well as in the negative side. More positive responses among the test group customers, on the one hand indicated that firms can increase customer satisfaction if they create an environment similar to the ESCC test days; on the other hand more negative responses among the same group of customers also showed that with only 'extra smile and attention' firms cannot fully compensate their other shortcomings. It appeared thus customer contacts create a strong momentum for building intense opinions about the contacted firms.

There was no difference found between the test and the control group customers in other satisfaction items, nor in terms of loyalty intentions.

Kruskal-Wallis H statistics, on the one hand indicated that product, service treatment, positive feelings, and loyalty intentions differed significantly among industries. On the other hand general satisfaction, prices, convenience, service quality, and satisfaction with last contact did not significantly differ among the firms, thus are considered as common denominators across industries.

Although the *book & music* firm showed relatively higher satisfaction scores, customer loyalty intentions were lowest in comparison with the other test firms. The *insurance* firm had the highest ratio of very negative contacts, but relatively high loyalty intentions. The *pension fund* customers were highly satisfied and also highly loyal to their firms. The *bank* customers demonstrated a high dissatisfaction, but also high loyalty intentions.

Based on the principal component analysis, positive feelings for the firm, service quality, service treatment, and convenience items are grouped under the 'emotional satisfaction' dimension; and prices and products under the 'cognitive satisfaction' dimension.

Cross-tabulation analyses with the dimensions of satisfaction showed that emotional dimension consistently plays a more important role than cognitive dimension in transactional satisfaction, in general satisfaction, and in loyalty. Despite the importance of emotional aspects it is, however, contradictory to observe that many firms still heavily rely on cognitive aspects like prices. Recent examples vary from Dutch supermarkets, that are struggling with 'price-wars', to publishing or telecom industries that constantly give large discounts for new subscribers.

Although loyalty appeared to be depending more on general satisfaction than on transactional satisfaction, the ESCC surveys indicated that transactional and general satisfaction are interrelated and require each other's presence to generate a stronger effect on both sides. It also appeared that *the more positive the customer contacts with firms, the stronger the general satisfaction and loyalty intentions*.

Furthermore, the length of the relationship with firms played no significant role in customer's general satisfaction process, but seemed to play a significant role in customer loyalty intentions. Finally, it appeared that customer contacts create a momentum for building strong opinions about firms, and customer perceptions about the last contact with firms fade and become more moderate when time passes.

# 6 THE ESCC OBSERVATIONS: TEST DAY RESULTS

As the previous chapter indicated, the emotional dimension plays a stronger role in customer satisfaction and loyalty process than the cognitive dimension. This chapter will now investigate whether the emotional satisfaction can be observed during customer contacts by customer service representatives (CSR). Therefore, this chapter will outline the results of the experimentations of the ESCC methodologies, as described in chapter 3, in test firms during the test days. It will also assess the accuracy of the ESCC observations, and will investigate the relationship between the observed ESCC, customer satisfaction, and loyalty intentions.

## 6.1 Survey Settings

During the test days, selected CSRs[103] evaluated all incoming (inbound) calls they received with the ESCC principles while doing their routine tasks. Prior to the ESCC evaluations, they received a very brief introduction to the research rather than an extensive training due to the limitations in using test firm resources. The ESCC evaluations are therefore made more or less with CSRs 'common sense' or 'gut-feelings,' rather than with a structural ESCC methodology.

The ESCC have not changed normal business day routines in test firms, except for the additional task of observing and evaluating customer satisfaction and related emotions. CSRs evaluated each call, rated them between 1 (very negative) to 5 (very positive) representing the red-orange-yellow-green-blue spectrum, and noted the ratings either on a spreadsheet or on a paper-form. They also noted the customer data like name, account number, and telephone number. Customers were neither aware of these evaluations, nor did they know about the pending survey.

At least a few hours after the customer contacts, or the next day, different CSRs called the test group customers as if they were randomly selected for a routine 'customer satisfaction survey.' Again no ESCC evaluations had been mentioned to customers. Outbound CSRs called *all* customers in the test group with no particular selection criteria. Therefore, everyone in the test group had equal chance to respond to the survey. Those customers, who were reached and who were willing to participate, were surveyed with the same questionnaire as the control group customers who were randomly selected from the firm database. Survey question (How would you evaluate your last telephone contact with the

[103] CSRs are selected during the test day by the test firm management. It is requested that the selected CSRs should represent the averages of their contact center in terms of age, education, and experience.

firm?)[104] is used for comparing the inbound CSRs' ESCC evaluations with customers ratings.

During the test days CSRs also observed their own feelings and self-rated them in a 5-point scale, from very negative to very positive, with 30 minutes intervals.

For more information about the general settings and descriptive statistics please refer to Survey Settings in chapter 5, on page (53).

## 6.2 Frequency Distribution in ESCC Observations

A total of 842 calls have been rated by 38 CSRs in 4 different firms during test days, and 300 of them could have been verified by customer surveys. As Figure 6-1 shows, CSR evaluations were mainly neutral and positive. The ESCC evaluations at the pension fund firm and the book & music firm were most positive, and at the insurance firm most negative. $\chi^2$ test showed a significant frequency distribution ($p< 0.01$); and differences among the firms were also significant (Kruskal-Wallis test, $p< 0.01$).

Figure 6-1: Observed ESCC Frequency Distribution

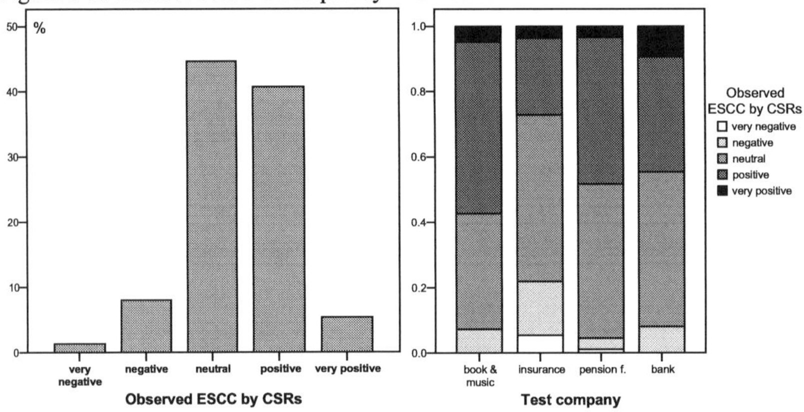


Frequency distributions both in verified calls and all calls were similar, indicating that evaluated customers formed a representative sample group, as shown in Table 6-1.

Table 6-1: CSRs' ESCC Evaluations

| The ESCC in 4 firms (Frequency Distribution in %) | Very Negative | Negative | Neutral | Positive | Very Positive |
|---|---|---|---|---|---|
| Among verified calls (N=300) | 1.3 | 8.0 | 44.7 | 40.7 | 5.3 |
| Among all evaluated calls (N=842) | 0.8 | 6.1 | 46.0 | 43.2 | 3.9 |

[104] Although customer responses were between very negative-very positive, they are tabulated as strongly agree-strongly disagree so that they are not confused with the ESCC ratings.

## 6.3 Research Question 6: What are the (emotional) satisfaction levels in customer contacts?

As shown in Figure 6-2, when CSR evaluations, test group evaluations and control group evaluations are compared, it appears that *test group* customers perceived their encounters most positively.[105] There might be two reasons for this. Firstly, CSRs indeed may have performed better because an interest is taken in their work, and they also knew that the customer would be surveyed soon -- the Hawthorne Effect (Mayo, 1933). Secondly, CSRs may have performed better because their awareness of customer satisfaction and emotions were stimulated by the research settings, that might be called the ESCC Effect.

*Control group* customers were also more positive than CSRs, however, their ratings were somewhat tempered with less extreme answers than test group customers. These less sharp evaluations might be either due to less positive service experiences or due to the fact that their last contacts were not recent and, therefore, their effects were diminished by time.

*CSRs* evaluated the majority of calls as 'neutral' or 'positive.' This is actually a conceivable scenario as the majority of customer contacts occur in 'neutral' circumstances like 'a straight question and a straight answer.' When customers show a little more appreciation than a habitual 'thank you,' then they might have been considered as a positive contact by CSRs during test days. Moreover, a neutral evaluation is also frequently used when customer contacts had positive as well as negative episodes during the same contact. Discrepancies therefore, mostly occurred in neutral CSR ratings. There was however, much less discrepancy in negative or very negative areas.

When the rough averages of CSRs, control and test group customers are taken into consideration it appears that about 10% of customer contacts are considered as negative and very negative, about 20% neutral, about 50% positive, and 20% very positive. Nevertheless, when specific sample groups are analyzed, then some sharp differences appear. For instance, the percentage of negative and very negative evaluations in the test group of insurance firm was 23.6%, whereas, the same percentage in book & music firm was only 2.4%.

These differences indicate that the ESCC may vary among industries and may even vary among firms, depending on their products, processes, customer contact and problem solving strategies, and available resources. For example, firms with customer friendly products and processes would less likely create customer frustrations; and when such frustrations would arise, then they would handle them without any further frustrations, at least, if they had proper strategy and resources for solving such issues.

---

[105] In the insurance firm, test group customers were primarily health insurance customers who called in the test day; whereas control group customers were health and non-health insurance customers from the Internet channel. As the health insurance calls are much more problematic than other insurance areas, the perception comparisons in this firm are different than the other firms.

Figure 6-2: The ESCC Perceptions among CSRs, Test and Control Group Customers

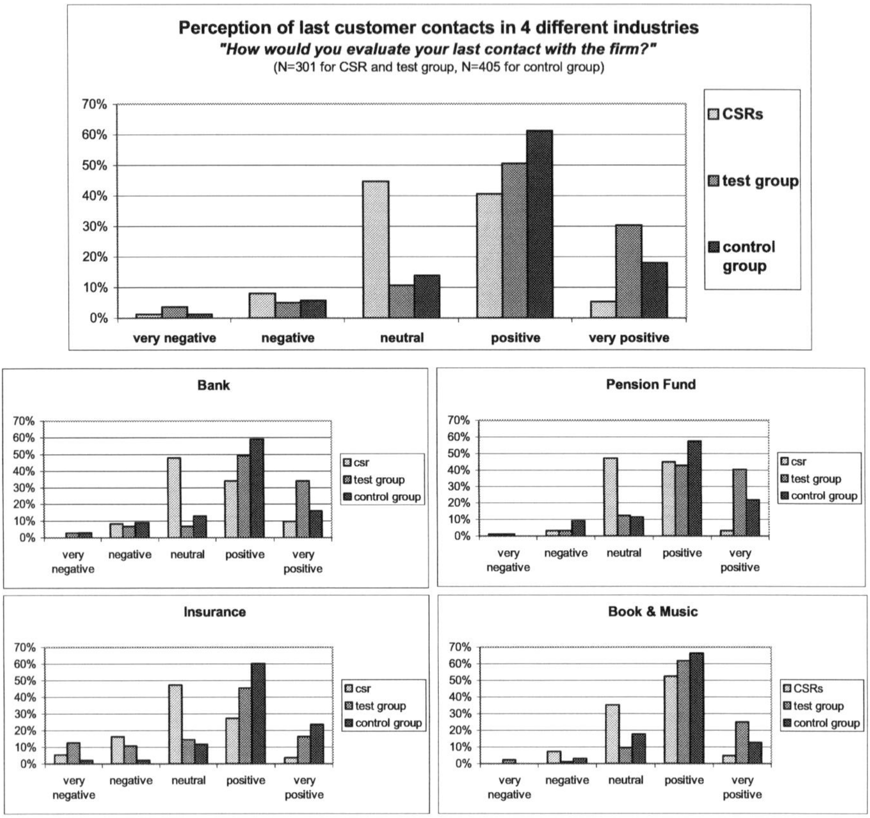


## 6.4 Accuracy of the ESCC Observations

Bitner, Booms and Mohr (1994:96) suggest that frontline personnel are a critical source of information about customers and such personnel have a better understanding of customer needs and problems than others in the firm. Nevertheless, "in some industries in which service encounters are less routine, contact employees may not be as accurate in their assessment of customer expectations and satisfaction" (ibid., p.103).[106] The ESCC research will provide some more empirical evidence on the above subject. As the test group service encounters are evaluated by CSRs, and as these customers are surveyed afterwards by different CSRs, it will be possible to compare these views.

Accuracy variables are calculated by taking the difference between 'customer evaluation' about the last contact (survey question 9) and the 'ESCC observations' of CSRs. As both variables are in a 5-point scale, the maximum deviation could be +/- 4. Survey results presented here, however, varied between

[106] As cited in Bitner, Booms & Mohr (1994:103): See Brown & Schwarz (1989). A Gap Analysis of Professional Service Quality. *Journal of Marketing*, 53 (April), 92-98.

-2 and +2. Positive differences in accuracy indicate that customers are more positive, and negative differences indicate that customers are more negative than CSRs. Positive differences can be interpreted as *safe deviations* as CSRs in the worst case scenario would give a false alarm, whereas, negative differences can be interpreted as *alarming deviations* as CSRs overestimate customer satisfaction or underestimate customer dissatisfaction.

As shown in Table 6-2 and Figure 6-3, customers on average evaluated 34% (ranging from 29% to 43%) of the calls the same as CSRs, 42% (ranging from 36% to 49%) of the encounters 1 scale more positive than CSRs, and 14% (ranging from 7% to 19%) of the encounters 2 scales more positive than CSRs. This positive tendency is in line with many customer satisfaction surveys where customers tend to give more "socially desirable" (positive) answers and tend to "yeah saying" (Nancarrow & Brace, 2000).[107] The critical zone, however, is where customer evaluations are less positive than CSRs. These ratings were on average less than 10% (ranging from 6% to 13%) and thus can be considered as acceptable, especially for the initial test days.

To offset the effects of 1-scale-difference, especially between neutral and positive evaluations, customer and CSR evaluations are re-grouped into three classes: Negative and very negative evaluations (1&2) formed one, neutral and positive evaluations (3&4) formed the other, and very positive evaluations (5) formed the last class. As shown in Figure 6-4, re-grouped accuracies increased sharply to about 60% for correct observations. With this grouped scales, on average about 30% of customers were still 1-scale more positive than the CSRs; and about 5% were less positive. When 1-scale-differences, where customers are 1-score more positive than CSRs, are tolerated and considered as correct, then the accuracy of observations reached near 80% (Figure 6-5).

Accuracy varied among the firms during test days. Book & music firm CSRs seem to be the most accurate, followed by the insurance firm. CSRs at the bank deviated in all directions and in all scales when assessing the ESCC. Finally, CSRs at the pension fund evaluated half of the calls as 1 scale less positive than their customers.

Table 6-2: ESCC Accuracy in Test Firms

| ESCC Accuracy (Frequency Distribution in %) | Book & music | Insurance | Pension F. | Bank | ALL firms |
|---|---|---|---|---|---|
| customer 2 scales less positive | 2.5 | 9.1 | 0 | 2.7 | 3.0 |
| customer 1 scale less positive | 3.7 | 3.6 | 6.1 | 11.0 | 6.4 |
| CSR Correct | 43.2 | 34.5 | 29.2 | 28.8 | 33.9 |
| customer 1 scale more positive | 35.8 | 45.5 | 49.4 | 38.4 | 42.3 |
| customer 2 scales more positive | 14.8 | 7.3 | 14.6 | 19.2 | 14.4 |

[107] They also refer to: Kalton & Schuman (1991). The Effect of the Question on Survey Responses: a review. *Journal of the Royal Statistical Society,* 145, Part 1, 42-73.

Figure 6-3: The ESCC Accuracy in test Firms

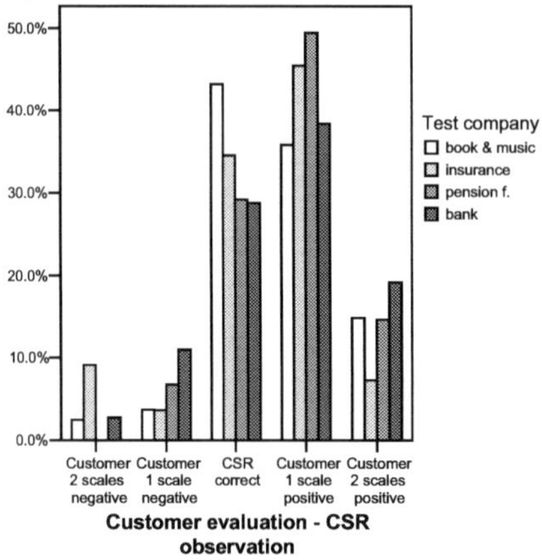


Figure 6-4: The ESCC Accuracy in Combined Scales: 1&2, 3&4, 5

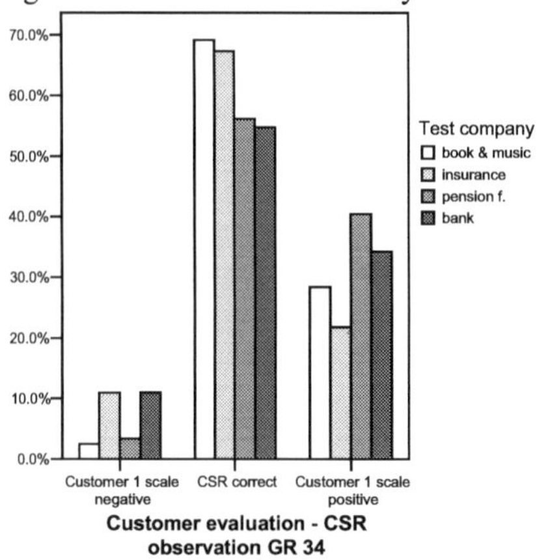


Figure 6-5: The ESCC Accuracy (+1 is tolerated)

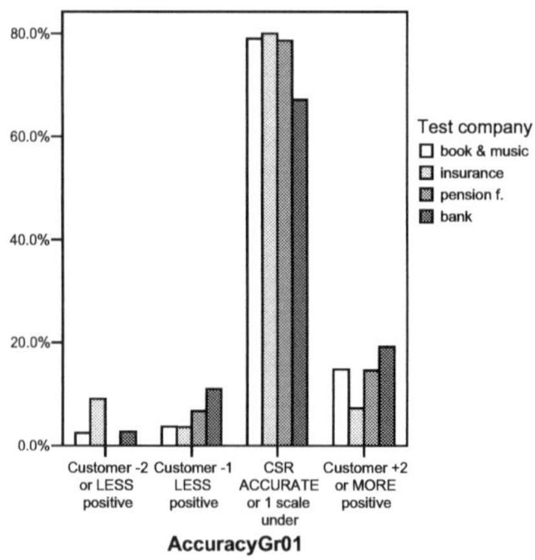

### *6.4.1 The ESCC Accuracy and Cross-tabulations*

Figure 6-6 is drawn from cross tabulations of CSR observations and customer evaluations about the same contact. This chart is particularly interesting as it also shows the proportion of the accuracy levels. For example, the column on the left side shows that when CSRs evaluate a 'very negative' contact it is also entirely true for customers; because all customers in this segment also 'strongly disagree' with the statement of 'last contact was satisfactory.' The proportion of disagreement also gradually declines in other columns representing more positive evaluations.

The column on the right side shows that when CSRs evaluate a 'very positive' contact, it is then mostly true for the customers; because the majority of the customers in this segment 'strongly agree' with the statement. The proportion of agreement again gradually declines in other columns representing less positive evaluations.

The column in the middle represents 'neutral' evaluation of CSRs, but contains mostly positive customer evaluations together with some negative evaluations. It seems that the ESCC accuracy decreases in neutral evaluations and increases with the intensity of the perceived satisfaction by CSRs. In other words, the more intense the customer contacts the more accurate the CSR evaluations in customer satisfaction.

Figure 6-6: The ESCC Accuracies with CSR's Perspective

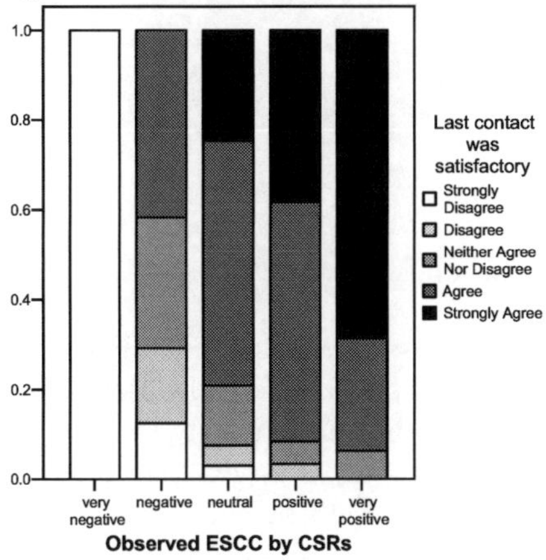


The previous chart sketched the situation when CSRs segment the calls. The following chart (Figure 6-7), sketching the same situation from a different angle, shows the proportion of the accuracy levels from the customer's perspective. For example, the column on the left side shows that when customers 'strongly disagree' with the statement 'last contact was satisfactory', about 1/3 of them are evaluated as 'very negative' by CSRs, about 1/3 as 'negative', and about 1/3 as 'neutral.' The proportion of negative evaluations gradually declines in other columns representing more positive evaluations.

The column on the right side shows that when customers 'strongly agree' with the statement 'last contact was satisfactory', about 1/10 of them are evaluated as 'very positive' by CSRs, about 1/2 as 'positive', and about 1/3 as 'neutral'. The proportion of positive evaluations declines gradually in other columns representing less positive customer evaluations.

The column in the middle shows that when customers 'neither agree, nor disagree' with the statement 'last contact was satisfactory', about half of them are evaluated as 'neutral' by CSRs, about 1/4 as 'negative', and about 1/4 as 'positive'.

It appears thus that CSRs do not capture all customers in a specific satisfaction segment that is based on customer evaluations; nevertheless, when CSRs segment the customers then their accuracies become more reliable.

Figure 6-7: The ESCC Accuracies with Customers' Perspective

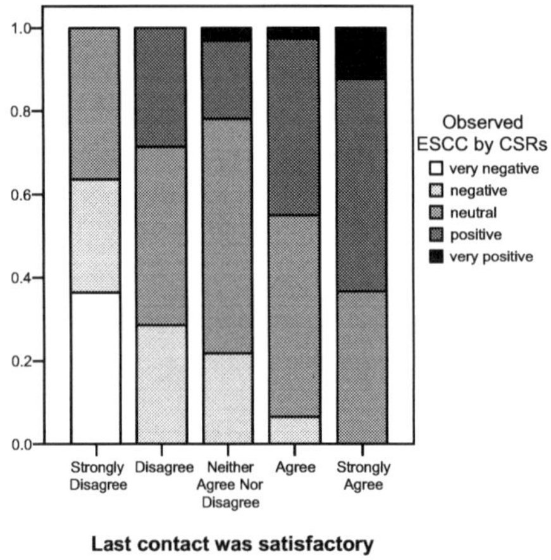


### *6.4.2 The ESCC Accuracy and Cohen's Kappa*

Cohen's Kappa is a statistic which is used to assess inter-rater reliability when observing or coding categorical variables. It calculates the equal observations [accuracy] of two raters [customer and CSR] on the same object [the ESCC]. Kappa has a range from 0.00 to 1.00 from which values larger than 0.70 are considered satisfactory. The calculated Kappa statistic for the ESCC observations is 0.09 which is very low.[108] This figure is low due to the fact that the majority of the ratings were not accurate but around the 1-scale differences. The important question that arises here is whether there are some patterns in those ratings and in their deviations. Therefore, further analyses are performed to investigate the ESCC observations and their accuracies.

[108] When the scales are grouped by (1&2, 3, 4&5) then the Kappa slightly increased to 0.159; also the grouping in 1&2, 3&4, 5 did not change the situation as the Kappa remained very low (0.147).

### *6.4.3 The ESCC Accuracy and Boxplot*

To analyse the accuracies[109] per observation scale (label) a boxplot is drawn (Figure 6-8). Boxplots are used for graphical analysis of quantitative variables (Bethlehem & De Gooijer, 1999). Bryman and Cramer (2005:112) describe the shapes in boxplots as follows: "The box comprises the middle 50 percent of observations. Thus, the lower end of the box, in terms of the measure to which it refers, is the first quartile and the upper end is the third quartile. In other words, the box comprises the inter-quartile range. The line in the box is the median. The broken lines (the whiskers) extend downwards to the lowest value in the distribution and upwards to the largest value excluding outliers, that is, extreme values which are separately indicated." Outliers are shown with their case numbers in the database; (o) indicates a single case, and a (*) indicates that there are more outliers.

Figure 6-8: The ESCC Accuracies with Boxplot

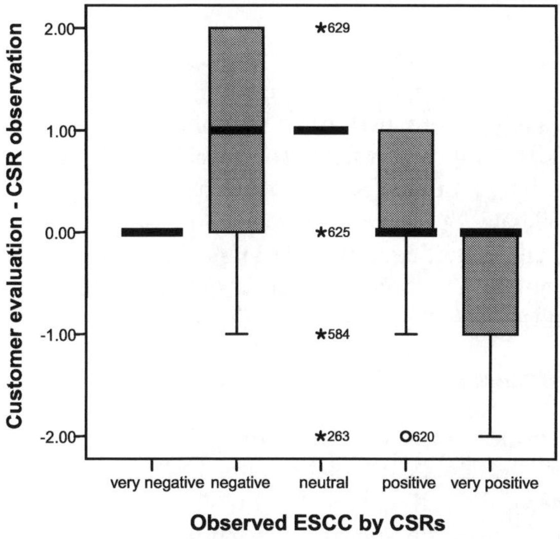


As shown in Figure 6-8:

- CSRs were always correct in their 'very negative' observations.
- 'Negative' observations were generally between accurate and two-scales more positive area with a median at +1, indicating that data is skewed towards the positive area, and customers were in more cases more positive than CSRs. There were also cases to a lesser extent where customers were one-scale under CSRs.

---

[109] Accuracy is calculated as 'customer evaluation' minus 'CSR evaluation.' Thus, zero means full accuracy, +1 means customer is one-scale more positive than CSR, and -1 means customer is one-scale less positive than CSR.

- 'Neutral' observations however, deviated in all directions in all scales and therefore formed the least accurate category. The median, at +1, indicates that data is skewed towards positive area, and customers were in many cases one-scale more positive than CSRs.
- 'Positive' observations were generally between the accurate (median) and one-scale more positive area, where customers were one-score more positive than CSRs. There were also, to a lesser extent, one-scale-negative cases where customers were 'neutral', and a single case (620) where a customer was even 'negative.'
- 'Very positive' observations were generally between the accurate (median) and one-scale-negative area, where customers were only 'positive' instead of 'very positive.' There were also, to a lesser extent, two-scales-negative cases where customers were 'neutral.'

### *6.4.4 The ESCC Accuracies and Associative Analysis*

To assess the strength as well as the direction of the associations between CSR observations and customer evaluations about the same calls, $\chi^2$ analysis, related Cramér's V, and correlation analyses are performed. Results of $\chi^2$ analysis indicate that there is a significant association between the ESCC ratings and customer evaluations; and the strength of this association according to Cramér's V figure (0.36, $p< 0.01$) is moderate. Spearman's correlation coefficient (0.39) also confirms this moderate and significant ($p< 0.01$) positive association between CSR observations and customer evaluations about the same calls representing transactional satisfactions.

### *6.4.5 Aspects That May Influence the ESCC Accuracies*

The aspects that may influence the accuracy level of the ESCC observations such as customer age, gender, the length of relationship, CSR age, gender, education, experience, and time of the call, are analyzed with cross-tabulations and correlations analysis. Nevertheless, no significant relationship was found. However, practicing the ESCC observations for a longer time, and calibrating it by frequently comparing them with customer evaluations enhance the accuracies. For example, accurate observations increased from 30% to 45% in one Dutch financial organization over a month period.[110]

[110] Such longer term implementations occurred in different conditions, and are thus not identically comparable with each other, as well as, with the test firms. Therefore, their results are not extensively used in this text.

### *6.4.6 Research Question 7: Can CSRs accurately observe (emotional) satisfaction during customer contacts?*

Previous sections analyzed the accuracy of the ESCC which is calculated by taking the difference between 'customer evaluation' on the last contact (survey question 9) and the 'ESCC observation' of CSRs on the same contact. In one-on-one comparisons, the average accuracy appeared to be only 34% on average. When the data was re-grouped into three classes (1&2, 3&4, 5), the average accuracy increased to about 60%. When 1-scale-differences, where customers are more positive than CSRs, were considered as accurate, then the accuracy of observations reached near 80%. Accuracy rates varied among the test firms being more accurate in book & music and in insurance firms, and less accurate in pension fund and in the bank.

*Cross-tabulation* analysis indicated that CSRs did not capture all customers in a specific satisfaction segment when this segment is based on customer evaluations. However, when CSRs segmented the customers with their ESCC evaluations, then their accuracies become more reliable. CSRs were more accurate in extreme scales and even more accurate in negative cases; thus, the more intense the customer contacts the more accurate the CSR evaluations in customer satisfaction. *Cohen's Kappa* statistic indicated a very low reliability due to high proportion of cases where customer evaluations were 1-scale more positive than CSRs. The *Boxplot* chart confirmed the accuracies in extreme-ends and inaccuracies in neutral zones. It also illustrated that the deviations were mostly in 'safe zones' where customer evaluations were more positive than CSRs. Results of $\chi^2$ *analysis* showed a significant and a moderately strong association between the ESCC ratings and customer evaluations (Cramér's V: 0.36, $p < 0.01$). Furthermore, Spearman's *correlation coefficient* (0.39) also confirmed this moderately strong, significant ($p < 0.01$), and positive association.

The ESCC thus appeared to be a reasonably accurate indicator, rather than a precise tool, for assessing satisfaction in customer contacts, and also has the potential to be more accurate when practiced for a longer period of time.

## 6.5 Research Question 8: What is the relationship between the ESCC and CSR's emotions?

In order to observe the relationship between the ESCC observations, and thus perceived customer emotions, and CSR's own emotions, two types of measurements have been experimented. In the first measurement, CSRs were asked about their own emotions every half-hour with the same scale as the ESCC. As the question "*how do you feel*?" was about the last half-hour, CSRs answers likely represented moods rather than specific emotions of those moments.[111] These measurements showed no significant correlations.

[111] Emotions are generally of short duration and are associated with a specific stimulus. Moods, in contrast, are more enduring, more diffuse, and less related to specific stimuli. The difference between,

However, in another measurement in a Dutch financial organization other than the test firms, CSRs were asked to rate their own emotions each time they rate an ESCC. The number of ratings, over 300, was this time thus equal to the number of ESCC ratings. This measurement showed a significant positive correlation (0.56, $p < 0.01$) between the ESCC ratings and CSR's own emotions.[112]

It appears thus, emotions in customer contact environment are continuously changing, and CSRs' own emotions are interrelated with how they perceive customer emotions (ESCC). Furthermore, CSRs are continually exposed to trembling customer emotions (or vice-versa); and these emotions have a clear impact on how CSRs feel immediately after calls, but no clear impact on how CSRs feel after several different calls.

## 6.6 Research Question 9a: What is the relationship between the ESCC and Emotional & Cognitive Satisfaction?

As the accuracy of the ESCC observations are reasonably established in the previous sections, other analyses can also be conducted. To start with, the relationship between the ESCC, emotional and cognitive satisfaction are investigated.

In the previous chapter, principal component analysis has indicated that emotional satisfaction includes the satisfaction elements of positive feelings for the firm, service quality, service treatment, and convenience; and cognitive satisfaction includes price and product. As also used in the previous chapter, emotional satisfaction was calculated by taking the arithmetic mean of the survey scores of positive feelings for the firm, service quality, service treatment, and convenience. Cognitive satisfaction was calculated by taking the arithmetic mean of the survey scores of price and products.

When cross tabulated, chi-square analysis reveals that the ESCC ratings and emotional satisfaction is significantly ($\chi^2$ $p < 0.01$) and moderately associated (Cramér's V: 0.35). Spearman's correlation coefficient (0.31) indicates a significant ($p < 0.01$) but a weak relationship between the ESCC ratings and emotional satisfaction. On the other hand, the association between the ESCC ratings and cognitive satisfaction is significant ($\chi^2$ $p < 0.01$) but weak (Cramér's V (0.24, $p < 0.01$) similar to its correlation (0.23, $p < 0.01$).

The ESCC observations thus associate more strongly with emotional satisfaction than with cognitive satisfaction. This result is inline with initial expectations. However, the strength of the association between the emotional satisfaction and the ESCC, weak to moderate, is less strong than initial expectations.

---

emotion and mood is that emotion is directed toward something, but mood is a general state (Frijda, 1993).

[112] Such longer term implementations occurred in different conditions, and are thus not identically comparable with each other, as well as, with the test firms. Therefore, their results are not extensively used in this text.

## 6.7 The ESCC Relationship with Transactional Satisfaction, General Satisfaction, and Loyalty

Previous sections displayed, albeit moderately, the accuracy of the ESCC and its association with the emotional dimension of customer satisfaction. This section will attempt to analyze the relationship between the ESCC and transactional satisfaction (with last contact), general satisfaction, and customer loyalty intentions. To do so, firstly correlation coefficients will be examined, and then correspondence analyses will be performed, finally cross-tabs and $\chi^2$ analyses will be carried out.

### *6.7.1 Correlation Analysis*

Spearman's correlation coefficients significantly ($p < 0.01$) indicate that there is a positive relationship between the ESCC observations of CSRs and general satisfaction (0.30), transactional satisfaction (0.39), and loyalty intentions (0.27) of customers. The strengths of coefficients however, indicate a weak relationship for general satisfaction and loyalty, and moderate relationship for the transactional satisfaction.

As the ESCC observations correlate relatively higher with transactional satisfaction than the other items in this survey (Table 6-3), it seems that the ESCC observations are more suitable for identifying transactional satisfaction of customer contacts than the other measured items in this research.

Table 6-3: The ESCC Correlations with Other Survey Items

| Survey Items | Correlations with ESCC (Spearman's rho*) |
|---|---|
| Generally satisfied | 0.30 |
| Prices are satisfactory | 0.13 |
| Products are satisfactory | 0.22 |
| It is convenient to be firm's customer | 0.28 |
| Satisfied the way the firm treats him/her | 0.28 |
| Reliable, accurate, and timely services | 0.28 |
| Positive feelings for the firm | 0.21 |
| Last contact was satisfactory | 0.39 |
| Loyalty Intention | 0.27 |

* All items are significant; prices at the 0.05 level, others at the 0.01 level

### *6.7.2 Correspondence Analysis: The ESCC & Customer Evaluations*

Correspondence analysis is a graphical procedure for representing associations in a table of frequencies or counts. The output charts actually make the relative positions of all items visible on a plot. The plot produced by this analysis contains two sets of points: a set of 'Observed ESCC' points corresponding to rows and a set of 'Customer Evaluation' points corresponding to columns. More specifically, one of the dimensions in the plot represents the ESCC observations of CSRs, whereas, the other dimension represents the customer evaluations on the related subject. The positions of the points then reflect the associations between the two variables: CSRs ESCC observations and customer evaluations. The output of correspondence analysis is the "best" two-dimensional representation of the data, along with the coordinates of the plotted points, and a measure (called the *inertia*) of the amount of information retained in each dimension (Johnson & Wichern, 2002:709).

This section will focus on the plots only. Cumulative inertia of two dimensions and p-values associated with chi-square analyses of contingency tables will also be noted under the plots. Correspondence tables and summary analyses, however, can be found in appendix (11.10).

#### 6.7.2.1 The ESCC and Transactional Satisfaction

As shown in Figure 6-9 CSRs ESCC observations (between very negative and very positive) and customer evaluations (between strongly disagree and strongly agree) about their last contacts (transactional satisfaction) are plotted according to their associations with each other. The plot shows that:

- 'Very negative' and 'strongly disagree' are separated from the rest.
- 'Negative' and 'disagree' are separated from all positive evaluations but close to neither/nor agreement area of the customers.
- 'Neutral' ESCC observations are located very close to 'agree' in customer evaluations which are 1-scale more positive.
- 'Positive' observations are located between 'agree' and 'strongly agree' evaluations which is the accurate area.
- Finally 'very positive' observations are separated from the rest, and are positioned close to 'strongly agree' and 'agree' area.

These associations suggest that the more extreme the CSR observations the closer their associations with customer's transactional satisfaction with their last contacts.

Figure 6-9: Correspondence Analysis: The ESCC and Transactional Satisfaction

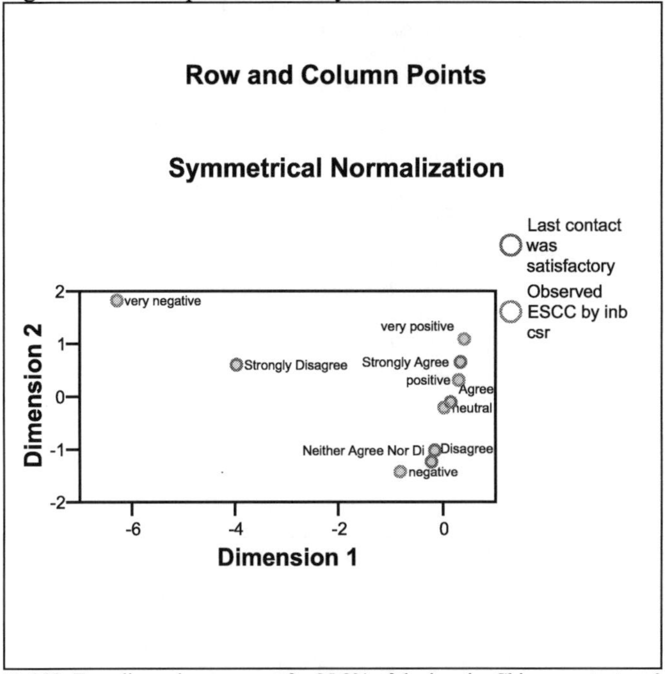


N=298; Two dimensions account for 95.8% of the inertia; Chi-square test p< 0.01.

#### 6.7.2.2 The ESCC and General Satisfaction

As shown in Figure 6-10, CSRs ESCC observations (between very negative and very positive) and customer evaluations (between strongly disagree and strongly agree) with general satisfaction are plotted according to their associations with each other. The plot shows that:

- 'Very negative' and 'strongly disagree' are clearly separated from neutral and positive evaluations and less clearly from 'negative' and 'disagree' evaluations.
- 'Neutral' ESCC observations are located between 'neither agree nor disagree' and 'agree' zones.
- 'Positive' and 'very positive' observations are located together with 'agree' and 'strongly agree' evaluations which is the accurate area.

These associations again suggest that the more extreme the CSR observations the closer their associations with customer's general satisfaction evaluations.

Figure 6-10: Correspondence Analysis: The ESCC and General Satisfaction

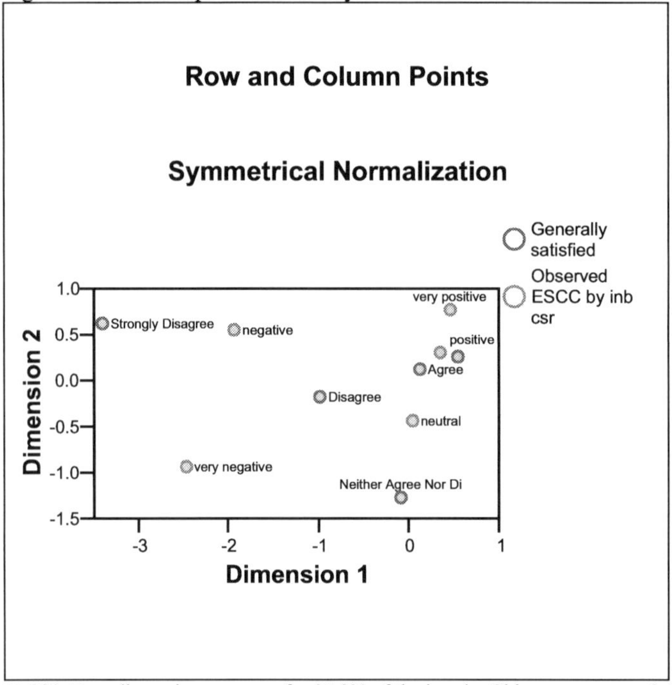


N=300; Two dimensions account for 97.8% of the inertia; Chi-square test $p < 0.01$.

#### 6.7.2.3 The ESCC and Loyalty Intentions

CSRs ESCC observations (between very negative and very positive) and customer loyalty intentions (between very unlikely and very likely) are plotted according to their associations with each other. As shown in Figure 6-11:

- 'Very negative' observations are clearly separated from the rest. 'Very negative' and 'negative' observations are on the same side with 'very unlikely' and 'somewhat unlikely.'
- 'Negative' observations are quite close to 'very unlikely' intentions, and again on the same side of 'somewhat unlikely.'
- 'Neutral' ESCC observations are located between 'somewhat likely' and 'very likely'.
- 'Positive' observations are located close to 'very likely', and also around 'neither likely nor unlikely' area.
- And finally, 'very positive' observations are separated from the rest, and are positioned close to 'somewhat likely' area.

These associations suggest that (very) negative ESCC observations are related to (very) negative loyalty intentions; neutral and (very) positive ESCC observations are related to neutral and (very) positive loyalty intentions. Although the distinctions are not crystal clear among negative observations and intentions as well as among positive observations and intentions, the ESCC observations separated the loyalty intentions into two groups: possible defectors (unlikely or somewhat unlikely to stay as customer) and the others.

Figure 6-11: Correspondence Analysis: The ESCC and Loyalty Intention

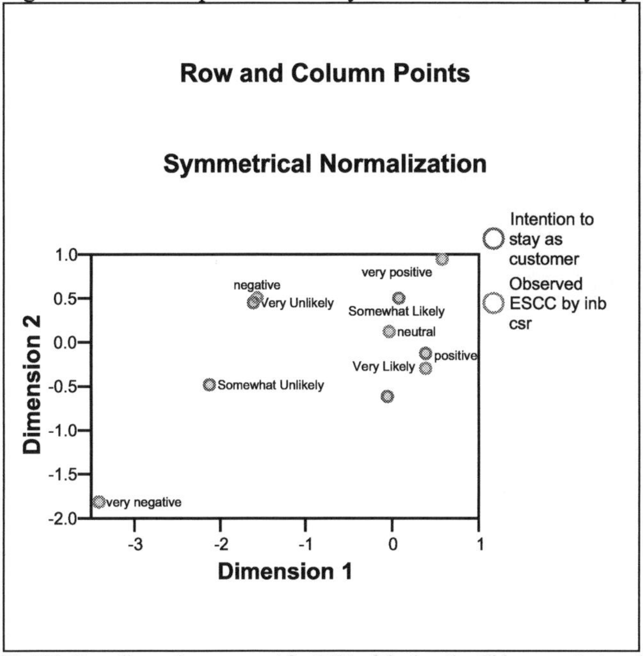


N=296; Two dimensions account for 94% of the inertia; Chi-square test $p< 0.01$.

### *6.7.3 Cross-Tabulation Analysis*

In the previous section, correspondence analyses graphically illustrated the relative positions and associations between the CSRs ESCC observations and customer evaluations on transactional satisfaction, general satisfaction, and loyalty intentions. This section will analyze the same combinations with cross-tabulations and bar charts to support the initial suggestions.

To assess the strength, as well as, the direction of association, $\chi^2$ tests, related Cramér's V, and correlation coefficients are computed.

#### 6.7.3.1 The ESCC and Transactional Satisfaction

The relationship between the ESCC and transactional satisfaction is already analyzed when dealing with the accuracies of the ESCC observations in section (6.4.1). The conclusion in that section was that the more intense (negative or positive) the customer contacts the more accurate the CSR evaluations in customer satisfaction.

With regard to the relationship between the variables in Figure 6-12, results of $\chi^2$ analysis indicate that there is a significant association between the ESCC ratings and customer's transactional satisfactions. The strength of this association, according to Cramér's V (0.36, $p< 0.01$), is moderate. Spearman's correlation coefficient (0.39) also confirms this moderate and significant ($p< 0.01$) positive association between the ESCC and transactional satisfaction.

Figure 6-12: Cross-tabs: The ESCC and Transactional Satisfaction

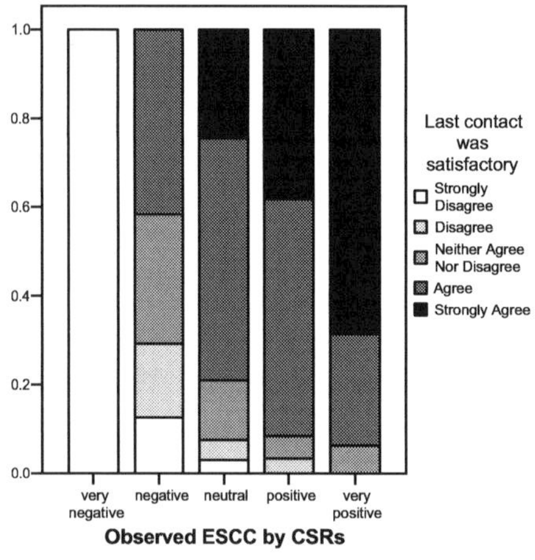


N=298; $\chi^2$ $p< 0.01$; Cramer's V: 0.36; Spearman Correlation: 0.39 $p< 0.01$.

#### 6.7.3.2 The ESCC and General Satisfaction

The variety of customer evaluations in each of the ESCC columns in Figure 6-13 indicates a weak association between the ESCC and general satisfaction. The only trend which is visible is the decreasing negative customer evaluations towards the right-side, and conversely, decreasing positive customers towards the left-side.

Results of $\chi^2$ analysis indicate that there is a significant association between the ESCC ratings and customer's general satisfactions. The strength of this association, according to Cramér's V (0.24, $p < 0.01$), is weak. Spearman's correlation coefficient (0.30) also confirms this weak but significant ($p < 0.01$) positive association between the two variables.

Figure 6-13: Cross-tabs: The ESCC and General Satisfaction

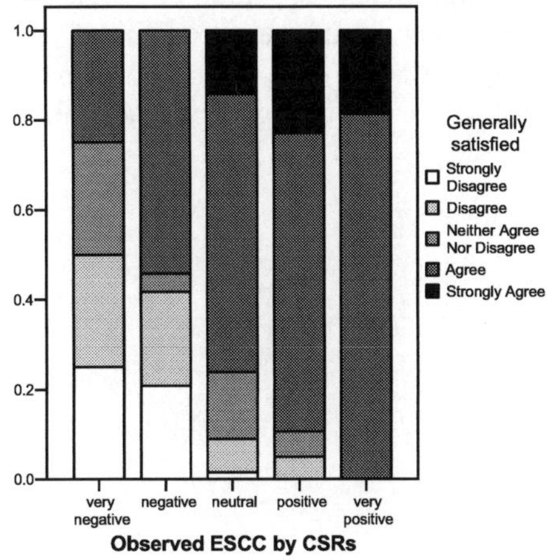


N=300; $\chi^2$ $p < 0.01$; Cramer's V: 0.24; Spearman Correlation: 0.30 $p < 0.01$.

#### 6.7.3.3 The ESCC and Loyalty Intentions

Correspondence analysis has already indicated that the distinctions were not crystal clear among negative, as well as, among positive CSR observations and customer loyalty intentions. This is also visible in the chart derived from cross-tabs (Figure 6-14). For example, the proportion of 'very likely' is almost equal both in 'positive' and 'very positive' columns; similarly, the proportion of 'very unlikely' is also almost equal both in 'negative' and 'very negative' columns. This finding thus confirms the result of correspondence analysis (in 6.7.2.3) stating that the ESCC observations actually separate the loyalty intentions into two groups: possible defectors, who would be (somewhat) unlikely to stay as customer, and the others.

Results of $\chi^2$ analysis indicate that there is a significant association between the ESCC ratings and customer loyalty intentions; and the strength of this association, according to Cramér's V (0.24, $p< 0.01$), is weak. Spearman's correlation coefficient (0.27) also indicates a weak but significant ($p< 0.01$) positive association between the two variables.

Figure 6-14: Cross-tabs: The ESCC and Loyalty Intentions

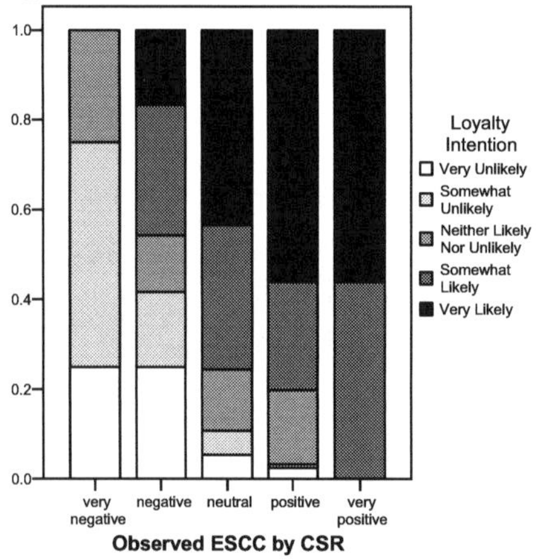


N=296; $\chi^2$ $p< 0.01$; Cramer's V: 0.24; Spearman Correlation: 0.27 $p< 0.01$.

In order to demonstrate a sharper representation, survey response scales are grouped into three classes in Figure 6-15: lowest two loyalty intention scales were grouped under 'Churn Intentions', middle scale is kept as 'Neutral', and top two scales were grouped under 'Loyalty Intentions'. These three classes indeed showed the relationship between the ESCC and loyalty more clearly. Churn Intentions, for example, were up to 75% in 'very negative' ESCC ratings, but gradually decreased in 'negative' and 'neutral' ESCC ratings, and (almost) disappeared in 'positive,' and 'very positive' ratings. Loyalty intentions had also similar patterns, but in reverse order. Neutral loyalty intentions were relatively small and more than half of them were concentrated in negative zones. The

ESCC observations thus segmented the customers into two main groups: customers with churn intentions and customers with loyalty intentions.

The results of $\chi^2$ analysis indicate that there is a significant association between the ESCC ratings and (the re-grouped) customer loyalty intentions; and the strength of this association, according to Cramér's V (0.31), is moderate. Spearman's correlation coefficient (0.26) indicates a weak but significant ($p < 0.01$) positive association between the two variables.

Figure 6-15: Re-grouped Cross-tabs: The ESCC and Loyalty Intentions

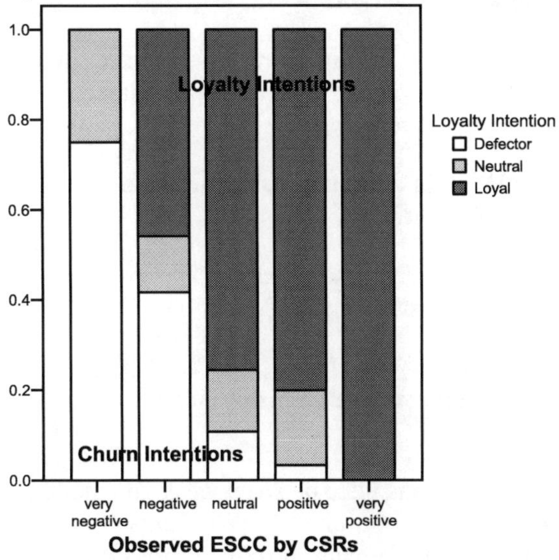


N=296; Loyalty Intentions: very likely & likely to stay as customer; Neutral Intentions: neither likely nor unlikely to stay as customer; Churn Intentions: very unlikely & unlikely to stay as customer. $\chi^2$ $p < 0.01$; Cramer's V: 0.31; Spearman's Correlation: 0.26, $p < 0.01$.

### *6.7.4 Summary of the ESCC Relationships*

The relationship between the ESCC and transactional satisfaction (with last contact), general satisfaction, and customer loyalty intentions are examined with correlation analyses, correspondence analyses, cross-tabs and $\chi^2$ analyses. Results indicated that:

#### 6.7.4.1 Research Question 9b: What is the relationship between the ESCC and Transactional Satisfaction?

The ESCC and transactional satisfaction are moderately associated. It also appeared, the more extreme the CSR observations the stronger their associations with customer satisfaction with their last contacts.

#### 6.7.4.2 Research Question 9c: What is the relationship between the ESCC and General Satisfaction?

The ESCC and general satisfaction are weakly associated. It appeared again, the more extreme the CSR observations the stronger their associations with customer's general satisfaction.

#### 6.7.4.3 Research Question 9d: What is the relationship between the ESCC and loyalty (intentions)?

The ESCC and customer loyalty associations were between weak and moderate. However, although the distinctions are not crystal clear among negative observations and intentions, as well as, among positive observations and intentions, the ESCC observations segmented the customers into two main groups: customers with churn intentions and customers with loyalty intentions.

## 6.8 Summary & Concluding Remarks on the ESCC Observations

The objective of this chapter was to experiment a basic implementation of the ESCC methodology, to assess the accuracy of the ESCC observations, and to investigate the relationship between the observed ESCC, customer satisfaction, and loyalty intentions.

During the test days, selected CSRs have evaluated all incoming calls with the ESCC methodology while doing their routine tasks. Test settings are briefly explained to CSRs who had no prior experience in such evaluations until test days. 842 calls are evaluated by 38 CSRs in four different firms, and about 300 of them could have been verified by customer surveys.

Results showed that test group customers perceived the contacts most positively, control group customers fairly positively, and finally the CSRs neutrally.

When the rough averages of CSRs, control and test group customers are taken into consideration it appeared that about 10% of customer contacts are considered as negative and very negative, about 20% neutral, about 50% positive and 20% very positive. Nevertheless, when specific sample groups are analyzed, then some sharp differences appeared. For instance, the percentage of negative and very negative evaluations in the test group of insurance firm was 23.6%, whereas, the same percentage in book & music firm was only 2.4%.

The accuracy of the ESCC observation is calculated by taking the difference between 'customer evaluation' on the last contact and the 'ESCC observation' of CSR. In one-on-one comparisons, the average accuracy was 34%; when the data was re-grouped into three classes (1&2, 3&4, 5), the average accuracy increased to 60%; when one-scale-differences where customers are more positive than CSRs were considered as accurate, then the accuracy of observations reached near 80%.

Accuracy rates varied among the test firms, being more accurate in book & music and insurance firms, and less accurate in pension fund and in the bank. No significant aspect is found that may influence the accuracy levels of the ESCC observations. However, practicing the ESCC observations for a longer time and calibrating it by frequently comparing them with customer evaluations enhanced the accuracies. For example, accurate observations increased from 30% to 45% in a Dutch financial organization over a month period.

CSRs did not capture all customers in a specific satisfaction segment based on customer evaluations, nevertheless, when CSRs segmented the customers then their accuracies sharply increased. CSRs were more accurate in extreme scales and even more accurate in negative cases; thus, the more intense the customer contacts the more accurate the CSR evaluations in customer satisfaction.

Results showed that despite the variations in accuracies per firm and even per employee, with the ESCC observations firms would be able to identify many more unsatisfied customers. These unsatisfied customers would normally be unknown to firms due to fact that the majority of unsatisfied customers do not complain to their firms but to their friends and relatives.

The ESCC observations, as expected, associated more strongly with emotional satisfaction than with cognitive satisfaction. The strength of this relationship has, however, appeared to be between weak and moderate.

Cohen's Kappa statistic, boxplot chart, cross-tabs, $\chi^2$ analysis and correlation coefficients signified the ESCC as a 'reasonable indicator' rather than a 'precise tool' for assessing satisfaction in customer contacts. It is also noted that when practiced for a longer period of time, the ESCC evaluations have the potential to be more accurate.

Positive correlations have been found between CSRs own emotions and their ESCC ratings, thus how CSRs perceive customer emotions. It also appeared that the ESCC significantly associated with how CSRs feel immediately after calls, but not with how they feel after several different calls.

The relationship between the ESCC and transactional satisfaction, general satisfaction, and customer loyalty intentions are examined with correlation analyses, correspondence analyses, cross-tabs and $\chi^2$ analyses. Results indicated that the ESCC associated moderately with transactional satisfaction, weakly with general satisfaction, and somewhat moderately with customer loyalty intentions. The ESCC observations effectively separated customers with churn intentions from customers with loyalty intentions.

It appeared thus, during customer contacts CSRs are able to observe and assess transactional satisfaction with a reasonable accuracy; and these observations seemed to be a reasonable predictor of customer loyalty intentions. More specifically, the more positive the ESCC, the stronger the customer satisfaction and loyalty!

# 7 EMPLOYING THE ESCC INFORMATION

The previous chapter showed that CSRs are able to observe and register the satisfaction that occurs during customer contacts with reasonable accuracy. Also the relationship between these observations, customer satisfaction, and customer's loyalty intentions are to some extent established. This chapter now will attempt to describe some preliminary practicalities of using the ESCC information.

## 7.1 Following up the ESCC

As shown in previous chapters, the accuracies of the ESCC observations were relatively higher in very positive and very negative areas than, for example, neutral ESCC areas. Also the proportions of these extreme areas were smaller than the other ESCC areas. Therefore, the following subsections will focus on these relatively small and accurate observations for designing some specific follow-up actions for both positive and negative ESCC observations.

### *7.1.1 The ESCC Cross/Up-Sales Process*

Increasing sales in contact centers is one of the 'hot topics' in recent industry events, and organizations demand more and more sales from their contact centers (Güngör, 2006). Sales in contact centers are primarily done by utilizing inbound calls or by initiating outbound calls. Nevertheless, recent surveys and many contact center professionals across Europe indicate that customers do not appreciate (exaggerated) sales push when they contact their firms; and the majority of customers particularly dislike it when they receive outbound (telesales) calls (Efma, 2005). It is therefore not surprising to see that banks even want customers back into their branch offices due to dissatisfactory sales performance of their contact centers (De Volkskrant, 21-12-2005).

Sales pressure can be annoying for customers, but can also be too premature for many contact centers that are not (yet) capable of organizing a sales environment, and are actually struggling with their primary responsibility: *customer services*. It is obviously a big customer service disappointment, if not a total marketing disaster, when organizations that cannot properly serve their customers try to sell more products to their existing customers, as well as, when they try to acquire more new customers (Güngör, 2006). The ESCC methodologies therefore, aim at identifying the best customers and the best moments for initiating sales actions.

There are three possibilities of using (very) positive ESCC information for increasing sales or its productivity.[113] The first possibility is a casual result of

[113] Sales increase in absolute terms is like increasing sales from 100 to 110. Sales productivity in relative terms is like creating about the same amount of sales with less effort and investment.

positive service experiences. It is thus expected that incoming service calls, which create positive emotions, would also create more sales opportunities. These opportunities vary from closing sales deals on the phone to creating sales leads, such as, sending new product brochures or making appointments with sales representatives.

The second possibility to promote new products or services is to design specific direct marketing or telemarketing actions for the blue customers, who have had a very positive contact with the firm. This option, however, seems to be most suitable for frequently purchased products like office supplies, or pizza delivery services, where satisfaction with the last product or interaction may easily lead to another transaction in the near future.

The third possibility is the elimination of the red and orange customers, who have had a recent negative contact with the firm, from direct mail and telemarketing campaigns. As dissatisfied customers would already have negative attitudes and intentions towards their firms, it would be useless to promote new products or services to those customers. Such sales calls would even create a reverse effect for the customers who were recently disappointed or upset with the firm. On the one hand, elimination of unsatisfied customers from direct marketing actions might decrease sales figures a little, due to the slight possibility of purchases among unsatisfied customers. On the other hand, this elimination would more sharply decrease direct marketing and telemarketing costs; and this would consequently increase sales productivities. Such eliminations have a considerable cost savings potential due to fact that about 500 million telemarketing calls are made yearly in The Netherlands alone (de Volkskrant, 4-6-05).

However, it is also important to note that sales increase not only depends on interactions between customers and CSRs, but also depends on product quality and price in comparison with the competition. This means that, the ESCC methodologies will have the potential to increase sales if firms have similar product quality and comparable prices with their competitors.

### *7.1.2 The ESCC Service Recovery Process*

Figure 7-1 illustrates the proposed ESCC service recovery flow, where CSRs continuously evaluate their calls with the ESCC methodology and *assign* colors to customer information systems. Senior CSRs or supervisors then sort and *analyze* the data according to the ESCC colors. They also review and *filter*[114] the negative (orange) and very negative (red) cases by reading the notes of the CSRs, checking the customer information, talking to the related CSRs, listening to the recorded conversation, etc. Then, the filtered cases are communicated to customer recovery CSRs who are capable of dealing with difficult customer circumstances and are also familiar with the firm's products and procedures.

Figure 7-1: The ESCC Service Recovery Process Flow

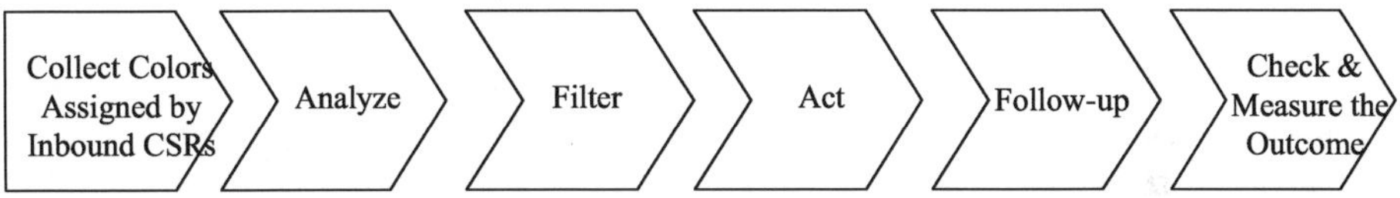


Recovery CSRs then proactively initiate *recovery actions* that can be analyzed in two main categories: recoveries and extras. Recoveries are the cases that are (satisfactorily) resolved by recovery interventions such as convincing customers who were not happy with a process or transaction, or, arranging special treatments like an express delivery of the documents needed. Extras are the gifts that customers receive alongside a letter, when for instance, a recovery attempt is not successful, and might vary from a pen with firm's logo to a box of candies. Recovery actions may require extra *follow-ups* such as arranging that customers are contacted by branch personnel. Finally, such actions may also require a *final check* in order to make sure that promised actions are done and customer satisfaction is regained.

Verifying the effectiveness of the proposed recovery process flow, customer surveys in the Dutch financial sector[115] showed that recovery customers, who were red and orange before the recovery attempt, scored in most cases significantly[116] higher than the red and orange customers who did not receive a recovery attempt. These (disappointed) orange and (angry) red customers became in most cases (positive) green or (very positive) blue after recovery attempts. Recovery customers also scored in satisfaction with last contact, and in

[114] Filter criteria for proactive recovery attempts may include the following: customers are not approached if they are already in contact with other departments, if they have been extremely rude towards CSRs, if they are already in legal conflict with the firm, etc.

[115] In an organization other than the test firms, the sample group contained over 150 customers with about 25 recovery cases.

[116] As Mann-Whitney U tests indicate, the differences between "red" and "recovery group" customers were significant ($p< 0.05$) in all survey items, except in price item. General satisfaction, satisfaction with the last contact, and loyalty intentions were also significantly ($p< 0.05$) differed between "orange" and "recovery group" customers.

loyalty intentions, significantly[117] higher than the randomly selected control group customers who represent the typical customers of the firm.

These results confirm the findings of other studies suggesting that recovery actions such as correcting the error, redressing the losses and offering sincere apologies after dissatisfactory service encounters can save the customer from defection and can even increase loyalty (Reinartz & Kumar, 2002 & 2001; Tax & Brown, 1998; Robinette et al., 2001; Reichheld, 1996; Jones & Sasser, 1995; Keaveney, 1995; Hart, Heskett, & Sasser, 1990; Reichheld & Sasser, 1990; Iacobucci, 1999; Lovelock & Wirtz, 2004; Freemantle, 1999:58, 66; IBM & Rochester Study, 1994; TARP research, 2001; Oliver, 1997:373; Zeithaml & Bitner, 2003:189; Smith & Bolton, 1998[118]).

The proactive ESCC approach can be used to complement (reactive) complaint management tools. The advantage of this proactive approach is that with the ESCC observations CSRs are able to identify many unsatisfied customers who would normally be unknown to firms since the majority of unsatisfied customers do not complain to their firms but to their friends and relatives. Indeed, unsatisfied customers can be a very strong source of negative word-of-mouth (Kotler, 1996:297; Katona, 1975:75), and proactive recovery actions can reverse this effect by creating even positive word-of-mouth and referrals. Reichheld (2003) suggests that the question of "would you recommend this company to a friend?" is one of the most important criteria to predict the company success, and proactive recovery actions seem to have the potential to create this effect.

---

[117] Mann-Whitney U tests, $p < 0.01$ for satisfaction with last contact, and $p < 0.037$ for loyalty intentions.

[118] As cited in Jones & Farquhar (2003): Smith, A. & Bolton, R. (1998). An experimental investigation of customer reactions to service failure and recovery encounters: paradox or peril. *Journal of Service Research*, Vol. 1, No. 1, 65-81.

## 7.2 The ESCC and Organizational Learning Process

Organizational learning is what comes after the follow up actions in the ESCC model. This step particularly emphasizes the importance of continuous improvement actions within firm's product and processes, which are constantly reviewed and revised inline with the follow up actions, as described in the previous section. In other words, rather than correcting the same mistake over and over again with recovery actions after negative ESCC evaluations, this step suggests to review and revise the products or processes so that the same mistakes will not occur again. It also suggests learning from positive ESCC evaluations and adapting similar processes and procedures to other areas of the firm's business.

The ESCC model thus prescribes the practicalities of a learning organization, and proposes a simple methodology that at least proactively feeds single-loop learning where errors are detected and corrected. In the ESCC model, CSRs proactively observe customer dissatisfactions and register them. Organizations can thus identify with the ESCC data their most delicate areas where frequent customer dissatisfactions arise. Recovery CSRs can then help in designing structural improvements (double-loop learning) as they repeatedly answer and apply similar solutions for such deficiencies. The ESCC model, however, not only aims at learning from negative examples, like in complaint management systems, but also from positive ones. With the ESCC model, organizations can identify their healthy processes that create positive customer experiences as these processes will be associated with very positive (blue) customer contacts. Organizations can thus make use of these positive experiences as examples for improving entire processes, underlying principles, and associated values (triple-loop learning).

As metaphorically illustrated in Figure 7-2 companies (saucepan) have many customers (water) and they would like to keep them. However, when product or process shortcomings (fire under the saucepan) reach the boiling level, customer dissatisfaction (steam) occurs. When such dissatisfactions are disregarded, customers switch to competitors (vaporized steam); conversely, when dissatisfactions are recovered, customers stay in the firm (recycled steam). The ESCC methodologies (the lid) thus make sure that customer frustrations are proactively observed, registered, and recovered while information is shared with other departments (utilized steam). When the lid is too open it loses all the steam, and when it is too tightly closed it pressurises customers and employees creating whistles and screams in the form of complaints. The ESCC (lid) with a correct angle finally helps to assure that recovery information is utilized and product and processes are continuously improved (extinguishing the fire) for more customer satisfaction and loyalty.

Figure 7-2: The ESCC and Organizational Learning Cycle

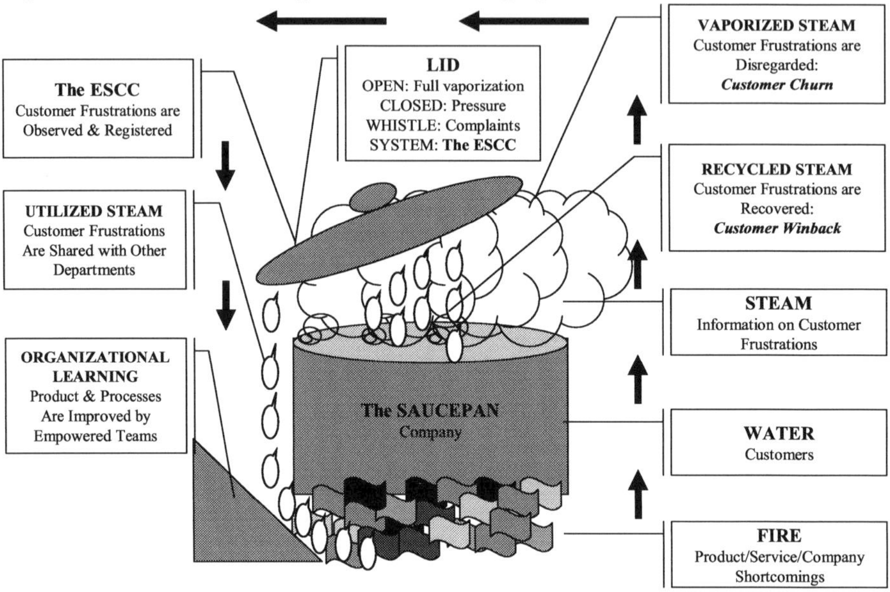


Cusack (1998:54-55, 67), points out that customer care facilities present a unique opportunity to gather data for recognizing opportunities for process improvements. However, although there is a desire for an ongoing mechanism that keeps senior managers permanently plugged into frontline customer feedback (e.g., Reichheld, 1996:69), CSRs commonly feel that their ideas and feedback are not utilized properly and sometimes not even taken seriously (cf. Cusack, 1998:56; Freemantle, 1999:256). It is thus important that the ESCC information proactively triggers the organization with 'continuous learning signals', nevertheless, it is even more important to utilize that information and make progress towards the next loops in organizational learning.

With the ESCC observations and recovery actions, CSRs become an important part of learning organizations where not only the things that go wrong are corrected but also the roots of the problems are analyzed. This cycle thus makes CSRs *conscious* of customer issues as well as system issues. This, however, will likely occur when employees are *empowered* to take decisions and make changes, and when management starts playing a "facilitator role" with "care" instead of a "controller role" in the organization (Ganzevoort, 1999). Through these changes CSRs observe customers and pro-act for improvements, instead of management observe CSRs and re-act for corrections.

Empowerment, according to Kotter and Cohen (2002:104), is not only about giving people new authority and responsibilities and then walking away; but it is also about removing barriers. Barriers can be the boss barrier within a rigid hierarchy, a system barrier within a rigid bureaucracy, barriers in the mind such as cynicism or skepticism, and finally information barriers which are traditionally restricted by hierarchical, physical, geographic boundaries but somewhat relaxed with new information technologies (Zmud, 1990).

Although organizations learn through individuals, "teams" are the fundamental learning unit in organizations (Senge, 1990: 10, 139). Teams of empowered employees, with the authority and autonomy to make changes in the way a company does business, are today the driving force behind efforts to attain total customer satisfaction (Hellinghausen, 1999). For example, Citibank aimed at creating defect-free (defect is anything that dissatisfies a customer) processes to increase customer loyalty. Methodologies like Cross Functional Process Mapping for Cycle Time Reduction have been implemented globally by using empowered teams. When these teams are challenged to reduce cycle times within their departments, they become empowered to make improvements that in turn improve the corporate culture (Rucker, 2000).

## 7.3 The ESCC, Customer Satisfaction and Loyalty

Customer satisfaction and loyalty are the anticipated results of using the ESCC methodologies and related activities such as proactive service recovery, adjusted sales actions and organizational learning.

As discussed in chapter 5, test group customer responses to survey questions were more positive than control group customers. Chapter 6 also showed that test group customers perceived their contacts with firms more positively than control group customers. Recovery customers were also more satisfied than randomly selected control group customers. These initial findings thus indicate that the ESCC settings at least have the potential to increase customer satisfaction in the customer contact environment.

Nevertheless, survey results discussed in chapter 5 showed that customers were more loyal than they were satisfied, indicating that customer satisfaction cannot be translated directly to customer loyalty. Moreover, despite the differences in satisfaction levels, there was no difference found between the test and the control group customers in terms of loyalty intentions.

Chapter 6 further indicated that the ESCC associated moderately with transactional satisfaction, weakly with general satisfaction, and somewhat moderately with customer loyalty intentions.

The above analyses, however, were cross-sectional in nature due to the fact that they only represent the test days. Longer term effects of the ESCC settings, which include emotionally conscious service environment with recovery procedures and continuous improvement actions, are not examined in this research. Therefore, future research is necessary to reveal the longer term effects of the ESCC implementations on customer satisfaction and loyalty.

## 7.4 Summary & Research Question 10: What can be done with the ESCC information?

Following the literature review in chapter 4, this chapter described what can be done with the ESCC information in practical terms and attempted to gather some evidence. Studies showed that positive customer experiences lead to more sales, and it is suggested that the ESCC information, indicating customer experience levels, can be utilized for increasing *sales*. This chapter proposed three possibilities in increasing sales (productivity) by utilizing the ESCC information. Firstly, it is expected that positive service experiences would increase sales. Secondly, it is proposed that special actions can be designed for (very) satisfied customers with very positive ESCC. Thirdly, it is suggested that elimination of disappointed and angry customers with (very) negative ESCC from direct marketing actions would decrease costs and consequently increase sales productivity.

Literature research confirmed the necessity and the effectiveness of proactive *service recoveries* in regaining customer satisfaction and loyalty, and the ESCC methodologies attempted to fill the gap of "how to make it operational". It is proposed that registered ESCC information can be analyzed, filtered for actionable customer disappointments, and that such customer problems can be recovered proactively. Limited empirical evidence indicated that the ESCC model is a reliable construction for a practical service recovery process.

The process of detecting and correcting error is examined under *organizational learning*. Studies suggested to grasp value from failures by learning from them, to translate them into improvements, and thereby to create customer satisfaction and loyalty. The saucepan (company) and water (customers) metaphor illustrated the ESCC process in organizational learning. In this metaphor, the ESCC lid (model) captured the steam (information on customer dissatisfaction) and simply utilized it by recovery actions for customer retention, and by process improvements for organizational learning and for more customer satisfaction. Finally, the importance of utilizing the feedback of CSRs (the ESCC information) and making progress towards the next loops in organizational learning is underlined.

Literature research verified the links between improvements in services and increases in customer satisfaction; however, what comes after satisfaction was not confirmed by all resources. Loyalty and profitability appeared to be reasonable extensions of customer satisfaction but with no guarantees. Test day survey results discussed in previous chapters had similar conclusions. The ESCC settings appeared to increase satisfaction among test group customers, however, no significant difference was found between test and control group customers in terms of loyalty intentions. Nonetheless, the ESCC observations were able to separate customers with churn intentions from customers with loyalty intentions; and this separation has the potential for increasing sales, service recoveries, customer satisfaction and consequently loyalty intentions.

# 8 SOME LAST REFLECTIONS ON THE SUBJECT

Based on the observations in test firms as well as in other contact center settings some principles are drafted as final reflections on the subject. These principles are complementary and at the same time pivotal for understanding the fundamentals of the ESCC model.

The ESCC model, first of all, aims at involving and empowering CSRs in customer satisfaction and organizational learning processes for more customer loyalty. The ESCC model aims at collecting information about each customer contact and consequently sketching a full transactional satisfaction picture of the customer contact environment. This is indeed a distinctive feature when compared with traditional satisfaction measurements, where information is acquired from thin sample groups. Although, such thin measurements may indicate statistically significant findings; these statistical findings do not solve specific problems when necessary. At best, some issues are improved after a considerable time lag, and maybe after losing many customers. The ESCC, however, aims at detecting and timely correcting specific problems, and thereby creating stronger customer relations.

The ESCC model does not exclude customer feedback from the satisfaction measurement process, as customer feedback is still needed to verify CSR observations periodically. Thus, the intention of the ESCC approach is not replacing existing systems or measurement methodologies but adding a new structure that would contribute to the overall customer satisfaction, as well as, quality improvements. Combining different methodologies and tools would indeed balance the strengths and weaknesses of different methods of measuring customer satisfaction (Lovelock & Wirtz, 2004:397;[119] Garver, 2001).

The ESCC approach does not propose starting (emotional) relationships with individual customers, but expect to improve service encounters with a genuine empathy. Masters (2001) suggests that "for many high-value customers, service implies efficiency, not dialogue... and there is scant evidence that customers want a relationship with a supplier." McKean (2003) similarly argues that customers don't want relationships. They simply want the best product or service at the right price and to be treated like a human being in the process.

The ESCC methodologies do not intend generalizing its scores for judging CSRs, organizations, or customers, but rather aim at identifying dissatisfactory issues for learning and continuous improvement actions. Quality monitoring systems and similarly the ESCC methodologies might have a contradictory role in their reason of existence. They can be discerned as a *treat* (or gift) for training and improvement purposes for customer and employee satisfaction, but they can also be discerned as a *threat* (or risk) for CSRs by sending the message of 'big

[119] As cited in Lovelock & Wirtz (2004:397): Berry, L.L. & Parasuraman, A. (1997). Listening to the Customer-The Concept of a Service Quality Information System. *Sloan Management Review,* Spring, 65-76.

brother is watching you!' It is therefore, very critical to determine and communicate the purposes of the ESCC in the very beginning as a dynamic customer satisfaction and learning tool rather than a control or a labeling tool.

Since CSRs determine a common ESCC color for both customers and themselves after each contact, it is very important to perceive that clicking the "orange" or "red" is not a blame on someone, but rather is a symbol that would help to identify development areas in the firm. Otherwise, CSRs would have a bias towards more positive colors misleading the outcomes. One of the pitfalls in the ESCC evaluations is indeed the (un)intentional bias of CSRs who would like to show a more positive picture about their contacts. This might occur in a working environment that explicitly or implicitly punishes CSRs when they select negative ESCC, and thus highlight customer dissatisfaction. A positive bias might also occur when positive ESCC colors are explicitly or implicitly rewarded. Therefore, another key in the ESCC implementation is to keep the ESCC as neutral as possible and to praise the accuracy of CSR evaluations.

The ESCC approach requires more emotional intelligence from employees for dealing successfully with customers and understanding distinctive situations (e.g., Skaggs & Youndt, 2004; Safizadeh, Field, & Ritzman, 2003); as well as, from management for dealing more successfully with employees (e.g., Dulewics & Higgs, 2004; Salovey, Hsee, & Mayer, 2001; Goleman, 1996).

Today's problems come from yesterday's solutions (cf. Senge, 1990:23). Thus, today's solutions might also create tomorrow's new problems. Therefore, continuous learning and improvements are crucial for organizations. Furthermore, for finding high-leverage changes organizations need to realize underlying "structures" rather than "events" (ibid., p.65). After all, "solutions that address only the symptoms of a problem, not fundamental causes tend to have short term benefits at best" (ibid., p.104). Therefore, the ESCC cannot be the ultimate solution in itself but can be an indicator of development areas.

Management (information systems) commonly tends to control CSRs' working hours, productivity figures, attitudes towards customers, etc. However, issues like customer satisfaction cannot be constantly supervised by the management (Ganzevoort, 1999:15). Therefore, the ESCC model aims at replacing the control tendency with responsibility. The ESCC model thus delegates the responsibility of customer satisfaction to CSRs who hopefully would stand up from the defendant chair, and sit down on the witness chair in the ongoing customer (dis)satisfaction trials.

Observed ESCC is not a static issue. It would fluctuate parallel to the nature of customer contacts, as well as, to the changes in CSR perceptions about these contacts. The accuracy of observations is therefore to be verified with random customer feedback surveys, done by peers, external parties, or even by (Completely) Automated Telephone Surveys with the help of IVR systems. However, outcomes of such surveys should be used for training purposes only. CSRs who receive customer feedback about their conversations will have the chance to review and adjust their performances while calibrating their ESCC accuracies. It is therefore, very important to neutralize the impact of these feedbacks as they can create unnecessary anxieties, called "feedback backlash" (Morse, 2004). Forwarding customer feedback information directly to the related CSRs, while facilitating a mild supervisory verification process, would be a balanced solution between learning and controlling concerns.

Recovery actions and subsequent process improvement actions are very critical due to the fact that they might require irregular interventions into the company's bureaucratic machinery. Therefore, such interventions should be very well coordinated from the beginning. Also, process improvements throughout the organization should be initiated after accumulating adequate information about the reasons and proven solutions of dissatisfactory issues.

One of the common worries in the ESCC implementation is whether interacting with customers by taking emotions into consideration would increase the duration of contacts, and thus would decrease CSR productivities. This is indeed a legitimate worry for contact center management who generally struggle with tight budgets and a limited number of CSRs. Although this factor was not measured during the test days, observations on longer term implementations other than the test firms initially indicate that working with the ESCC slightly increase the duration of calls in the very beginning, but duration of calls return to normal levels after a few weeks of learning process.

Hatch (1997:109) argues that measurements like customer satisfaction tend not to receive the same weight, as do financial indicators; and even may not be regarded as legitimate by many within the organization. This view seems to be softening in recent years. For example, in a Dutch bank, customer satisfaction ratings will play a more important role in evaluating the success of managers (de Volkskrant, 18-2-05). However, evaluating managers by customer satisfaction scores, on the one hand, would explicitly reward customer satisfaction measurements; on the other hand, would implicitly punish activities that might expose additional customer dissatisfaction, like the ESCC information.

Indeed, the ESCC observations may expose a less positive customer satisfaction picture as this information represents 'critical' opinions of CSRs rather than 'socially correct' opinions of customers. Such observations may also identify many unsatisfied customers who would normally be unknown to organizations. This can be a major confrontation and therefore, starting the ESCC evaluations requires a courageous first step that should be backed by the management who would like to see the customer contacts through the eyes of their own CSRs. Otherwise the ESCC would be discerned as threatening information against the *status quo*, and long-term effects would be jeopardized from the beginning.

Perils of many strategies, according to Jay (1998:209), are the "emphasis on short term goals only" and the "lack of commitment from top management." Short-term strategies and related success can indeed be at the expense of financial health in longer-term. One major European company, for example, pulled off an impressive turnaround in short-term financial performance with a severe cost emphasis. Nevertheless, its financial success was accompanied by a fall in customer service levels and increase in staff turnover resulting in severe financial consequences afterwards (Davis, 2005).

Regarding the commitment of top-management, an effective strategy with customer obsession should start with the CEO and then it extents to other employees (Etheredge, 1999). As Teerling, Gragg and Bisgaard-Bohr (2003) put it: “How can the people on the front lines think about customer service when all of the people supporting them don’t...”

Organizations are caught between two conflicting needs: one for managers to maintain the balance of operations, and one for leaders to create new approaches and imagine new areas to explore (Zaleznik, 1977:67). According to Covey companies are managing too much while leading too little (Het Financieele Dagblad, 25-4-2002). The ESCC approach, however, aims at introducing new structures while keeping the existing ones, and therefore requires a balanced approach.

When new technologies or systems are introduced, especially ones that alter normal social structures, it takes quite a while for organizations to adapt. For example, in early days a fire department refused to accept a phoned-in-report of a fire because it was not according to the official routine, and waited (10 minutes) until an official alarm was finally received (Norman, 1993:191). As the ESCC is a new way of approaching customer relations, it would eventually require some changes and improvements. Therefore, the ESCC should be introduced if there is also an intention to improve the underlying structures of customer and employee dissatisfactions. Otherwise, raising awareness in issues like customer and employee emotions, and subsequently not improving any conditions would even create more friction in organizations.

Kotter and Cohen (2002:179-183) describe organizational change process as “we see, we feel, and we change.” “Seeing” thus helps people to visualize and experience the problems similar to the ESCC evaluations. The dramatic visualizations and examples similar to recovery actions catch people’s attention, and these “feelings” transform behavior. It is, however, pivotal that the changes diffuse into the company culture and stay there. According to Kotter and Cohen (2002:165) “in a change effort, culture comes last not first. Enterprises often try to shift cultures first... a culture truly changes only when a new way of operating has been shown to succeed over some minimum period of time” (ibid., p.175).

Marketing is the art of attracting and keeping profitable customers; and it is widely suggested that a company should not try to pursue and satisfy every customer (Kotler, 1996:453; Curry, 1994; Treacy & Wiersema, 1995; Peppers & Rogers; 1997:30; Braff, Passmore, & Simpson, 2003). Brady (2000) describes such attitudes as “the new consumer apartheid.” The ESCC approach in fact challenges this consumer apartheid and aims at increasing customer advocacy by suggesting that "the best customers are not only the profitable ones, but also the ones who like the company and who would recommend it to others" (Güngör, 2002; cf. Reichheld, 2003). After all, one company's unprofitable customers can be some other companies' profitable customers, and the real challenge in marketing is the "customer alchemy," in other words, "turning less profitable customers into more profitable customers" (Rust, Zeithaml, & Lemon, 2000:217).

Finally, the ESCC methodologies can be most supportive if firms have similar product quality and comparable pricing with their competitors. Then a superior customer service can be utilized as a competitive advantage where customers are ready to tolerate some product inferiority or some price differences. However, the ESCC is not expected to compensate severe product deficiencies or very high price differences vis-à-vis competition. As Robinette and colleagues (2001) similarly put it, "the price and the product offering have to be at least on par with competitors –otherwise, don't even bother trying to establish a relationship based on emotion."

# 9 IMPLICATIONS & LIMITATIONS

## 9.1 Theoretical Implications

Several findings in this research were in line with the existing literature. For example, the finding of "customer satisfaction cannot be translated directly to customer loyalty" was parallel to Reichheld's studies (1993:71; 1996:58). Also the findings of "there is no straight line relationship between satisfaction and loyalty… and only very satisfied customers can be considered as loyal" were similar to the conclusions of Jones and Sasser (1995), and Heskett et al. (1997:83). Finally, the finding of "recovery actions after dissatisfactory service encounters can save the customer from defection and can even increase loyalty" confirmed numerous studies (e.g., Reinartz & Kumar, 2002 & 2001; Tax & Brown, 1998; Robinette et al., 2001; Reichheld, 1996; Jones & Sasser, 1995; Keaveney, 1995; Hart, Heskett, & Sasser, 1990; Reichheld & Sasser, 1990; Iacobucci, 1999; Lovelock & Wirtz, 2004; Freemantle, 1999:58, 66; IBM and Rochester Study, 1994; TARP research, 2001; Oliver, 1997:373; Zeithaml & Bitner, 2003:189; Smith & Bolton, 1998).

The conclusion "loyalty depends more on emotional dimensions than on cognitive dimensions" was in line with the studies of Wetzels (1999), and somewhat more explicit than other studies that tend to consider the weight of emotion and cognition equally in terms of loyalty intentions (Oliver, 1997:316; Mano & Oliver, 1993:451; Jones & Sassers, 1995:90).

This research found that general satisfaction is more important than transactional satisfaction in loyalty. Nevertheless, transactional and general satisfactions are interrelated and require each other's presence. These findings are complementary to the previous studies of Parasuraman, Zeithaml and Berry (1994:122) who argue that global evaluations are the aggregation of transaction experiences; Anderson, Fornell and Lehman (1994) who advocate 'cumulative satisfaction'; and Rust, Zahorik and Keiningham (1995:64) who suggest that both evaluations are equally useful.

Prior studies investigated customer emotions and frontline employee feedback with, for example, critical incident techniques (Bitner, Booms, & Mohr, 1994; van Dolen et al., 2001; Edwardson, 1998). This research, however, sets a practical methodology for assessing (emotional) satisfaction of customer contacts, and for comparing frontline employee's view with customer's view on customer (contact) satisfaction.

## 9.2 Managerial Implications

This research underlined the importance of emotions evoked during customer contacts, and suggested to engage frontline employee feedback in (emotional) satisfaction and loyalty processes. Therefore, a simple measurement and registration process is designed which can be used alongside various customer satisfaction measurement tools.

Surveys results suggested that CSRs are able to observe and assess transactional satisfaction with a reasonable accuracy during customer contacts, and these observations are a reasonable predictor of customer loyalty intentions.

It appeared that customer contact satisfaction can be particularly important close to the decision making moments of customers. For instance, when a customer contacts a firm a few days before the renewal date of a yearly subscription, then the (emotional) impact of this contact would likely be strong on the decision. The impact would, however, be less strong if the decision moment would be, for example, a few months ahead. Since such decision moments can be specified and traced with customer information systems, such customer contacts could be treated differently. For instance, with the help of technology such customers could be connected to expert (sales) employees, and they could even be served quicker than the other customers whose decision moments are more distant. Consequently, a rapid service with expert assistance would increase the chances that the contact is more positively experienced, and this positive contact experience would increase customer satisfaction and loyalty intentions.

Results showed that despite the variations in accuracies per firm and even per employee, with the ESCC observations firms would be able to identify many unsatisfied customers who would normally be unknown, since the majority of unsatisfied customers do not complain to the firms but to their friends and relatives.

Positive correlations have been found between CSRs own emotions and their ESCC evaluations, thus how CSRs perceive customer emotions. Although this relationship requires a specific (future) research, it initially appears that the emotional tone in customer contacts (the ESCC) influence CSRs immediate emotions, and therefore may influence the ESCC of the following calls. Maybe, it is a good idea to give CSRs an extra break, or, emotionally neutral tasks like archiving, after a series of (very) negative contacts.

Since the ESCC observations were able to separate customers with churn intentions from customers with loyalty intentions, it is suggested that having a general view of the emotional level on customer contacts would provide timely and tangible information that could be translated into specific actions. Hence, this research proposed several possibilities in increasing sales (productivity) by utilizing the ESCC information, drafted a construction for a practical and proactive service recovery process, and also suggested an organizational learning cycle.

Furthermore, the paradigmatic shift towards recognizing emotional values and 'emotionally conscious' service experiences would have some positive effects on stakeholders:

*Customers* would discern more "human touch" where a positive emotion factor is added to services. *CSRs*, whose emotional levels are also very critical for service encounters, would observe their own, as well as, customer's (emotional) satisfactions and would pro-act for service recovery, rather than management observing CSRs and re-acting for corrections. Then *management* would only have to facilitate, rather than control, the CSR-led recovery actions and preventive measures. Finally, *top executives* would be able to obtain regular, if not daily, feedback from their contact center's emotional satisfaction levels. And they would not have to wait for the results of their annual customer surveys in order to know what the hindrances of their firms are or what kind of emotion their product or services are creating. Since the ESCC information is constantly registered even the questions like *"How satisfied are our customers NOW?"* would promptly be available to executives.

Last but not least, as Rust, Zeithaml and Lemon (2000:34) suggested, "for an accurate gauge of the health of the organization, the company must now consider not only the current performance of its products, but also the future performance of its customer relationships"; and the ESCC model has the potential to provide this very information.

## *9.3* Limitations & Future research

- This research focused on test days of the ESCC implementation. Longer term effects of the ESCC model could be a subject for future research.
- Loyalty in this research is analyzed as "intention to stay as customer." Nevertheless, whether customer intentions are parallel with their future behavior is not examined. Therefore, it may be a subject for a further (longitudinal) research in which customer loyalty intentions are observed over time and compared with actual behavior.
- In this research, 'general satisfaction' is used to define the 'overall satisfaction' of customers. The term 'cumulative satisfaction' is reserved for a future research which will analyze the aggregation effect of 'transactional satisfactions.'
- Factors that may influence accuracy levels (customer age, gender, the length of relationship; CSR age, gender, and education, experience mood; time of the call) are analyzed, however, no significant relationship was found. More research seems to be needed to refine these issues.

- This research focused on in-house contact centers of commercial organizations that deal with incoming calls of individual customers. Outsourced contact centers, not-for-profit organizations, outbound (telesales) calls, and business customers remained as a subject for future research.
- In cross border outsourcing local CSRs serve customers from different countries and cultures. The effects of such multicultural settings could also be a subject for future research.
- In this research emotions are represented in a range between very negative and very positive. Specific emotions are not investigated. Further research can explore the relationship between customer contacts and specific emotions such as anger, surprise, or happiness.
- CSRs own emotions and the ESCC evaluations appeared to have a significant association immediately after calls, but not after several different calls. Specific dynamics behind this relationship can be investigated with a specific research setting.
- Reasons of customer dis/satisfactions are outside of the main focus of this research. However, it would be a subject for future research, such as "the elements in customer contacts that make customer dis/satisfied?"
- Organizational issues such as strategy, culture, emotional climate, principles in the organizations, leadership, control, change, etc. are not only very important aspects for potential implementations of the ESCC model but also very broad disciplines. Although related literature about these subjects is basically screened, and although these issues are shallowly discussed throughout the text, a detailed analysis supported with some empirical evidence is reserved for future research.

# 10 SUMMING UP

This chapter will review the previous chapters, and will summarize their main conclusions. In order to outline the full picture, conceptual and empirical parts will be combined in the next sections. Section 10.1 will summarize the introduction (Chapter 1). In section 10.2, the elements and dimensions of customer satisfaction and loyalty (Chapter 2) will be combined with survey results (Chapter 5). In section 10.3, the theory behind emotional satisfaction of customer contacts (ESCC) (Chapter 3) will be combined with the results of implementations in test firms (Chapter 6). In section 10.4, theoretical background of the steps from the ESCC observations to loyalty (Chapter 4) will be combined with the proposed models for using the ESCC information (Chapter 7). Finally, in section 10.5 some last reflections, implications, and limitations will be recapitulated.

## 10.1 Introduction

The introductory chapter 1 underlined the growing importance of contact centers and their growing presence in the daily lives of 21$^{st}$ century consumers. Despite the growing importance and presence, contact centers and their IVR systems seem to have become a center for customer "frustrations" and regularly associated with negative comments in the media.

Therefore it is suggested that positive customer experiences need to be increased in the contact center environment. Various studies indicated that customers want 'human touch' when dealing with their firms, and the expected growth in elderly people in western societies signified the necessity of more human touch in service environment and contact centers in particular. The Human Touch is the positive emotion that is created around services and work environment. Contact centers play a pivotal role in creating positive service experiences and the human touch in the entire customer journey from pre-acquisition to post-sales phases.

There are four parties identified as stakeholders of the contact center environment in this research. (1) *Top executives* in many firms seem not to be aware of or not fully concerned with the contact center dynamics; but demand more sales and profit from contact centers. (2) *Contact center management* appear to reside between conflicting goals such as increasing quality, customer satisfaction, employee motivation, and profitability with usually very limited resources given by the upper management. Therefore, contact centers are commonly discerned as the factory floors of the 21st century and labeled as high-tech sweat shops. Despite their obvious importance, (3) contact center jobs, i.e., *customer service representatives* (CSRs), are considered to be "low quality" and heavily routine; and not surprisingly CSRs have higher job related depression or job-related anxiety, and lower job satisfaction than most other jobs. Therefore, CSRs appeared to be the "Achilles' heel" of contact centers.

While (4) *customers* have many choices in a very competitive market place, they frequently experience frustration in contact centers and they even switch firms due to negative call center experiences; nevertheless, companies seemed not to fully comprehend these circumstances.

One of the reasons for this incomprehension appeared to be the traditional customer satisfaction measurements that are not adequate to capture such frustrations due to the limited number of customers that are contacted for surveys, low respond rates among unsatisfied customers, and positive influence of surveys on respondents. Also complaints seemed to be inadequate to identify many unsatisfied customers. In short, rather than filling in satisfaction surveys or complaint forms, many customers simply switch to competitors when they are unsatisfied, and firms seemed to be ineffective in dealing with these issues. Consequently, proactively identifying customer dissatisfaction appeared to be a necessity in marketing literature as well as in marketing practice.

On the one hand, customer dissatisfaction increases especially with contact centers, but firms are not able to fully capture this information. On the other hand, customer service representatives (CSR) in contact centers continuously observe whether or not customers are satisfied. It is, therefore, envisaged that CSRs can observe, evaluate and instantly register information about customer satisfaction. Examples from literature and business practices indicated that it is desirable as well as realistic to involve frontline personnel such as CSRs in the customer satisfaction (measurement) process.

*This research therefore attempted to analyze the customer satisfaction and loyalty process and proposed a model that could be used in the customer contact environment for observing customer satisfaction through the eyes of CSRs. As customer contacts can be a source of frustration (negative emotions), and as it appeared to be necessary to increase positive experiences (positive emotions) in the contact center environment, this research focused on emotional aspects of customer satisfaction, and emotional satisfaction of customer contacts (ESCC) in particular. It is envisaged that these observations would provide timely and tangible information for recovering service failures by following up dissatisfactions, for increasing sales productivity by following up satisfactions, and for organizational learning by continuous improvement actions. It is also envisaged that these actions would increase the internal and external quality and satisfaction, which in turn would increase customer loyalty (and profitability) as described in "the service profit chain" by Heskett et al. (1997).*

## 10.2 Elements, Dimensions, and Correlations in Customer Satisfaction and Loyalty

In chapter 2, based on literature review, six items are selected as the basic elements of customer satisfaction: Price, Product, Convenience, Service quality, Service treatment, and Positive feelings towards the firm or brand. Also four dimensions are identified as part of the customer satisfaction process: Emotional, Cognitive, Transactional, and General Satisfaction. Cognitive satisfaction represented the rational and thinking side of the satisfaction, whereas emotional satisfaction represented the experiential and feeling side. General satisfaction represented the overall satisfaction of customers, whereas transactional satisfaction' represented the last transactions, namely the satisfaction with last contact with firms. Finally, customer loyalty is investigated with the intention to stay as customer.

As described in chapter 5, customer surveys done in four different test firms, namely from book & music, insurance, pension fund, and banking sectors in The Netherlands, showed that customers are least satisfied with prices, convenience, and service quality issues. These low scores vis-à-vis other satisfaction areas indicated that customers expect lower prices, better services and more convenience. Low scores in service and convenience also confirmed the initial ideas that inspired this research: customers are not fully satisfied with the services they receive. Customers, however, appeared to be more loyal than they are satisfied, indicating that customer satisfaction cannot be translated directly to customer loyalty.

Almost all satisfaction items[120] used in this research, as common denominators of numerous studies, were moderately associated with general satisfaction, somewhat weaker with transactional satisfaction, and finally weakly with loyalty intention. Selected satisfaction elements and constructs thus appear to be more suitable in measuring general satisfaction than in measuring transactional satisfaction or loyalty intentions. This outcome confirmed the effectiveness of adding a transactional dimension in customer satisfaction measurement process, as well as, the necessity of analyzing customer loyalty with more specific constructs (cf. Reichheld, 1993:71; 1996:58).

Relatively positive responses to survey questions among test group customers, especially about their last contacts, signified that firms actually have the potential to increase customer satisfaction if they create an environment similar to the ESCC test days in which customer satisfaction is continuously observed and surveyed. However, more extreme dissatisfaction among test group customers also showed that with only 'extra attention' on customer satisfaction during service encounters firms cannot fully compensate their other shortcomings.

It appeared thus that customer contacts create a strong momentum for building intense opinions about the contacted firms. This fact, however, seemed not to be fully recognized in many organizations that regularly frustrate their customers in their contact centers.

However, there is no difference found between the test and control group customers in terms of loyalty intentions. This might indicate that test day settings with the ESCC have the potential to increase satisfaction, but on

[120] Price, Product, Convenience, Service quality, Service treatment, and Positive feelings towards the firm or brand.

average have no immediate impact on customer loyalty intentions, except in extreme cases where customers are severely dissatisfied.

On the one hand, products, service treatments, positive feelings, and loyalty intentions differed significantly among test firms; on the other hand, general satisfaction, prices, convenience, service quality, and satisfaction with last contact did not significantly differ, thus appeared as common denominators across industries.

Based on the principal component analysis, positive feelings for the firm, service quality, service treatment, and convenience are grouped under the 'emotional satisfaction' dimension; and prices and products under the 'cognitive satisfaction' (*Research Question 1*).

Cross-tabulation analyses with the dimensions of satisfaction showed that emotional dimension consistently plays a stronger role than cognitive dimension in transactional satisfaction, in general satisfaction, and in loyalty (*Research Questions 2a, b, c*). Despite the importance of emotional aspects, it was however contradictory to observe that many firms still heavily rely on cognitive aspects like prices in their marketing strategies.

Survey results showed that loyalty depends more on general satisfaction than on transactional satisfaction (*Research Question 3*). In other words, when customers are generally satisfied a single transactional incident, such as a disappointing customer contact, seems on average to be tolerable by customers. Conversely, a single transactional satisfaction seems not to have a big impact on general dissatisfaction. This finding, however, does not undermine the importance of transactional satisfaction, since the general satisfaction is a consequence of a series of transactional satisfactions. The ESCC surveys indicated that transactional and general satisfactions are interrelated and require each other's presence to generate a stronger effect on both sides. The survey results also indicated that the more positive the customer contacts with firms, the stronger the general satisfaction and loyalty intentions of customers (*Research Question 4a, b*).

The length of relationship with firms seemed to play no significant role in customer's general satisfaction process, but seemed to play a significant role in customer loyalty intentions. It appeared thus that customer satisfaction is an issue that plays a continuous and stable role during customer lifetime, whereas, customer loyalty appears to be strengthened in time. Survey results also pointed out that customer perceptions about the last contact with firms fade and become more moderate when time passes (*Research Question 5*), indicating that customer contact satisfaction can be particularly important close to the (re)purchase decision-making moments.

## 10.3 The Emotional Satisfaction of Customer Contacts (ESCC)

Chapter 3 basically examined the definition, measurement, and the role of emotions in customer satisfaction and in the contact center environment. On the one hand, customer emotions are linked to CSR emotions; on the other hand, CSR emotions are linked to organizational issues like emotional climate, emotional labor and emotional intelligence. These links indicated that organizational settings influence employee emotions and moods, and consequently influence customer emotions.

Chapter 3 also proposed a simple methodology for observing customer's (emotional) satisfaction during customer contacts by CSRs. In the ESCC model, a color range of 'red-orange-yellow-green-blue' represented CSR observations on customer's emotional states ranging from very negative to very positive. In order to help CSRs when assigning a color to a customer contact, two rough guidelines are designed. In the first one, the red represented most unpleasant and problematic calls to one extreme, and the blue represented most pleasant and easy-going calls to the other. In the second guideline, energy and pleasantness of calls are divided into high and low categories in a table with some specific emotions similar to the affect circumplex model, and these group of emotions are linked to the ESCC colors. It was however, not aimed to restrict the evaluations of CSRs with any guidelines. These colors, representing transactional satisfaction, are also linked to the emotional and cognitive dimensions, as well as, to churn and to loyalty as a cumulative effect.

During the test days, selected CSRs have evaluated all incoming calls with the ESCC methodology while doing their routine tasks. The ESCC model and research settings are briefly explained to CSRs who had no prior experience in such evaluations until test days.

Chapter 6 described the basic implementation of the ESCC methodology in test firms, examined the accuracy of the ESCC observations, and explored the relationship between observed ESCC, customer satisfaction, and loyalty intentions. As the results indicate, the test group customers perceived their contacts most positively, control group customers fairly positively, and finally the CSRs neutrally (*Research Question 6*). When the rough averages of CSRs, control and test group customers are taken into consideration it appeared that about 10% of customer contacts are evaluated as negative and very negative, about 20% neutral, about 50% positive, and 20% very positive. Nevertheless, when specific sample groups are analyzed, then some sharp differences have appeared. For instance, negative and very negative evaluations in the test group of insurance firm was 23.6%, whereas, the same percentage in book & music firm was only 2.4%.

The critical issue, however, was whether CSR observations are accurate. The accuracy is calculated by taking the difference between 'customer evaluation' on the last contact (survey question 9) and the 'ESCC observation' of CSR about the same contact. In one-on-one comparisons, the average accuracy was 34%; when the data was re-grouped into three classes (1&2, 3&4, 5), the average accuracy increased to about 60%; and when one-scale-differences where customers are more positive than CSRs were considered as accurate, then the accuracy reached near 80%.

Cohen's Kappa statistic, Boxplot chart, cross-tabs, $\chi^2$ analysis, and correlation coefficients signified the ESCC as a 'reasonable indicator' rather than a 'precise tool' for assessing satisfaction in customer contacts (*Research Question 7*).

Accuracy rates varied among the test firms, being more accurate in book & music and in insurance firms, and less accurate in pension fund and in the bank. CSRs were more accurate in extreme scales and even more accurate in negative cases; hence, the more intense the customer contacts the more accurate the CSR evaluations in customer satisfaction. Although, no significant aspects are found that may influence the accuracy levels of the ESCC observations, practicing the ESCC observations for a longer time, and calibrating it by frequently comparing them with customer evaluations enhanced the accuracies. For example, accurate observations increased from 30% to 45% in a Dutch financial organization over a month period.

Positive correlations have been found between CSRs own emotions and their ESCC evaluations, thus how CSRs perceive customer emotions. It also appeared that the ESCC significantly associated with how CSRs feel immediately after calls, but not with how they feel after several different calls (*Research Question 8*).

As correlation and $\chi^2$ analysis indicated, the ESCC observations associated more strongly with emotional satisfaction than cognitive satisfaction (*Research Question 9a*). In other words, the ESCC observations represented the customer satisfaction with convenience, service quality, service treatment, and positive feelings towards the firm, more strongly than the satisfaction with price and products. The statistical strength of this relationship has however, appeared to be between weak and moderate.

The relationship between the ESCC and transactional satisfaction, general satisfaction, and customer loyalty intentions are examined with correlation coefficients, correspondence analyses, cross-tabs and $\chi^2$ analyses. Results indicated that the ESCC associated moderately with transactional satisfaction, weakly with general satisfaction, and somewhat moderately with customer loyalty intentions (*Research Questions 9b, c, d*).

Moreover, the ESCC observations effectively separated customers with churn intentions from customers with loyalty intentions. In other words, CSRs were able to observe and assess transactional satisfaction with a reasonable accuracy during customer contacts; and these observations were a reasonable predictor of customer loyalty intentions. More specifically, the more positive the ESCC, the stronger the customer satisfaction and loyalty!

## 10.4 Employing the ESCC

Chapter 4 started with the assumption that information is valuable when it is actionable, and suggested the next steps in the ESCC process by reviewing related literature. Chapter 7 described these steps within the ESCC framework and with some, albeit very limited, empirical evidence. These steps included following up positive ESCC for more sales, following up negative ESCC for service recovery, learning from failures and improvements, and consequently increasing satisfaction and loyalty (*Research Question 10*).

Studies showed that positive customer experiences lead to more sales, and it is suggested that the ESCC information, indicating customer experience levels, can be utilized for increasing sales performance and productivity which is one of the 'hot topics' in the contact center industry.

Sales in contact centers are primarily done by utilizing inbound calls, or by initiating telesales calls. Nevertheless, the majority of customers neither appreciate an exaggerated sales push when they contact their firms, nor would they like to receive telesales calls. Moreover, sales pressure can even be annoying for customers when organizations cannot properly serve them in the first place.

The ESCC methodologies therefore, aimed at identifying the best customers and the best moments for initiating sales actions which can be summarized in three possibilities. Firstly, it is expected that more positive service experiences would increase customer satisfaction and consequently propensity for (re)purchase. Secondly, it is proposed that special actions can be designed for (very) satisfied customers with very positive ESCC. Thirdly, it is suggested that elimination of disappointed and angry customers with (very) negative ESCC from direct marketing actions would decrease costs and would consequently increase sales productivity.

Literature research confirmed the necessity, as well, as the effectiveness of proactive service recoveries in regaining customer satisfaction and loyalty, and the ESCC methodologies attempted to fill the gap of "how to make it operational!" Therefore, it is proposed that registered ESCC information can be analyzed, filtered for actionable customer disappointments, and such customer problems can be recovered proactively. Limited empirical evidence indicated that recovery actions are very effective in regaining customer satisfaction and loyalty, and proved that the ESCC is a reliable construction for a practical service recovery process.

The process of detecting and correcting error is examined under organizational learning. Studies suggested to grasp value from failures by learning from them, to translate them into improvements, and thereby to create customer satisfaction and loyalty. Also three learning loops are identified: single-loop learning where errors are detected and corrected; double-loop learning where processes and products are improved; and triple-loop learning where systems learn how to learn, and norms, principles and associated values are adjusted.

The ESCC model prescribed the practicalities of a learning organization, and proposed a simple methodology that at least proactively feeds single-loop learning where errors are detected and corrected. The saucepan (company) and water (customers) metaphor illustrated the ESCC process in organizational learning. In this metaphor, the ESCC lid (model) captured the steam (information on customer dissatisfaction) and simply utilized it by recovery actions for customer retention, and by process improvements for organizational learning and customer satisfaction.

The importance of utilizing the ESCC information and making progress towards the next loops in organizational learning is also underlined. Employee empowerment, team learning, as well as, a shift from "control" to "care" in management styles were seen as the few initial building blocks of learning organizations.

Finally, literature research and survey results verified the links between improvements in services and increases in customer satisfaction; however, what comes after satisfaction was not confirmed. Loyalty and profitability appeared to be reasonable extensions of customer satisfaction but with no guarantees.

## 10.5 Some last reflections, implications, and limitations

A few principles drafted as the final reflections on the subject. The ESCC model, first of all, is described as a tool that collects information about each customer contact by involving and empowering CSRs in customer satisfaction, loyalty, and organizational learning processes. Secondly, the ESCC approach appeared to be an instrument that could sketch a full transactional satisfaction picture of the customer contact environment.

The ESCC model, however, did not propose to start (emotional) relationships with customers; did not intend to generalize its scores for judging CSRs, organizations, or customers; and also did not imply to compensate severe product quality deficiencies, or, very high price differences vis-à-vis competition.

Several findings in this research such as "customer satisfaction cannot be translated directly to customer loyalty", "loyalty depends more on emotional dimensions than on cognitive dimensions", and "recovery actions after dissatisfactory service encounters can save the customer from defection and can even increase loyalty" were in line with the existing literature. This research also revealed the relationship between transactional and general satisfaction dimensions, which appeared to be interrelated and require each other's presence.

Prior studies investigated customer emotions and frontline employee feedbacks with, for example, critical incident techniques. This research, however, set a practical methodology for assessing emotional satisfaction of customer contacts, and for comparing frontline employee's view with customer's view on customer (contact) satisfaction.

For managerial implications, this research sketched a simple observation and registration process in assessing emotions evoked during customer contacts through the eyes of CSRs. With these observations firms would be able to identify many unsatisfied customers who would normally be unknown to them, since the majority of unsatisfied customers do not complain to the firms but to their friends and relatives. This research also proposed several possibilities in increasing sales (productivity) by utilizing the ESCC information, drafted a construction for a practical and proactive service recovery process, and also suggested an organizational learning cycle. Last but not least, as Rust, Zeithaml and Lemon, (2000:34) suggested, "for an accurate gauge of the health of the organization, the company must now consider not only the current performance of its products, but also the future performance of its customer relationships." The ESCC model has appeared to have the potential to provide this very information.

Limitations of this research were mainly related to longer term effects of the ESCC model. Moreover, this research focused on in-house contact centers of commercial organizations that deal with incoming calls of individual customers. Outsourced contact centers, not-for-profit organizations, outbound (telesales) calls, and business customers remained a subject for future research. Lastly, in this research emotions were represented in a range between very negative and very positive, rather than specific emotions. Further research can explore the relationship between customer contacts and specific emotions such as anger, surprise, or happiness.

# 11 APPENDIX

## 11.1 List of Abbreviations

**ATM**: Automated Teller Machine or cash dispensers of banks.

**CC** or **CCC**: Call Center, Contact Center, Customer Contact Center.

**cf.**: Abbreviation for the Latin word “confer” means “compare”.

**CRM**: Customer Relationship Management

**CSR**: Customer Service Representative, Call Center Agent, Frontline Employee.

**ESCC**: Emotional Satisfaction of Customer Contacts

**IVR**: Interactive Voice Response

**p<**: Probability of obtaining the statistic by chance, indicating statistical significance. Values lower than 0.05 are commonly considered as significant.

**Sig.**: Statistical Significance, see also p<

## 11.2 Customer Survey Script & Questionnaire

Introduction: Good morning/afternoon/evening, my name is……., and I am calling from XYZ as part of a quality program to assess our customer's satisfaction levels. Would you be willing to answer a few questions which would take only a few minutes of your time? Please also note that you are randomly selected for this survey, and results will be analyzed anonymously.

1. *When was your last contact with XYZ Telephone Center?*

   Today (or few days) - A week ago - A month ago - Few months ago - Longer than 6 months ago

I will read a few statements about XYZ, and will ask whether or not you agree with these statements. You can choose between (1) Strongly Disagree, [Disagree, Neither agree nor disagree, Agree] and (5) Strongly Agree.

If this is okay with you, I would like to start with the first statement…

2. *I am a satisfied customer of XYZ in General.*

   Strongly Disagree - Disagree - Neither agree nor disagree – Agree - Strongly Agree

3. *I am satisfied with XYZ's prices (interest rates), and other charges like fees and commissions.*

   Strongly Disagree - Disagree - Neither agree nor disagree – Agree - Strongly Agree

4. *I am satisfied with XYZ's products. [E.g.: variety, their term and conditions…]*

   Strongly Disagree - Disagree - Neither agree nor disagree – Agree - Strongly Agree

5. *It is very easy and convenient to be a customer of XYZ.*

   Strongly Disagree - Disagree - Neither agree nor disagree – Agree - Strongly Agree

6. *I am satisfied with the way XYZ treats me.*

   Strongly Disagree - Disagree - Neither agree nor disagree – Agree - Strongly Agree

7. *I am satisfied with the service quality of XYZ. [E.g.,: Reliable, accurate, timely]*

   Strongly Disagree - Disagree - Neither agree nor disagree – Agree - Strongly Agree

8. *I have positive feelings towards XYZ [as a company].*

   Strongly Disagree - Disagree - Neither agree nor disagree – Agree - Strongly Agree

9. *How would you evaluate your (last) telephone contact with XYZ?*

   Very Negative - Negative - Neutral - Positive - Very Positive

The last question is about your intentions about the future relations with XYZ. Please note that your answers are anonymously analyzed. The question is:

10. *In the future, would you stay as a customer of XYZ? Is it…*

    Very Unlikely - Unlikely - Neither unlikely nor likely - Likely - Very Likely

Do you have any remarks that I can note? ……………..………………………

Finally I have two general questions: When did you become a customer of XYZ? (year…….) What is your year of birth? [Note customer gender: M / F]

EXIT: Thank you very much for your time. XYZ will be acting upon this survey to ensure the highest quality of service is maintained.

## 11.3 Customer Survey Script & Questionnaire (Dutch Version)

Introductie: Goedemiddag, u spreekt met ......van XYZ. Wij zijn bezig met een tevredenheids onderzoek onder onze klanten. Wij hebben u willekeurig geselecteerd uit het XYZ bestand. Uw antwoorden zullen vertrouwelijk en anoniem (dus niet op naam) verwerkt worden. Heeft u een paar minuten voor 10 korte vragen?

*1) Wanneer was uw laatste contact met XYZ contact center?*

Deze week - een week geleden - een maand... - enkele maanden... - langer dan 6 maanden...

Ik ga u een aantal stellingen over XYZ voorlezen en de vraag is dan in hoeverre u het met deze stelling eens bent. U kunt dan kiezen uit (1) helemaal mee oneens, [mee oneens, niet mee eens/niet mee oneens, mee eens] of (5) helemaal mee eens.

Is dit voor u duidelijk? Dan nu de eerste stelling.

*2) Ik ben een tevreden klant van XYZ.*

Helemaal mee oneens - mee oneens - niet mee eens / niet mee oneens - mee eens - helemaal mee eens

*3) Ik ben tevreden over de prijzen (rentevergoeding) en overige tarieven van XYZ.*

Helemaal mee oneens - mee oneens - niet mee eens / niet mee oneens - mee eens - helemaal mee eens

*4) Ik ben tevreden met de producten van XYZ.*

Helemaal mee oneens - mee oneens - niet mee eens / niet mee oneens - mee eens - helemaal mee eens

*5) Het is erg handig en makkelijk om klant te zijn van XYZ.*

Helemaal mee oneens - mee oneens - niet mee eens / niet mee oneens - mee eens - helemaal mee eens

*6) Ik ben tevreden met de manier waarop XYZ mij behandelt.*

Helemaal mee oneens - mee oneens - niet mee eens / niet mee oneens - mee eens - helemaal mee eens

*7) Ik vind dat XYZ goede service geeft. [Bijvoorbeeld: betrouwbaar, accuraat en op tijd.]*

Helemaal mee oneens - mee oneens - niet mee eens / niet mee oneens - mee eens - helemaal mee eens

*8) Ik heb een goed gevoel bij XYZ als bedrijf.*

Helemaal mee oneens - mee oneens - niet mee eens / niet mee oneens - mee eens - helemaal mee eens

*9) Hoe beoordeelt u het laatste contact dat u met XYZ heeft gehad? (ENQ. Lees voor)*

Zeer negatief – negatief - niet negatief, niet positief – positief - zeer positief

De laatste vraag gaat over het voortzetten van uw relatie met XYZ. Deze vraag is uitsluitend bestemd voor dit onderzoek en niet voor commerciële doeleinden. De vraag is:

*10) Blijft u in de toekomst klant van XYZ, is dat (ENQ. Lees voor)*

Zeker niet - Waarschijnlijk niet - Misschien wel, misschien niet - Waarschijnlijk wel - Zeker wel

Heeft u nog opmerkingen die ik kan noteren? ........................................

Tenslotte heb ik nog twee algemene vragen aan u. [ENQ. Noteer geslacht: M / V]. Sinds wanneer (welk jaar) bent u klant bij XYZ? ... ... ...Wat is uw geboortejaar? ....... ......

Ik dank u voor uw tijd en medewerking. Met behulp van dit onderzoek zullen wij proberen onze klanten nog beter van dienst te zijn.

## 11.4 Survey Table: Comparison of means between test and control group

| Test or Control Group | Generally satisfied | Prices are satisfactory | Products are satisfactory | convenient to be firm's customer | Satisfied the way the firm treats him/her | Reliable, accurate, and timely services | Positive feelings for the firm | Last contact was satisfactory | Intention to stay as customer |
|---|---|---|---|---|---|---|---|---|---|
| **TEST GROUP Mean** | **3.85** | **3.43** | **3.84** | **3.67** | **3.78** | **3.76** | **3.82** | **3.99** | **4.06** |
| N | 303 | 293 | 300 | 301 | 302 | 301 | 299 | 301 | 299 |
| Std. Deviation | .878 | .932 | .791 | .943 | .985 | .963 | .829 | .969 | 1.144 |
| **CONTROL GROUP Mean** | **3.92** | **3.54** | **3.84** | **3.76** | **3.95** | **3.87** | **3.90** | **3.89** | **4.08** |
| N | 406 | 399 | 404 | 403 | 406 | 404 | 404 | 405 | 406 |
| Std. Deviation | .734 | .873 | .666 | .793 | .786 | .770 | .660 | .804 | 1.094 |
| **TOTAL Mean** | **3.89** | **3.49** | **3.84** | **3.72** | **3.88** | **3.82** | **3.86** | **3.93** | **4.07** |
| N | 709 | 692 | 704 | 704 | 708 | 705 | 703 | 706 | 705 |
| Std. Deviation | .799 | .899 | .721 | .861 | .880 | .858 | .737 | .879 | 1.115 |

## 11.5 Survey Table: Comparison of means among test firms

| Test company | Generally satisfied | Prices are satisfactory | Products are satisfactory | convenient to be firm's customer | Satisfied the way the firm treats him/her | Reliable, accurate, and timely services | Positive feelings for the firm | Last contact was satisfactory | Intention to stay as customer |
|---|---|---|---|---|---|---|---|---|---|
| **book & music Mean** | **3.88** | **3.55** | **3.71** | **3.72** | **3.99** | **3.92** | **3.79** | **3.97** | **3.61** |
| N | 210 | 210 | 210 | 210 | 210 | 210 | 210 | 208 | 209 |
| Std. Deviation | .699 | .853 | .741 | .826 | .634 | .673 | .661 | .680 | 1.383 |
| **insurance Mean** | **3.84** | **3.55** | **3.82** | **3.66** | **3.72** | **3.71** | **3.82** | **3.79** | **4.05** |
| N | 148 | 148 | 148 | 148 | 148 | 148 | 148 | 148 | 148 |
| Std. Deviation | .878 | .950 | .791 | .930 | 1.017 | .964 | .789 | 1.032 | .957 |
| **pension f. Mean** | **4.01** | **3.45** | **3.93** | **3.84** | **3.99** | **3.91** | **3.99** | **4.05** | **4.35** |
| N | 177 | 176 | 177 | 177 | 177 | 177 | 177 | 177 | 176 |
| Std. Deviation | .754 | .739 | .699 | .791 | .872 | .841 | .666 | .855 | .822 |
| **bank Mean** | **3.81** | **3.42** | **3.92** | **3.66** | **3.76** | **3.71** | **3.86** | **3.88** | **4.37** |
| N | 174 | 158 | 169 | 169 | 173 | 170 | 168 | 173 | 172 |
| Std. Deviation | .876 | 1.060 | .631 | .906 | .982 | .959 | .835 | .957 | .937 |

## 11.6 Survey Table: Test Firms Frequency Distribution (colon %)

| | | book & music | insurance | pension f. | bank |
|---|---|---|---|---|---|
| Generally satisfied | Strongly Disagree | .5% | 2.7% | 1.1% | 2.9% |
| | Disagree | 7.6% | 6.8% | 3.4% | 6.9% |
| | Neither Agree Nor Disagree | 5.2% | 10.8% | 10.7% | 11.5% |
| | Agree | 76.7% | 62.8% | 62.7% | 63.8% |
| | Strongly Agree | 10.0% | 16.9% | 22.0% | 14.9% |
| Prices are satisfactory | Strongly Disagree | 1.0% | 2.7% | 1.1% | 5.7% |
| | Disagree | 16.2% | 10.1% | 7.4% | 18.4% |
| | Neither Agree Nor Disagree | 14.8% | 31.1% | 40.3% | 12.7% |
| | Agree | 63.3% | 41.9% | 47.2% | 55.1% |
| | Strongly Agree | 4.8% | 14.2% | 4.0% | 8.2% |
| Products are satisfactory | Strongly Disagree | 1.0% | 2.0% | .6% | .6% |
| | Diasgree | 7.6% | 4.7% | 2.3% | 4.7% |
| | Neither Agree Nor Disagree | 17.1% | 15.5% | 18.1% | 6.5% |
| | Agree | 67.6% | 64.9% | 62.1% | 78.7% |
| | Strongly Agree | 6.7% | 12.8% | 16.9% | 9.5% |
| It is convenient to be firm's customer | Strongly Disagree | 1.4% | 3.4% | 1.1% | 1.8% |
| | Disagree | 10.0% | 6.1% | 5.1% | 14.2% |
| | Neither Agree Nor Disagree | 13.3% | 27.0% | 18.6% | 10.1% |
| | Agree | 65.7% | 48.0% | 59.3% | 63.9% |
| | Strongly Agree | 9.5% | 15.5% | 15.8% | 10.1% |
| Satisfied the way the firm treats him/her | Strongly Disagree | 1.0% | 4.7% | 1.7% | 3.5% |
| | Disagree | 2.4% | 10.1% | 6.8% | 9.8% |
| | Neither Agree Nor Disagree | 7.6% | 10.8% | 7.9% | 12.7% |
| | Agree | 74.8% | 57.4% | 58.2% | 55.5% |
| | Strongly Agree | 14.3% | 16.9% | 25.4% | 18.5% |
| Reliable, accurate, and timely services | Strongly Disagree | .5% | 2.7% | .6% | 1.8% |
| | Disagree | 4.3% | 10.8% | 7.9% | 14.7% |
| | Neither Agree Nor Disagree | 11.0% | 16.2% | 13.0% | 10.0% |
| | Agree | 71.0% | 53.4% | 57.1% | 58.2% |
| | Strongly Agree | 13.3% | 16.9% | 21.5% | 15.3% |
| Positive feelings for the firm | Strongly Disagree | .5% | | .6% | 1.8% |
| | Disagree | 5.2% | 7.4% | 3.4% | 7.7% |
| | Neither Agree Nor Disagree | 16.2% | 18.9% | 9.0% | 8.9% |
| | Agree | 71.4% | 57.4% | 70.6% | 66.1% |
| | Strongly Agree | 6.7% | 16.2% | 16.4% | 15.5% |
| Last contact was satisfactory | Strongly Disagree | .5% | 6.1% | .6% | 2.9% |
| | Disagree | 2.4% | 5.4% | 6.2% | 8.1% |
| | Neither Agree Nor Disagree | 14.4% | 12.8% | 11.9% | 10.4% |
| | Agree | 64.9% | 54.7% | 50.3% | 54.9% |
| | Strongly Agree | 17.8% | 20.9% | 31.1% | 23.7% |
| Intention to stay as customer | Very Unlikely | 14.4% | 2.0% | 1.1% | 2.3% |
| | Somewhat Unlikely | 7.2% | 4.7% | .6% | 2.9% |
| | Neither Likely Nor Unlikely | 14.8% | 16.9% | 13.6% | 9.3% |
| | Somewhat Likely | 30.6% | 39.2% | 31.3% | 26.2% |
| | Very Likely | 33.0% | 37.2% | 53.4% | 59.3% |

## 11.7 **Survey Table: Test & Control Group Frequency Distribution** (colon %)

| | | Test Group | Control Group |
|---|---|---|---|
| Generally satisfied | Strongly Disagree | 2.6% | 1.0% |
| | Disagree | 7.3% | 5.4% |
| | Neither Agree Nor Disagree | 9.6% | 9.1% |
| | Agree | 63.7% | 69.7% |
| | Strongly Agree | 16.8% | 14.8% |
| Prices are satisfactory | Strongly Disagree | 4.1% | 1.3% |
| | Disagree | 13.0% | 13.3% |
| | Neither Agree Nor Disagree | 24.6% | 24.1% |
| | Agree | 52.6% | 52.9% |
| | Strongly Agree | 5.8% | 8.5% |
| Products are satisfactory | Strongly Disagree | 2.0% | .2% |
| | Diasgree | 5.7% | 4.5% |
| | Neither Agree Nor Disagree | 11.7% | 16.6% |
| | Agree | 68.0% | 68.6% |
| | Strongly Agree | 12.7% | 10.1% |
| It is convenient to be firm's customer | Strongly Disagree | 4.0% | .2% |
| | Disagree | 9.0% | 8.9% |
| | Neither Agree Nor Disagree | 15.6% | 17.6% |
| | Agree | 59.1% | 60.5% |
| | Strongly Agree | 12.3% | 12.7% |
| Satisfied the way the firm treats him/her | Strongly Disagree | 4.3% | 1.2% |
| | Disagree | 8.6% | 5.7% |
| | Neither Agree Nor Disagree | 10.3% | 9.1% |
| | Agree | 58.6% | 65.0% |
| | Strongly Agree | 18.2% | 19.0% |
| Reliable, accurate, and timely services | Strongly Disagree | 2.7% | .2% |
| | Disagree | 11.3% | 7.4% |
| | Neither Agree Nor Disagree | 11.0% | 13.4% |
| | Agree | 57.1% | 63.4% |
| | Strongly Agree | 17.9% | 15.6% |
| Positive feelings for the firm | Strongly Disagree | 1.7% | |
| | Disagree | 7.0% | 5.0% |
| | Neither Agree Nor Disagree | 14.0% | 12.6% |
| | Agree | 62.5% | 70.3% |
| | Strongly Agree | 14.7% | 12.1% |
| Last contact was satisfactory | Strongly Disagree | 3.7% | 1.2% |
| | Disagree | 5.0% | 5.7% |
| | Neither Agree Nor Disagree | 10.6% | 13.8% |
| | Agree | 50.5% | 61.2% |
| | Strongly Agree | 30.2% | 18.0% |
| Intention to stay as customer | Very Unlikely | 5.7% | 5.4% |
| | Somewhat Unlikely | 4.7% | 3.4% |
| | Neither Likely Nor Unlikely | 14.4% | 13.1% |
| | Somewhat Likely | 28.8% | 33.5% |
| | Very Likely | 46.5% | 44.6% |

## 11.8 Survey Charts: Differences among Test Firms; and between Test and Control Group

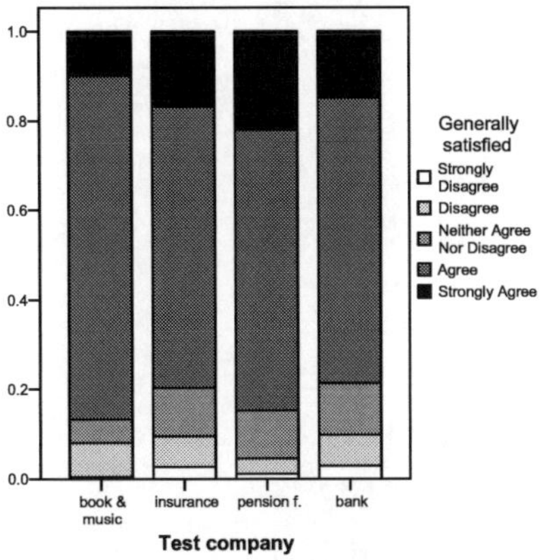


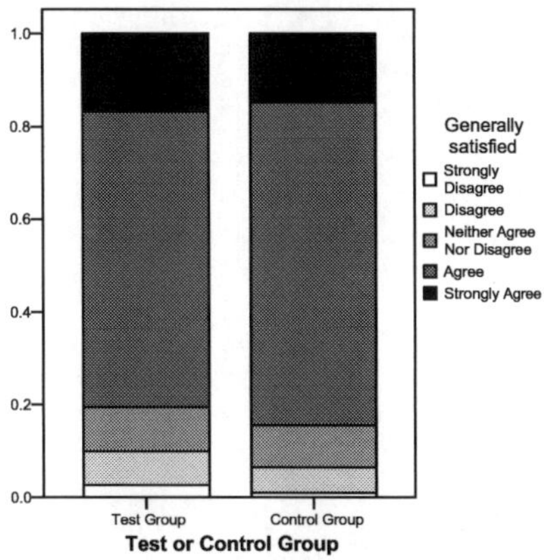


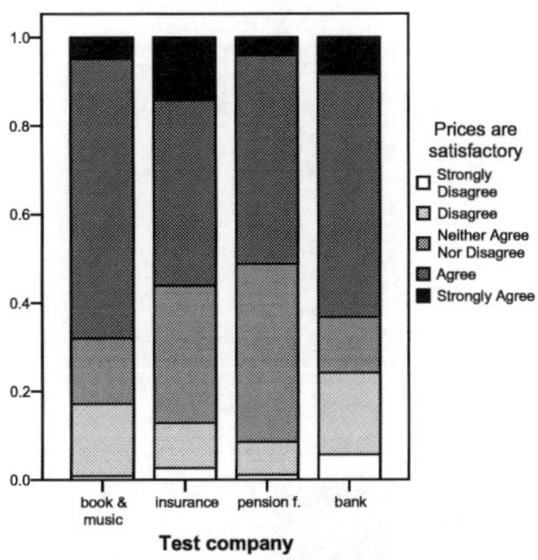


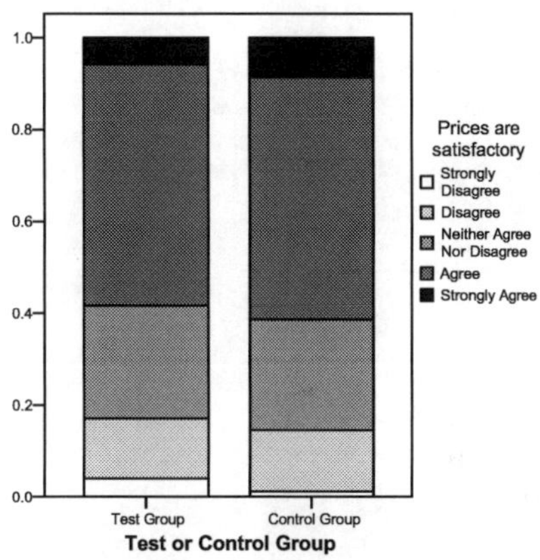


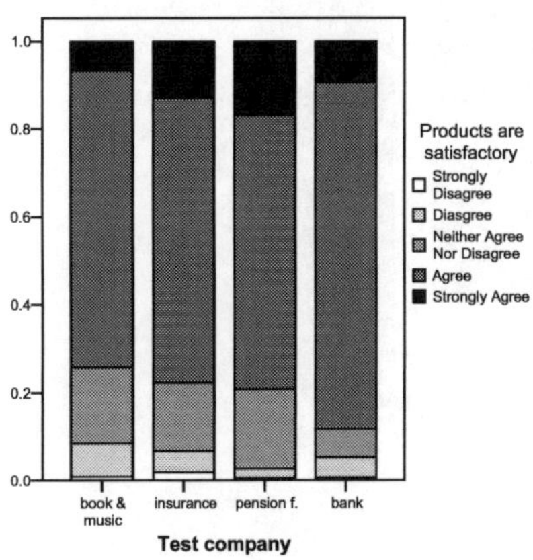


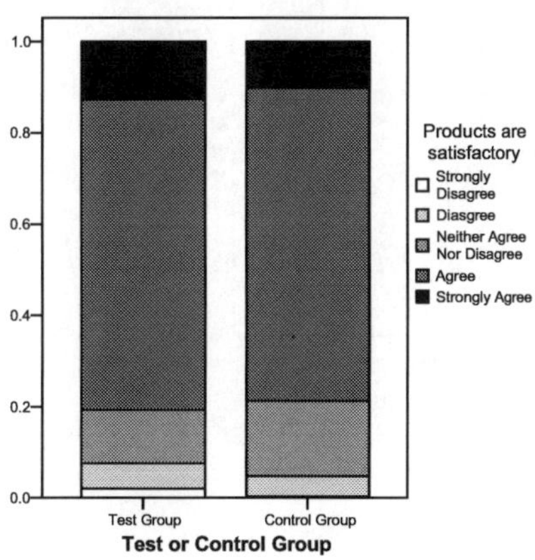

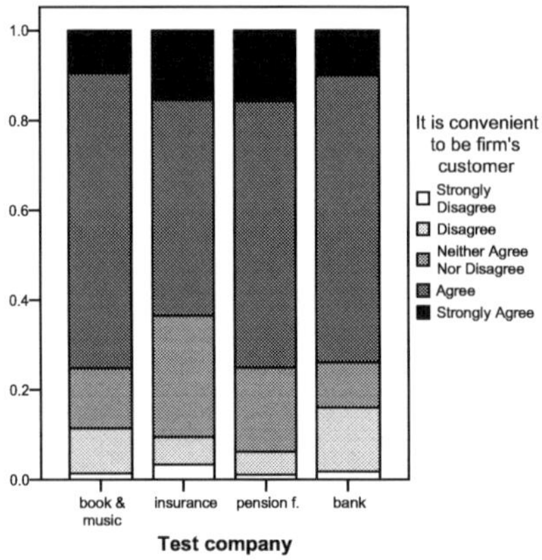
1.0
0.8
0.6
0.4
0.2
0.0
book & music
insurance
pension f.
bank
Test company
It is convenient to be firm's customer
Strongly Disagree
Disagree
Neither Agree Nor Disagree
Agree
Strongly Agree

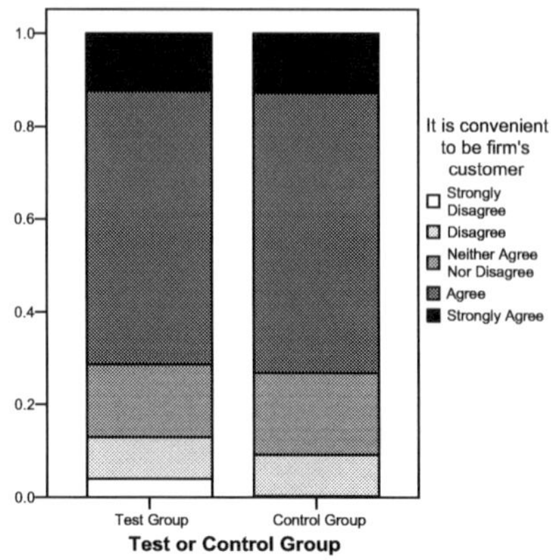
1.0
0.8
0.6
0.4
0.2
0.0
Test Group
Control Group
Test or Control Group
It is convenient to be firm's customer
Strongly Disagree
Disagree
Neither Agree Nor Disagree
Agree
Strongly Agree

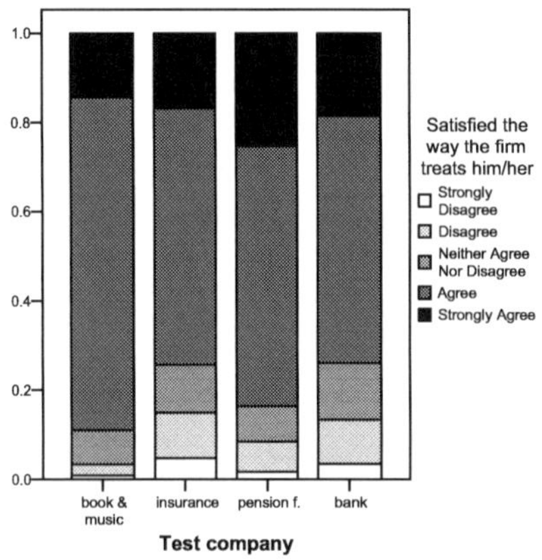
1.0
0.8
0.6
0.4
0.2
0.0
book & music
insurance
pension f.
bank
Test company
Satisfied the way the firm treats him/her
Strongly Disagree
Disagree
Neither Agree Nor Disagree
Agree
Strongly Agree

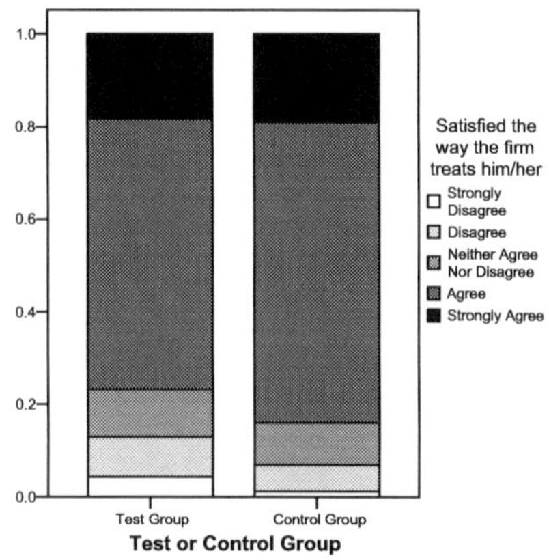
1.0
0.8
0.6
0.4
0.2
0.0
Test Group
Control Group
Test or Control Group
Satisfied the way the firm treats him/her
Strongly Disagree
Disagree
Neither Agree Nor Disagree
Agree
Strongly Agree

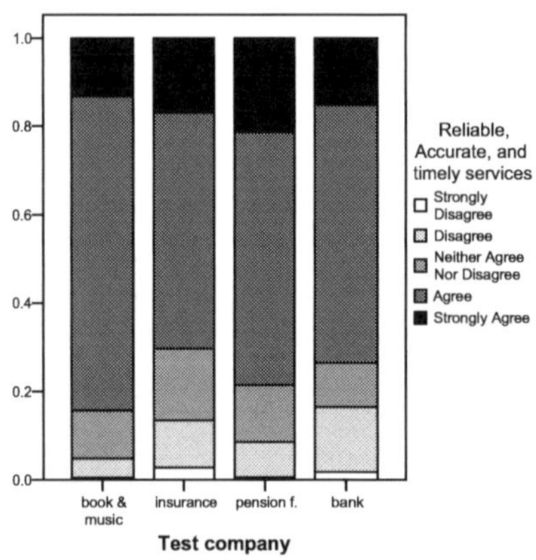
1.0
0.8
0.6
0.4
0.2
0.0
book & music
insurance
pension f.
bank
Test company
Reliable, Accurate, and timely services
Strongly Disagree
Disagree
Neither Agree Nor Disagree
Agree
Strongly Agree

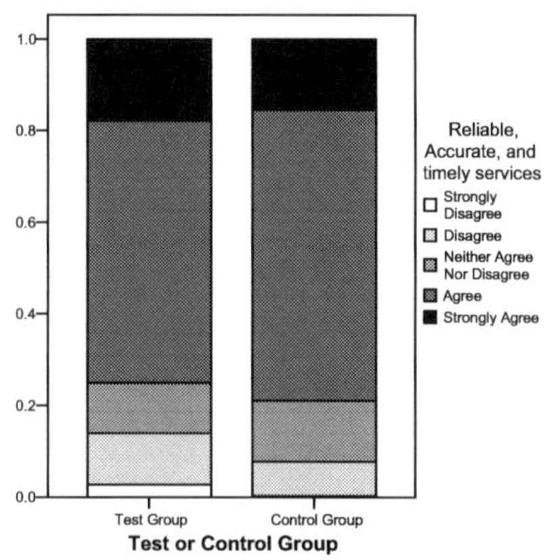
1.0
0.8
0.6
0.4
0.2
0.0
Test Group
Control Group
Test or Control Group
Reliable, Accurate, and timely services
Strongly Disagree
Disagree
Neither Agree Nor Disagree
Agree
Strongly Agree

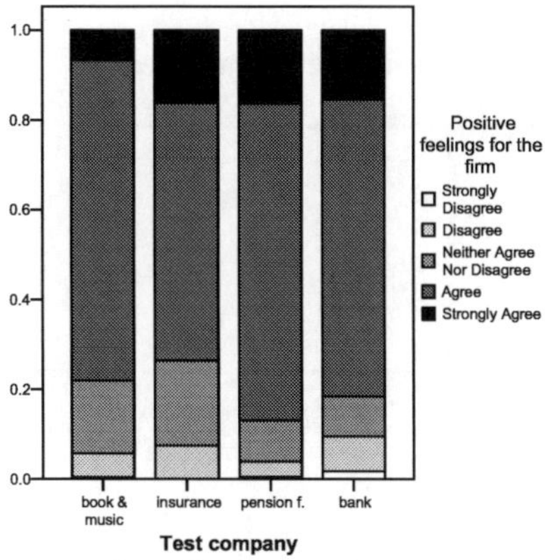
1.0
0.8
0.6
0.4
0.2
0.0
book & music
insurance
pension f.
bank
Test company
Positive feelings for the firm
Strongly Disagree
Disagree
Neither Agree Nor Disagree
Agree
Strongly Agree

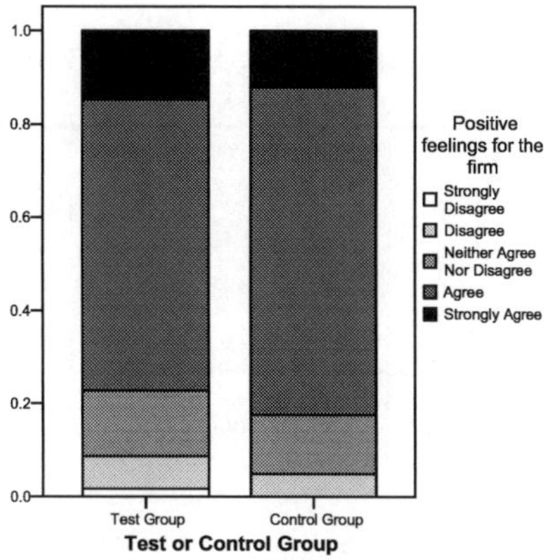
1.0
0.8
0.6
0.4
0.2
0.0
Test Group
Control Group
Test or Control Group
Positive feelings for the firm
Strongly Disagree
Disagree
Neither Agree Nor Disagree
Agree
Strongly Agree

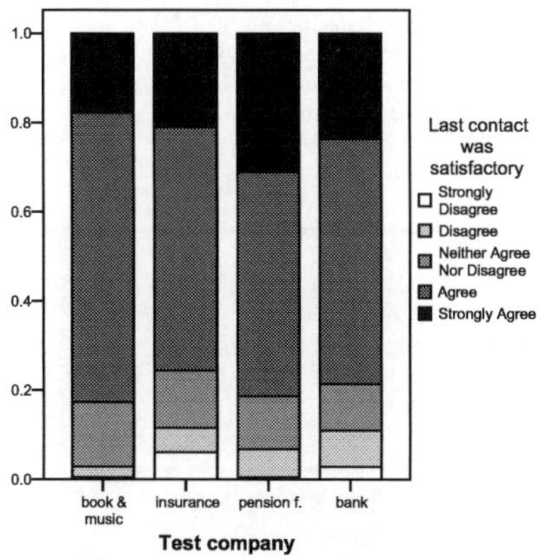
1.0
0.8
0.6
0.4
0.2
0.0
book & music
insurance
pension f.
bank
Test company
Last contact was satisfactory
Strongly Disagree
Disagree
Neither Agree Nor Disagree
Agree
Strongly Agree

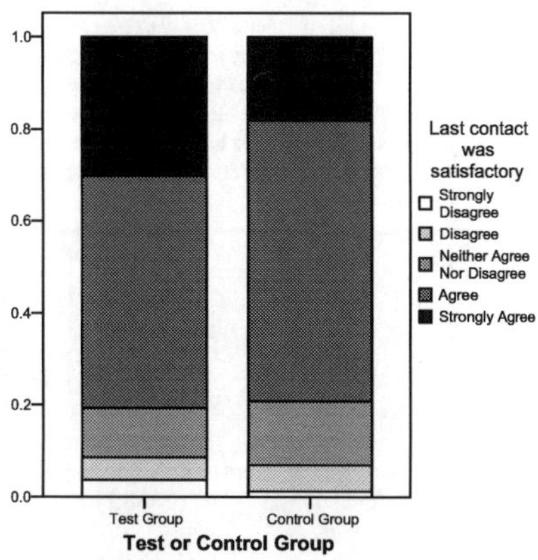
1.0
0.8
0.6
0.4
0.2
0.0
Test Group
Control Group
Test or Control Group
Last contact was satisfactory
Strongly Disagree
Disagree
Neither Agree Nor Disagree
Agree
Strongly Agree

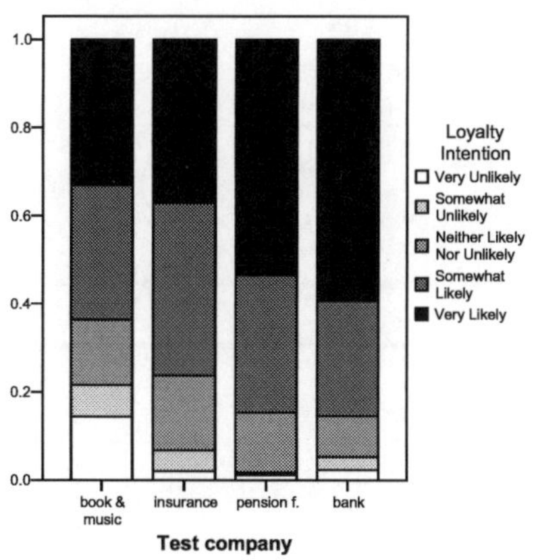
1.0
0.8
0.6
0.4
0.2
0.0
book & music
insurance
pension f.
bank
Test company
Loyalty Intention
Very Unlikely
Somewhat Unlikely
Neither Likely Nor Unlikely
Somewhat Likely
Very Likely

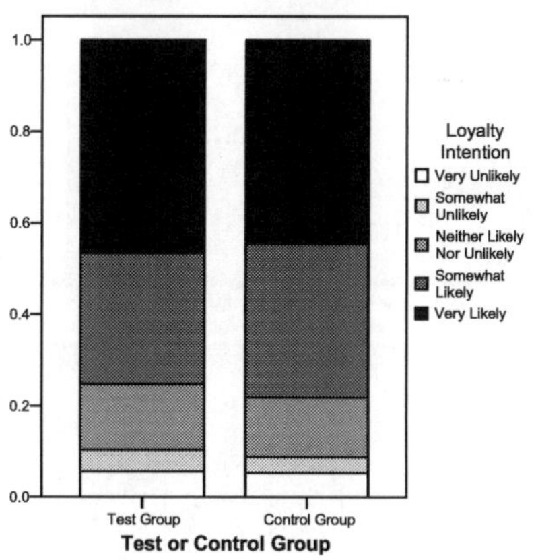
1.0
0.8
0.6
0.4
0.2
0.0
Test Group
Control Group
Test or Control Group
Loyalty Intention
Very Unlikely
Somewhat Unlikely
Neither Likely Nor Unlikely
Somewhat Likely
Very Likely

## 11.9 Chi-Square, Mann-Whitney U, Kruskal-Wallis Test Statistics

| Chi-Square | Generally satisfied | Prices are satisfactory | Products are satisfactory | It is convenient to be firm's customer | Satisfied the way the firm treats him/her | Reliable, accurate, and timely services | Positive feelings for the firm | Last contact was satisfactory | Intention to stay as customer |
|---|---|---|---|---|---|---|---|---|---|
| Chi-Square a,b,c,d,e,f,g | 1021 | 555 | 1066 | 744 | 840 | 774 | 1009 | 684 | 452 |
| df | 4 | 4 | 4 | 4 | 4 | 4 | 4 | 4 | 4 |
| Asymp. Sig. | .000 | .000 | .000 | .000 | .000 | .000 | .000 | .000 | .000 |

a 0 cells (.0%) have expected frequencies less than 5. The minimum expected cell frequency is 141.8.
b 0 cells (.0%) have expected frequencies less than 5. The minimum expected cell frequency is 138.4.
c 0 cells (.0%) have expected frequencies less than 5. The minimum expected cell frequency is 140.8.
d 0 cells (.0%) have expected frequencies less than 5. The minimum expected cell frequency is 141.6.
e 0 cells (.0%) have expected frequencies less than 5. The minimum expected cell frequency is 141.0.
f 0 cells (.0%) have expected frequencies less than 5. The minimum expected cell frequency is 140.6.
g 0 cells (.0%) have expected frequencies less than 5. The minimum expected cell frequency is 141.2.

| Mann-Whitney U* | Generally satisfied | Prices are satisfactory | Products are satisfactory | It is convenient to be firm's customer | Satisfied the way the firm treats him/her | Reliable, accurate, and timely services | Positive feelings for the firm | Last contact was satisfactory | Intention to stay as customer |
|---|---|---|---|---|---|---|---|---|---|
| Mann-Whitney U | 60281 | 55316 | 58818 | 58834 | 56984 | 59213 | 58650 | 54688 | 60637 |
| Wilcoxon W | 106337 | 98387 | 140628 | 104285 | 102737 | 104664 | 103500 | 136903 | 105487 |
| Z | -.547 | -1.320 | -.812 | -.772 | -1.853 | -.677 | -.788 | -2.608 | -.024 |
| Asymp. Sig. (2-tailed) | .584 | .187 | .417 | .440 | .064 | .498 | .431 | **.009** | .981 |

*Grouping Variable: Test or Control Group

| Kruskal-Wallis Test** | Generally satisfied | Prices are satisfactory | Products are satisfactory | It is convenient to be firm's customer | Satisfied the way the firm treats him/her | Reliable, accurate, and timely services | Positive feelings for the firm | Last contact was satisfactory | Intention to stay as customer |
|---|---|---|---|---|---|---|---|---|---|
| Chi-Square | 5.799 | 3.934 | 11.126 | 3.621 | 10.623 | 6.674 | 10.607 | 5.820 | 48.442 |
| df | 3 | 3 | 3 | 3 | 3 | 3 | 3 | 3 | 3 |
| Asymp. Sig. | .122 | .269 | **.011** | .305 | **.014** | .083 | **.014** | .121 | **.000** |

**Grouping Variable: 4 Test companies

## 11.10 Correspondence Tables and Summary Correspondence Analysis Tables

Correspondence tables are contingency tables or cross-tabulations of the variables. Summary tables show whether there is a relationship between the row (ESCC) and column (transactional, general, loyalty) variables, and how many dimensions are needed to display this relationship. The singular values are measures of association by dimension between the row and column variables, with larger values indicating stronger relationships. The squares of the singular values equal the inertias, which are summable over dimension. Proportion of Inertia shows how well the data is represented with the number of dimensions. As correspondence analysis is a two-dimensional representation, the cumulative inertia for 2 dimensions is important for assessing how well the data fits the representation. For example, in transactional satisfaction & the ESCC (section 11.10.1) cumulative inertia for 2 dimensions is 95.8% which means two-dimensional plotting represents the 95.8% of the data, and thus representation fits data well. The chi-square statistics and related p-values represent the significance of the relationship between the row and column variables.

### *11.10.1 Transactional Satisfaction and The ESCC*

Contingency Table

| Observed ESCC by CSR | Last contact was satisfactory | | | | | |
|---|---|---|---|---|---|---|
| | Strongly Disagree | Disagree | Neither Agree Nor Disagree | Agree | Strongly Agree | Active Margin |
| very negative | 4 | 0 | 0 | 0 | 0 | 4 |
| negative | 3 | 4 | 7 | 10 | 0 | 24 |
| neutral | 4 | 6 | 18 | 73 | 33 | 134 |
| positive | 0 | 4 | 6 | 64 | 46 | 120 |
| very positive | 0 | 0 | 1 | 4 | 11 | 16 |
| Active Margin | 11 | 14 | 32 | 151 | 90 | 298 |

Summary

| Dimension | Singular Value | Inertia | Chi Square | Sig. | Proportion of Inertia | | Confidence Singular Value | |
|---|---|---|---|---|---|---|---|---|
| | | | | | Accounted for | Cumulative | Standard Deviation | Correlation |
| | | | | | | | | 2 |
| 1 | .631 | .398 | | | .752 | .752 | .098 | .276 |
| 2 | .330 | .109 | | | .206 | .958 | .054 | |
| 3 | .134 | .018 | | | .034 | .993 | | |
| 4 | .063 | .004 | | | .007 | 1.000 | | |
| Total | | .529 | 157.78 | .000 (a) | 1.000 | 1.000 | | |

a 16 degrees of freedom

## *11.10.2 General Satisfaction and The ESCC*

Contingency Table

| Observed ESCC by CSR | Generally satisfied | | | | | |
|---|---|---|---|---|---|---|
| | Strongly Disagree | Disagree | Neither Agree Nor Disagree | Agree | Strongly Agree | Active Margin |
| very negative | 1 | 1 | 1 | 1 | 0 | 4 |
| negative | 5 | 5 | 1 | 13 | 0 | 24 |
| neutral | 2 | 10 | 20 | 83 | 19 | 134 |
| positive | 0 | 6 | 7 | 81 | 28 | 122 |
| very positive | 0 | 0 | 0 | 13 | 3 | 16 |
| Active Margin | 8 | 22 | 29 | 191 | 50 | 300 |

Summary

| Dimension | Singular Value | Inertia | Chi Square | Sig. | Proportion of Inertia | | Confidence Singular Value | |
|---|---|---|---|---|---|---|---|---|
| | | | | | Accounted for | Cumulative | Standard Deviation | Correlation |
| | | | | | | | | 2 |
| 1 | .441 | .195 | | | .825 | .825 | .080 | .078 |
| 2 | .190 | .036 | | | .153 | .978 | .053 | |
| 3 | .068 | .005 | | | .020 | .997 | | |
| 4 | .025 | .001 | | | .003 | 1.000 | | |
| Total | | .236 | 70.781 | .000 (a) | 1.000 | 1.000 | | |

a 16 degrees of freedom

### *11.10.3 Loyalty Intentions and The ESCC*

Contingency Table

| Observed ESCC by CSR | Intention to stay as customer | | | | | |
|---|---|---|---|---|---|---|
| | Very Unlikely | Somewhat Unlikely | Neither Likely Nor Unlikely | Somewhat Likely | Very Likely | Active Margin |
| very negative | 1 | 2 | 1 | 0 | 0 | 4 |
| negative | 6 | 4 | 3 | 7 | 4 | 24 |
| neutral | 7 | 7 | 18 | 42 | 57 | 131 |
| positive | 3 | 1 | 20 | 29 | 68 | 121 |
| very positive | 0 | 0 | 0 | 7 | 9 | 16 |
| Active Margin | 17 | 14 | 42 | 85 | 138 | 296 |

Summary

| Dimension | Singular Value | Inertia | Chi Square | Sig. | Proportion of Inertia | | Confidence Singular Value | |
|---|---|---|---|---|---|---|---|---|
| | | | | | Accounted for | Cumulative | Standard Deviation | Correlation |
| | | | | | | | | 2 |
| 1 | .434 | .189 | | | .832 | .832 | .074 | -.003 |
| 2 | .156 | .024 | | | .108 | .940 | .057 | |
| 3 | .107 | .012 | | | .051 | .991 | | |
| 4 | .046 | .002 | | | .009 | 1.000 | | |
| Total | | .227 | 67.058 | .000(a) | 1.000 | 1.000 | | |

a 16 degrees of freedom

## 12 REFERENCES


Agarwal, A., Harding, D.P., & Schumacher, J.R., (2004). Organizing for CRM. *The McKinsey Quarterly*, Number 3.

Ajzen, I., & Fishbein, M. (1980). *Understanding Attitudes and Predicting Social Behavior*. Englewood Cliffs, NJ: Prentice-Hall.

Ajzen, I. (1991). The Theory of Planned Behavior. *Organizational Behavior and Human Decision Process*. 50, pp.179-211.

Allen, D.R., & Wilburn, M. (2002). *Linking Customer and Employee Satisfaction to the Bottom Line*. Milwaukee, Wisconsin: ASQ Quality Press.

Ammerlaan, G. (2002). Charisma: Tussen Charme en Waanzin. *Psychologie Magazine*, Februari, pp.24-27.

Anderson, E.W., & Sullivan, M. (1993). The Antecedents and Consequences of Customer Satisfaction for Firms. *Marketing Science,* vol. 12, no. 2, p. 125-143.

Anderson, E.W., Fornell, C., & Lehman, D.R. (1994). Customer Satisfaction, Market Share And Profitability: Findings From Sweden. *Journal of Marketing,* 58, 53-65.

Antila, J., & Ylostalo, P. (2002). *The Proactive Approach: The Joint Interest of Companies and Employees?* A paper for SASE 2002 Work and Labor in the Global Economy, University of Minnesota June 27-30.

Applegarth, M., Guttridge, A., & Posner, K. (2001). *The E-Customer Care Pocketbook,* UK: Management Pocketbooks.

Argyris, C. (1977). Double Loop Learning in Organizations. *Harvard Business Review,* 55: 115-125.

Argyris, C. (1998). Empowerment: The Emperor's New Clothes. *Harvard Business Review,* May-June, 98-105.

Armstrong, G., & Kotler, P. (2003). *Marketing: An Introduction,* 6th edition, Prentice Hall.

Arussy, L. (2002). *The Experience! How to Wow Your Customers and Create a Passionate Workplace,* CMP Books.

Ashforth, B.E., & Saks, A.M. (2002). Feeling Your Way: Emotion and Organizational Entry. In: Lord, R.G., Klimoski, R.J., and Kanfer, R., (Eds.), *Emotion in the Work Place: Understanding the Structure and Role of Emotions in Organizational Behavior*. (pp.331-369). San Francisco: Jossey-Bass.

Autry, J.A., & Mitchell, S. (1998). *Real Power: Business Lessons from the Tao Te Ching,* NY: Riverhead B.

Averill, J.R. (2001). Studies on Anger and Aggression: Implications for Theories of Emotion. In: Parrott, W.G., (ed.), *Emotions in Social Psychology: Essential Readings*, Psychology Press. Also in: *American Psychologist*, 38, 1145-1160.

Bach, H. (1998). *Human Resources in Call Centers*. F&G Publishing.

Barkema, H.G. (1995). Do Job Executives Work Harder When They are Monitored? *Kyklos,* 48:19-42.

Barlow, J., & Maul, D. (2000). *Emotional Value: Creating Strong Bond with Your Customers*. Berrett-Koehler Publishers, Inc.

Barsade, S.B. (2001). *The Ripple Effect: Emotional Contagion in Groups*. Working Paper Series Organizational Behavior, YALE School of Management.

Bartlett, C.A., & Ghoshal, S. (1992). What is a Global Manager? In: Leadership in a Changed World, *Harvard Business Review Special Issue*, August 2003.

Barton, D., & Park, J. (2003). Asia's banking Maveric. *The McKinsey Quarterly*, Nr.1.

Bateman, T.S., & Crant, J.M. (2001). *Intrinsic and Extrinsic Motivation*. Viginia University Research Papers. Retrived 18-10-2005 from www.commerce.virginia.edu/

BCG (1999). *Breaking Compromises: Opportunities for Action in Consumer Markets*. The Boston Consulting Group Inc.

BearingPoint (2004). *Wake-Up Call: To Fix CRM, Fix Customer Experiences Now!* White Paper, Retrieved from www.bearingpoint.com.

Beaujean, M., Davidson, J., & Madge, S. (2006). The 'moment of truth' in customer service. *The McKinsey Quarterly*, Number1.

Beniger, J.R. (1990). Conceptualization of Information Technology as Organization, and Vice Versa. In: Fulk, J., & Steinfield, C (Eds.), *Organizations and Communication Technology*. London: Sage Publications Inc.

Berkowitz, L. (2001). On the Formation and Regulation of Anger and Aggression: A Cognitive-Neoassociationistic Analysis. In: Parrott, W.G., (ed.), *Emotions in Social Psychology: Essential Readings*, Psychology Press. Also in: *American Psychologist*, 45, 494-503.

Bethlehem, J., & de Gooijer, J. (1999). *Syllabus Data-Analyse*. Versie 2. Afdeling Kwantitative Economie, FEE, Universiteit van Amsterdam.

Bilsen, van, J. (2002). De Customer Balanced Scorecard. In: Tricht, van, E., (ed.), *De Essentie van Customer Relationship Management*. F&G Publishing.

Birgelen, M. van, Ruyter, K. de, & Wetzels, M. (2000). *The Impact of Attitude Strength on the Use of Customer Satisfaction Information: An Empirical Investigation*. MAXX Working Paper Series, 3: Maastricht Academic Center for Research in Services.

Bisschop, J.S. (2002). IT-Paradox in bankwereld. *Het Financieele Dagblad*, 5 Januari.

Bitner, M.J., Booms, B.H., & Mohr, L.A. (1994). Critical Service Encounters: The Employee's Viewpoint. *Journal of Marketing, 58*: 95-106.

Bitner, M.J., Booms, B.H., & Tetreault, M.S. (1990). The Service Encounter: Diagnosing Favorable and Unfavorable Incidents. *Journal of Marketing*, 54: 71-84.

Blackard, K., & Gibson, J.W. (2002). Capitalizing on Conflict: Strategies and Practices for Turning Conflict to Synergy in Organizations. In: *Soundview Executive Book Summaries*, Vol.24, No.10. Part 1, October.

Bless, H., Bohner, G., Schwarz, N., & Strack, F. (2001). Mood and Persuasion: A Cognitive response Analysis. In: Parrott, W.G., (ed.), *Emotions in Social Psychology: Essential Readings*, Psychology Press. Also in: 1990, *Personality and Social Psychology Bulletin, 16* 331-345.

Bloemer, J., Odekerken-Schroder, G., & Martens, H. (2002). *The Psychology Behind Commitment and Loyalty: An Empirical Study in a Bank Setting*. Maastricht Research School of Economics of Technology and Organization. Research Memoranda: 076.

Boot, A.W.A. (2002). Concurrentie van Banken ter Discussie. *Het Financieele Dagblad*, 26 September.

Booz Allen Hamilton. (2003). When Art Meets Science: The Challenge of ROI Marketing. *Strategy+ Business & Knowledge@Wharton*, 17 Dec.

Borsboom, M., & Zoete, R. de (2001). *Financien Callcenter Management: Financieel Management van Callcenters*. F&G Publishing.

Braff, A., Passmore, W.J., & Simpson, M. (2003). Going the distance with telecom customers. *The McKinsey Quarterly*, Number 4.

Brady, D. (2000). Why Service Stinks. *Business Week*, 23 October. Also in Lovelock &Wirtz (2004), pp.466-473.

Brealey, R.A., Myers, S.C., & Marcus, A.J. (1995). *Fundamentals of Corporate Finance*, Int'l Edition, McGraw-Hill.

Brewster, C., Dowling, P., Grobler, P., Holland, P., & Warnich, S. (2001). Human Resources and Leadership. In: *Contemporary Issues in Human Resources Management: Gaining a Competitive Advantage*. Oxford University Press.

Brink, M.V. van den (1999). *De Opzet, Implementatie en Organisatie van een Call Center*. F&G Publishing.

Bugel, M. (2002). Klantenloyaliteit. In: Tricht, van, E., (ed.), *De Essentie van Customer Relationship Management*. F&G Publishing.

Bugel, M. (2003). Loyaliteit in de Uitgeefbranche: Wie Durft? In: *CustomerBase*, Nummer 1.

Burns, A.C., & Bush, R.F. (2003). *Marketing Research*. 4th ed. NJ: Prentice Hall.

Buzan, T. (2000). *Head First: 10 ways to tap into your natural genius*. Thorsons.

Bryman, A., & Cramer, D. (2005). *Quantitative Data Analysis with SPSS 12 and 13: A guide for social scientists*. Routledge.

Castaneda, C. (1968). *The Teachings of Don Juan: A Yaqui Way of Knowledge*. Washington Square Press.

Chase, R.B., & Dasu, S. (2001). Want to Perfect Your Company's Service? Use Behavioral Science. *Harvard Business Review*, June, pp.78-84.

Child, P., Dennis, R.J., Gokey, T.C., Mcguire, T.I., Sherman, M., & Singer, M. (1995). Can Marketing Regain the Personal Touch? *The McKinsey Quarterly*, Number 3, pp. 112-125. Also in: *Personal Financial Services: Industries in Collision,* McKinsey Quarterly Anthologies, 1997.

Christophe, V., & Rime, B. (2001). Exposure to the Social Sharing of Emotion: Emotional Impact, Listener Responses and Secondary Social Sharing.. In: Parrott, W.G., (ed.), *Emotions in Social Psychology: Essential Readings*, Psychology Press. Also in: 1997, *European Journal of Social Psychology, 27,* 37-54.

Cleveland, B., & Mayben, J. (2002). *Call Center Management in Volle Vaart Vooruit,* 2nd Edition, F&G Publishing.

Cleveland, B. (2003). Understanding First Call Resolution. *Call Center Magazine*, nr:4.

Cohen, A.R., & Bradford, D.L. (1991). *Influence Without Authority: The Use of Alliances, reciprocity, and Exchange to Accomplish Work.* John Wiley & Sons Inc.

Cornelius, R.R. (2000). *Theoretical Approaches to Emotion*. ISCA Workshop on Speech & Emotion, Belfast.

Covey, S.R. (1989) *The 7 Habits of Highly Effective People: Restoring the character Ethic.* Simon and Schuster.

Covey, S.R. (1997). *The 7 Habits of Highly Effective Families*. Franklin Covey Co.

Cowie, R., Douglas-Cowie, E., Savvidou, S., McMahon, E., Sawey, S., & Schröder, M. (2000a). *Describing The Emotional States Expressed in Speech*", ISCA Workshop on Speech & Emotion, Belfast.

Cowie, R., Douglas-Cowie, E., Savvidou, S., McMahon, E., Sawey, M., & Schroder, M. (2000b). *'Feeltrace': An Instrument for Recording Perceived Emotion in Real Time.* ISCA Workshop on Speech & Emotion, Belfast.
Cox, R.W. (1987). *Production, Power, and World Order: Social Forces in the Making of History.* New York: Columbia University Press.
Coyles, S., & Gokey, T.C. (2002). Customer Retention is Not Enough. *The McKinsey Quarterly,* Number 2.
Coyne, J.C. (2001). Depression and the Response of Others. In: Parrott, W.G., (ed.), *Emotions in Social Psychology: Essential Readings*, Psychology Press. Also in: 1976, *Journal of Abnormal Psychology, 85*, 186-193.
Curry, J. (1994). *Know Your Customers: How Customer Marketing Can Increase Your Profits.* Great Britain: Kogan Page.
Cusac, M. (1998). *Online Customer Care: Strategies for Call Center Excellence*, ASQ press.
Datamonitor (2002). *Regulation in European Call Centers: Striking Balance Between Rights and Flexibility.*
Davis, I. (2005). How to escape the short-term trap. *The McKinsey Quarterly*, Web exclusive, April.
Dawson, K. (2001). *The Call Center Handbook.* New York: CMP Books.
Day, J. D., Mang, P. Y., Richter, A., & Roberts, J. (2002). Has Pay for Performance had its day? *McKinsey Quarterly,* No: 4, 46-55.
Deci, E.L., & Ryan, R.M. (1985). *Intrinsic Motivation and Self-Determination in Human Behavior.* New York: Plennum Press.
Deloitte Consulting (2002a). *Rules of the CRM Road: Field Guide to Tracking True North.*
Deloitte Consulting (2002b). *Customer Relationship Management for Financial Institutions.*
Desmet, P.M.A. (2002). *Designing Emotions.* Dissertation-TU Delft.
Desmet, P.M.A. (2003). Measuring Emotion: Development And Application Of An Instrument To Measure Emotional Responses To Products. In: M.A. Blythe, A.F. Monk, K. Overbeeke, & P.C. Wright (Eds.), *Funology: From Usability To Enjoyment.* (pp. 111-123). Dordrecht: Kluwer Academic Publishers.
Dick, A., & Basu, K. (1994). Customer loyalty: Toward and integrated conceptual framework. *Journal of Marketing Science*, Vol. 22, No. 2, pp. 99-113.
Dickson, T., & Hawcock, N., (Eds.) (1999) *Financial Times Mastering Marketing.* London :Financial Times & Prentice Hall.
Dolen, W. van, Lemmink, J., Mattsson, J., & Rhoen, I. (2001). Affective consumer responses in consumer responses in service encounters: The emotional content in narratives of critical incidents. *Journal of Economic Psychology*, 22, 359-376.
Doyle, M.E., & Smith, M.K. (1999). *Born and Bred? Leadership, Heart and Informal Education.* London: YMCA George Williams College/The Rank Foundation.
Doyle, M. E., & Smith, M. K. (2001). *Classical leadership.* Retrieved from www.infed.org/leadership/
Dulewics, V., & Higgs, M. (2004). Can Emotional Intelligence be developed? *Int. Journal of Human Resource Management 15:1,* February, pp 95-111. (www.tandf.co.uk/journals).

Dull, S.F. (2001). *A Breed Apart.* CRM Project, Volume 2. Retrieved from www.accenture.com

E.Piphany (2003) *The Human Touch: How Customers Choose Between You and Your Competitiors.*

Earley, P.C., & Francis, C.A. (2002). International Perspectives on Emotion and Work. In: Lord, R.G., Klimoski, R.J., and Kanfer, R., (Eds.), *Emotion in the Work Place: Understanding the Structure and Role of Emotions in Organizational Behavior*, (pp.370-401). San Francisco: Jossey-Bass.

Ebner, M., Hu, A., Levitt, D., & McCrory, J. (2002). How to Rescue CRM. *The McKinsey Quarterly*, Number 4, Technology.

Edwardson, M. (1998). Measuring consumer emotions in service encounters: An exploratory analysis. *Australian Journal of Market Research*, 6, 34-48.

EFMA (2004). Changes in the number of bank branches in Europe. *The European Financial Management & Marketing Association*. September.

EFMA (2005). Customer Contact Centres - What is their potential in a multichannel strategy? *The European Financial Management & Marketing Association.* September.

Elzinga, L. (2002). *CRM, Sturen op Klantentevredenheid.* www.crmmarketplace.nl, newsletter 6/6/2002.

Engel, J.F., Blackwell, R.D., & Miniard, P.W. (1990). *Consumer Behavior,* 6th edition. USA:Dreyden Press.

Erol, M. (2002). *Customer Satisfaction as an Indicator of CRM Competencies.* Unpublished Master's Thesis in Business Administration, Katholieke Universiteit Nijmegen.

Etheredge, J.O. (1999). *Human Performance in the Customer Driven Enterprise.* Retrieved from www.accenture.com.

Fishbein, M., & Ajzen, I. (1975). *Belief, attitude, intention, and behavior: An introduction to theory and research.* Reading, MA: Addison-Wesley. (www.people.umass.edu/aizen/f&a1975.html).

Fiske, J. (1990). *Introduction to Communication Studies*. London: Routledge Inc.

Forgas, J.P., & Bower, G.H. (2001). Mood Effects on Person-Perception Judgments. In: Parrott, W.G., (ed.), *Emotions in Social Psychology: Essential Readings*, Psychology Press. Also in: *Journal of Personality and Social Psychology*, *53*, 53-60.

Fournier, S., Dobscha, S., & Mick, D.G. (1998). Preventing the Premature Death of Relationship Marketing. *Harvard Business Review*, Jan-Feb.

Fradette, M., & Michaud, S. (1999). *Corporate Kinetics*. Simon & Schuster.

Frank, R., Mihas, E.A., & Narasimhan, L. (2003). Value-Driven Shopping. *The McKinsey Quarterly,* Nr: 3.

Fredrickson, B.L. (1998). What Good are Positive Emotions? *Review of General Psychology*, 2, 173-186.

Freemantle, D. (1999). *What Customers Like About You: Adding Emotional Value for Service Excellence and Competitive Advantage*. London: Nicholas Brealey Publishing.

Freemantle, D. (2001). The Psychology of CRM: Creating a customer relations buzz - The stimulus factor. *International Journal of Customer Relationship Management*, 4(1), 79-86.

Frey, B.S. (1997). *Not Just for the Money: An Economic Theory of Personal Motivation,* Cheltenham, UK and Brookfield, USA: Edward Elgar.
Frey, B.S. (2000). *Performance Pay and Employee Motivation.* Institute for Economic research, University of Zurich.
Frijda, N.H. (1993). Moods, Emotion Episodes, and Emotions. In M.Lewis & J.M.Haviland (Eds.), *Handbook of Emotions* (pp.381-403). New York: Guilford Press.
Frijda, N.H. (2001). The Laws of Emotion. In: Parrott, W.G., (ed.), *Emotions in Social Psychology: Essential Readings*, Psychology Press. Also in: *American Psychologist* (1988), *43-349-358.*
Froehle, C.M., & Roth, A.V. (2004). New measurement scales for evaluating perceptions of the technology-mediated customer service experience. *Journal of Operations Management*, 22, 1-21.
Fry, L.F., Stoner, C.R., & Hattwick, R.E. (2004). *Business: An Integrative Approach*, 3rd edition, Irwin/McGraw-Hill.
Fulk, J., & Steinfield, C. (Eds.) (1990). *Organizations and Communication Technology.* London: Sage Publications Inc.
Ganzevoort, J.W. (1999). *Organiseren als menselijk leven: Contouren van een nieuw paradigma*, Amsterdam: Vossiuspers AUP.
Ganzevoort, J.W. (2001). *Bedrijfsmodellering: een model voor businessmodeling.*
Gartner Group (2000). *Calculating Potential CRM Benefits.* www.gartner.com
Garver, M.S. (2001). Listening to Customers. *Mid-American Journal of Business*, Vol. 16, No.2. 41-54.
George, J.M. (2002). Affect Regulation in Groups and Teams. In: Lord, R.G., Klimoski, R.J., & Kanfer, R., (Eds.), *Emotion in the Work Place: Understanding the Structure and Role of Emotions in Organizational Behavior*, (pp.183-217) San Francisco: Jossey-Bass.
Geus, A.P., de (1988). Planning as Learning. *Harvard Business Review*, March/April, 70-74.
Ghoshal, S., & Bartlett, C. (1999). *The Individualized Corporation. A Fundamentally New Approach to Management.* London: William Heinemann.
Giese, J.L., & Cote, J.A. (2000). Defining Consumer Satisfaction. *Academy of Marketing Science Review, 1,* 1-24.
Gilson, K.A., & Khandelwal, D.K. (2005). Getting more from call centers : Used properly, they can be strategic assets. *The McKinsey Quarterly*, Web exclusive, April.
Gobe, M. (2001). *Emotional Branding: the new paradigm for connecting brands to people.* New York: Allworth Press.
Goleman, D. (1996). *Emotional Intelligence: Why It Can Matter More Than IQ.* Bloomsburry.
Goleman, D. (1998) What Makes a Leader. *Harvard Business Review*, Nov-Dec. Reprinted in: *Best of HBR*, Jan-2004, pp. 82-91.
Goodman, J., & Ward, D. (2001). The Payoff of Employing A Professional Call Center Manager. Retrieved from *www.TARP.com.*
Gordon, T. (1976). *Luisteren Naar Kinderen: De Nieuwe Methode voor Overleg in het Gezin.* Amsterdam: Elsevier.

Gordon Training International (2003). *Productivity & Profitability: The Case for Participation in the Workplace and the People Productivity Process*. Retrieved from www.gordontarining.com.

Grabbe, J.O. (1990). *International Financial Markets*, Amsterdam: Elsevier.

Grahl J., & Teague, P. (1990). *1992-The Big Market: The Future of the European Community*. London: Lawrence & Wishard Ltd.

Grandey, A.A., & Brauburger, A.L. (2002). The Emotion Regulation Behind the Customer Service Smile. In: Lord, R.G., Klimoski, R.J., & Kanfer, R., (Eds.), *Emotion in the Work Place: Understanding the Structure and Role of Emotions in Organizational Behavior*, (pp.260-294). San Francisco: Jossey-Bass.

Green, P.E., & Krieger, A.M. (1999). Slicing and Dicing the Market. In: Dickson, T. & Hawcock, N., (Eds.), *Financial Times Mastering Marketing*, (pp.55-59). London: Financial Times & Prentice Hall.

Griffin, J., & Lowenstein, M.W. (2001). *Customer WinBack: How to Recapture Lost Customers- and Keep them loyal*. San Francisco: Jossey-Bass.

Griffin, J. (2002). *Customer Loyalty: How to Earn It, How to Keep It*, 2nd edition. San Francisco: Jossey-Bass.

Grougiou, V., & Wilson, A. (2003). Financial service call centers: Problems encountered by the grey market. *Journal of Financial Services Marketing*, Vol. 7, no. 4, 360-369.

Güngör, H. (2002). *Human Factor in Call Centers; No Fancy Software Required.* Contactcenterworld.com.

Güngör, H. (2003). The Human Touch in Call Centers: Geen Fancy Software Nodig!" in: *Call Center Magazine*, nr:4, pp.30-34.

Güngör, H. (2004). *Operational Performance of Contact Center Agents and Linking This to Customer Satisfaction & Loyalty*. The 4th Annual European Contact Center Exchange, 1-2 March, Amsterdam.

Güngör, H. (2005). Emotional Satisfaction of Customer Contacts (ESCC) and its effects on customer loyalty. *8th Ph.D. Conference on Business Economics, management and Organization Science*, 26-January. Abstract, pp.7-8.

Güngör, H. (2006). Issues in Customer Contacts: Sales and Emotions. *EfMag*. European Financial Management & Marketing Association. Number 201, pp.26-28.

Güngör, H. (2006a). Dimension of Customer Satisfaction & Loyalty: Cognitive Vs. Emotional & General Vs. Transactional. *Italian Banking Association Magazine MK.* Number 6-2006, pp.20-26.

Hackman R.J., & Oldham, G.R. (1980). *Work Redesign.* Reading, MA: Addision-Wesley.

Harrel, G.D. (2002). *Marketing: Connecting with Customers*, 2nd edition. Prentice Hall

Hart, C.W.L., Heskett, J.L., & Sasser, W.E. Jr. (1990). The profitable Art of Service Recovery. *Harvard Business Review*, 68, 148-156.

Hatch, M.J. (1997). *Organization Theory: Modern, Symbolic, and Postmodern Perspectives*. Oxford University Press.

Hayes, B.E. (1998). *Measuring Customer Satisfaction: Survey Design, Use, and Statistical Analysis Methods*, Second Edition. Wilwaukee, Wisconsin: ASQ Quality Press.

Hegebarth, K.G. (2001). Quality Monitoring Captures Center Stage in the Enterprise. In: *Real Market*, Oct.

HELA (2001). Advice regarding call centre working practices. *Local Authority Circular.* 94/1 (Rev.). Issued December 2001, reviewed September 2005. Retrieved from: http://www.hse.gov.uk/lau/lacs/94-1.HTM

Hellinghausen, M.A. (1999). Empowered Employees: A New Team Concept for Total Customer Satisfaction. *European Quality*, March. Retrieved from www.masetllc.com/pdfs/129.pdf.

Heskett J.L, Sasser, W.E.jr., & Schlesinger, L.A. (1997). *The service profit chain: How leading companies link profit and growth to loyalty, satisfaction, and value.* The Free Press.

Heskett J.L., Jones, T.O., Loveman, G.L., & Sasser, W.E. jr. (1994). Putting the Service Profit Chain to Work. *Harvard Business Review*, 72, 164-174.

Hill, T., & Lewicki, P. (2006). *Statistics: Methods and Applications.* StatSoft, Tulsa, OK; Electronic Version: http://www.statsoft.com/textbook/stathome.html

Hochschield, A. (1983). *The Managed Heart.* Berkeley, CA: University of California Press.

Hoff, B. (1982). *The Tao of Pooh.* Penguin Books.

Holman, D. (2002). Employee wellbeing in call centers. *Human Resource Management Journal*, 12,4,35-50.

Howcroft, B. (2001). Editorial: Bank Branch Networks and Direct Delivery Channels. *Journal of Financial Services Marketing*, Vol.5, 202-204.

Howcroft, B., Hewer, P., & Durkin, M. (2003). Banker-Customer Interactions in Financial Services. *Journal of Marketing Management*, 19, 1001-1020.

Huber, G.P. (1990). A Theory of the Effects of Advanced information Technologies on Organizational Design, Intelligence, and Decision Making. In: Fulk, J., & Steinfield, C., (Eds.), *Organizations and Communication Technology.* London: Sage Publications Inc.

Huy, Q.N. (2002). Emotional Balancing of Organizational Change: The Contribution of Middle Managers. *Admin.Science Quarterly*, Cornell University. Also summarized in: http://knowledge.insead.edu.

Iacobucci, D. (1999). Golden Rules for Customer Service. In: Dickson, T., & Hawcock, N., (Eds.), *Financial Times Mastering Marketing* (pp.221-225). London: Financial Times & Prentice Hall.

Inzerilli, G. (1990). The Italian Alternative: Flexible Organization and Social Management. *International Studies of Management & Organization*, Vol.20, No:4, pp.6-21. M.E. Sharpe, inc.

Jahrmarkt, M. (1990). *Tau Management:Een Effectieve Methode om een Holistisch Manager te Worden.* Cothen: Servire Uitgevers bv.

Jansen, M., & Akgun, M. (2002). Meer Sturing is gewenst. *Banking Review*, February.

Jay, R. (1998). *The Essential Marketing Sourcebook,* 2nd Edition. Financial Times – Pitman Publishing.

Johnson, R.A., & Wichern, D.W. (2002). *Applied Multivariate Statistical Analysis*, 5th ed. NJ: Prentice Hall.

Jones, H., & Farquhar, J.D. (2003). Contact management and customer loyalty. *Journal of Financial Services Marketing*, Volume 8, Number 1, 71-78.

Jones, G.R., & George, J.M. (2003). *Contemporary Management*, 3rd edition. McGraw Hill.

Jones, T.O., & Sasser, W.E. Jr. (1995). Why Satisfied Customers Defect. *Harvard Business Review*, November-December, vol. 73, no. 6, 88-99.

Jong, A. de., Ruyter, K. de, & Lemmink, J. (2004). Antecedents and Consequences of the Service Climate in Boundary-Spanning Self-Managing Service Teams. *Journal of Marketing*, vol.68, 18-35.

Katona, G. (1975). *Psychological Economics.* NY & Amsterdam: Elsevier Scientific Publishing Company.

Kaya, N., & Epps, H.H. (2004). Relationship between color and emotion: a study of college students. *College Student Journal*, September. Retrieved from www.highbeam.com/library/

Keaveney, S. (1995). Customer Switching Behavior in Service Industries. *Journal of Marketing*, 59, 71-82.

Keen, P.G.W. (1990). Telecommunications and Organizational Choice. In: Fulk, J. & Steinfield, C (Eds.), *Organizations and Communication Technology*, London: Sage Publications Inc.

Kennedy, P. (1993). *Preparing for the Twenty-first century.* New York: Random Hause.

Kervin, J.B. (1992). *Methods for Business Research.* Harper Collins Publishers Inc.

Ketz de Vries, M. (2002). *Can CEOs Change? Yes, but only if they want to.* INSEAD Working Paper Series, 2002/36/ENT.

Ketz de Vries, M. (2003). *Global Leadership Life Inventory:Iinterpreting the Twelve Dimensions of Global Leadership.* Pfeiffer Publishing.

Kim, W.C., & Mauborgne, R. (2003). Fair Process: Managing in the Knowledge Economy, *Harvard Business Review*, January, 3-11.

Kleijssen, A.M.P., & Scheers, D.A.G. (2001). *CRM-markttrends.* Cap Gemini, Ernst & Young.

Knowledge@Wharton, Various issues of the Newsletter of the Wharton School of the University of Pennsylvania (http://www.wharton.upenn.edu/)

Kotler, P., Armstrong, G., Saunders, J., & Wong, V. (1996). *Principles of Marketing*, European Edition. London: Prentice Hall.

Kotler, P. (2003). *Marketing Management*, 11th International Edition. Prentice Hall.

Kotter, J.P., & Cohen, D.S. (2002). *The Heart of Change: Real-Life Stories How People Changed Their Organizations.* Boston: Harvard Business School Press.

Krause, D.G. (1997). *The Way of the Leader: Applying the principles of Sun Tzu and Confucius- Ancient Strategies for Modern Business World.* NY: Perigee Books.

Kreitner, R., & Kinicker, A. (2001). *Organizational Behavior,* 5th edition. McGraw Hill.

Kroon, E.W. (2003). *Projectverslag: Inspectieproject Callcenters 2001/2002, A502 / A521.*

Kshirsagar, A.E., McNamara, P.G., & Weir, J. (2001). A Broadband Future for Financial Services. *The McKinsey Quarterly*, Number 2 On-line tactics.

Larsen, R.J., Diener, E., & Lucas, R.E. (2002). Emotion: Models, Measures, and Individualk Differences. In: Lord, R.G., Klimoski, R.J., & Kanfer, R. (Eds.), *Emotion in the Work Place: Understanding the Structure and Role of Emotions in Organizational Behavior*, (pp.64-105). San Francisco: Jossey-Bass.

LaSalle, D., & Britton, T.A. (2003). *Priceless: Turning Ordinary Products Into Extraordinary Experiences,* Harvard Business School Press.

Laverie, D.A., Kleine, R.E. III, & Schultz Kleine, S. (1993). Linking emotions and values in consumption experiences: an exploratory study. *Advances in Consumer Research,* Volume 20, 70-75.
Leavitt, H. (1972). *The Volatile organization: Everything triggers everything else.* Managerial Psychology, Chicago Univ. of Chicago Press.
Leszinski, R., & Marn, M.V. (1997). Setting Value, Not Price. *The McKinsey Quarterly*, No.1, pp.98-115.
Levering, R., & Moskowitz, M. Great Place To Work Model, greatplacetowork.com accessed on 26-8-2004.
Lewis, M., & Haviland-Jones, J.M. (Eds.) (2000). *Handbook of Emotions*, 2nd edition, The Guilford Press.
Liljander, V., & Bergenwall, M. (1999). *Consumption-Based Emotional Responses Related to Satisfaction.* Working Papers, No 398, Swedish School of Economics and Business Administration.
Liu, A.H., Bernhardt, K.L., & Leach, M.P. (1999). *Examining Customer Value, Satisfaction, and Switching Costs in Multiple-Sourcing Purchase Decisions for Business Services.* ISMB Report 6, Institute for the Study of Business Markets, The Pennsylvania State University.
Lord, R.G., & Kanfer, R. (2002). Emotions and Organizational Behavior. In: Lord, R.G., Klimoski, R.J., & Kanfer, R. (Eds.) (2002). *Emotion in the Work Place: Understanding the Structure and Role of Emotions in Organizational Behavior*, (pp. 5-19). San Francisco: Jossey-Bass.
Lord, R.G., Klimoski, R.J., & Kanfer, R. (Eds.) (2002). *Emotion in the Work Place: Understanding the Structure and Role of Emotions in Organizational Behavior.* San Francisco: Jossey-Bass.
Lovelock, C.H., & Wirtz, J. (2004). *Services Marketing: People, Technology, Strategy*, 5th International Edition. Pearson Prentice Hall.
Luarn, P., & Lin, H.H. (2003). A customer loyalty model for e-service context. *Journal of Electronic Commerce Research*, Vol. 4, No. 4. 156-167.
Luttwak, E.N. (1999). *Turbo-Capitalism: Winners and Losers in the Global Economy.* London: Orion Business Books.
MacDermid, S.M., Seery, B.L., & Weiss, H.M. (2002). An Emotional Examination of the Work-Family Interface. In: Lord, R.G., Klimoski, R.J., & Kanfer, R. (Eds.). *Emotion in the Work Place: Understanding the Structure and Role of Emotions in Organizational Behavior.* San Francisco: Jossey-Bass.
Malaviya, P., & Spargo, S. (2002). *Relating to Customers: How and When to Strengthen Your Customer Relationships.* INSEAD Working Papers, 2002/41/MKT.
Mano, H., & Oliver, R.L. (1993). Assesing the Dimensionality and Structure of Consumption Experience: Evaluation, Feeling, and Satisfaction. *Journal of Consumer Research*, 20:451-466.
Maria, A.N., & Thomas, J.R.(1998). Organizing on the Edge: Meeting the Demand for Innovation and Efficiency. In: *Prism,* 3rd quarter.
Markus, H.R., & Kitayama, S. (2001). The Cultural Construction of Self and Emotion: Implications for Social Behavior. In: Parrott, W.G. (Ed.). *Emotions in Social Psychology: Essential Readings*, Psychology Press.
Maslow, A. (1970). *Motivation and Personality.* New York: Harper & Row

Masters, T. (2001). Have we lost our way with CRM? *International Journal of Customer Relationship Management*, vol. 3, no. 4, 287-290.

Mayo, E. (1933). *The Human Problems of an Industrial Civilization*. Macmillan.

Mazur, G. (1996). *Voice of Customer Analysis: A Modern System of Front-end QFD Tools, with Case Studies*. Retrieved from www.qfdi.org.

McClave, J.T., Benson, P.G., & Sincich, T. (2001). *A First Course in Business Statistics*, 8th edition. Prentice Hall.

McKean, J. (2003). *Customers Are People: The Human Touch*. UK: John Wiley & Sons.

McQuail, D. (1987). *Mass Communication Theory: an introduction,* 2nd ed. London: Sage Publications.

Mihelis, G., Grogoroudis, E., Siskos, Y., Politis, Y., & Malandrakis, Y. (2001). Customer Satisfaction Measurement in Private Bank Sector. *European Journal of Operational Research*, no. 130, 347-360.

Mintzberg, H. (1983). *Structures in Fives: Designing Effective Organizations.*New Jersey: Prentice-Hall.

Molineux, P. (2002). *Exploiting CRM: Connecting with Customers. UK:* Hodder & Stoughton.

Moorst, van, A. (2001). *Help een Klant!: Ontwerp en implementatie van klantencontactcenters*. F&G Publishing.

Morell, S., & Philonenko, L. (2001). *20:20 CRM: A Visionary insight into unique Customer Contact*. Genesys Telecommunications Laboratories Inc.

Morgan, G. (1997). *Images of Organization*. London: Sage Publications.

Morse, G. (2004). Feedback Backlash. *Harvard Business Review*, October-2004, p.28.

Mullins, L.J. (1996). *Management and Organizational Behavior*. London: Pitman Publishing.

Nabi, R.L. (1999). A Cognitive-Functional Model for the Effects of Discrete Negative Emotions on Information Processing, Attitude Change, and Recall. *Communication Theory*, 9, 292-320.

Nancarrow, C., & Brace I. (2000). Saying the “right thing”: Coping with Social Desirability Bias in Marketing Research. *British Business School Teaching and Research Review*, Issue 3.

NCCBP (2003). Nationaal Contact Center Benchmark Platform (www.nccbp.nl), *Contact Center Benchmark Rapport*.

Norman, D.A. (1993). *Things That Makes Us Smart: Defending Human Attributes in the Age of the Machine*. Perseus Books.

Nunez, M., & Yulinsky, C.M. (2005). Better customer service in banks. *The McKinsey Quarterly*, Nr. 1.

Olazabal, N.G. (2002). Banking: The IT Paradox. *The McKinsey Quarterly*, Nr. 1.

Oliver, R.L. (1997). *Satisfaction: A Behavioral Perspective on the Consumer.* Irwin/McGraw Hill

Oliver, R.L., Rust, R.T., & Varki, S. (1997). Customer Delight: Foundations, Findings, and Managerial Insight. *Journal of Retailing*, 73(3), 311-336.

Oundhakar, S., & Dutta, S. (2002). *ING Direct – Redefining Banking*. Case Study, Fontainebleau, INSEAD.

Ouwersloot, H., & Lemmink, J. (1999). *Integrating Feelings of Warmth Measures During Service Encounters and Ex-post Evaluations.* MAXX Working Paper Series, 1999-06; Maastricht Academic Center for Research in Services.

Page, M., Pitt, L., & Berthon, P. (1996). Analyzing and Reducing Customer Defections. *Longe RangePlanning,* 29 (6), 821-834.

Parasuraman, A., Zeithaml, V.A., & Berry, L.L. (1988). SERVQUAL: a Multiple-Item Scale for Measuring Customer Perceptions of Service Quality. *Journal of Retailing,* 64, 12-40.

Parasuraman, A., & Grewal, D. (2000). Serving Customers and Consumers Effectively in the Twenty-First Century: A Conceptual Framework and Overview. *Journal of the Academy of Marketing Science,*Vol. 28, No. 1, 9-16.

Parasuraman, A., Zeithaml, V.A., & Berry, L.L. (1994). Reassessment of Expectations as a Comparison Standard in Measuring Service Quality: Implications for Further Research. *Journal of Marketing,* 58, 111-124.

Parmenter, D. (1997). *First Direct: Branchless Banking.* Case Study, Fontainebleau, INSEAD.

Parrott, W.G., (Ed.) (2001). *Emotions in Social Psychology: Essential Readings,* Psychology Press.

Peccei, R. (2004). *Human Resources Management and the Search for the Happy Workplace.* Inaugural at Erasmus University, Rotterdam, 15 January.

Peppers, D., & Rogers, M. (1997). *Enterprise One-to-One: Tools for Building Unbreakable Customer Relationships in the Interactive Age.* Paperback edition, UK: Piatkus.

Peppers, D., Rogers, M., & Dorf, B. (1999). Is Your Company Ready for One-To-One Marketing? *Harvard Business Review,* Jan-Feb, 77, 3-12.

Peters, T., & Waterman, R.H., (1982). *In Search of Excellence: Lessons from America's Best-run Companies.* Harper & Row.

Pfeffer, J. (1995). *Rekabette üstünlüğün Sırrı: İnsan.* İstanbul: Gençlik Yayınları.

Pfeffer, J. (1998). Six Dangerous Myths About Pay. *Harvard Business Review,* May-June, 109-119.

Pine, B.J. II, & Gilmor, J.H. (1999). *The Experience Economy: Work Is Theatre & Every Business a Stage.* Harvard Business School Press.

Polito, T., & Watson, K. (2002). Toward an interdisciplinary organizational learning framework. *The Journal of American Academy of Business,* 2 (1), 162-166.

Prokesch, S.E. (1995). Competing on Customer Service: An Interview with British Airways' Sir Colin Marshall. *Harvard Business Review,* 73, 6, Nov-Dec, 100-113.

Pugh, S.D. (2001). Service with a Smile: Emotional Contagion in the Service Encounter. *Academy of Management Journal,* 44 (5), 1018-1027.

Raimondo, M.A. (1999). *The Measurement of Trust in Marketing Studies: A Review of Models and Methodologies.* Working Paper, University of Milan.

Reichheld, F.F., & Sasser, W.E. Jr. (1990). Zero Defections: Quality Comes to Services. *Harvard Business Review,* Sep-Oct, 105-111.

Reichheld, F.F. (1993). Loyalty Based Management. *Harvard Business Revie*w, 71, Mar-Apr, 64-73.

Reichheld, F.F. (1996). Learning From Customer Defection. *Harvard Business Review,* Mar-Apr, 59-60.

Reichheld, F.F. (2001). Lead for Loyalty. *Harvard Business Review*, July-Aug, 76-84.
Reichheld, F.F. (2001b). *Loyalty Rules! How today's leaders build lasting relationships.* Boston: Harvard Business School Press.
Reinartz, W.J., & Kumar, V. (2001). *The Impact of Customer Relationship Characteristics on Profitable Lifetime Duration.* INSEAD Working Papers 2001/108/MKT.
Reinartz, W.J., & Kumar, V. (2002). The Mismanagement of Customer Loyalty. *Harvard Business Review*, July 2002.
Riley, M., Wood, R., Clark, M., Wilkie, E., & Szivas, E. (2000). *Researching and Writing Dissertations in Business and Management.* London: Thomson Learning.
Ritzer, G. (2000). *The McDonaldization of Society: An Investigation Into the Changing Character of Contemporary Social Life.* University of Maryland, Pine Forge Press.
Robinette, S. (2001). Get Emotional, best practice. *Harvard Business Review*, May 2001.
Robinette, S., Brand, C., & Lenz, V. (2001). *Emotion Marketing: The Hallmark way of winning customers for life.* New York: McGraw-Hill.
Romme, A.G.L., & Witteloostuijn, A. v. (1999). Circular Organizing and Triple Loop Learning. *Journal of Organizational Change,* 12 (5), 439-453.
Rona, L. (2003). *Önce Ben, Sonra Müşteri: Mükemmel Müşteri Memnuniyeti Kavramına Yeni Bir Bakış.* İstanbul: Epsilon Yayınevi.
Rucker, R. (2000). City bank increase customer loyalty with defect free processes. *The Journal of Quality and Participation*, Vol. 23 No.4, pp.32-36.
Russel, J.A. (1980). A Circumplex Model of Affect. *Journal of Personality and Social Psychology*, 39, 1161-1178.
Rust, R.T., Zahorik, A.J., & Keiningham, T.L. (1995). Return on Quality (ROQ): Making Service Quality Financially Accountable. *Journal of Marketing,* 59, 58-70.
Rust, R.T., Zeithaml, V.A., & Lemon, K.N. (2000). *Driving Customer Equity: How Customer Lifetime Value Is Reshaping Corporate Strategy.* Free Press.
Rust, R.T., Moorman, C., & Dickson, P.R. (2002). Getting Returns from Service Quality: Revenue Expansion, Cost Reduction, or Both? *Journal of Marketing*, 66 (October), 7-24.
Safizadeh, M.H., Field, J.M., & Ritzman, L.P. (2003). An Empirical Analysis of Financial Services Processes with a Front-Office or Back-Office Orientation. *Journal of Operation Management*, 21, 557-576.
Salovey, P., Hsee, C.K., & Mayer, J.D. (2001). Emotional Intelligence and the Self-Regulation of Affect. In: Parrott, W.G., (Ed.), *Emotions in Social Psychology: Essential Readings.* Psychology Press, (pp.185-197). Also in: Wegner, D.M. & Pennebaker J.W. (Eds.), (1993). *Handbook of mental control*, (pp.258-277). Prentice Hall.
Shapiro, B., Rangan, K., Moriarty, R., & Ross, E. (1987). Manage customers for Profits (not just sales). *Harvard Business Review*, Sept.-Oct, 65(5), 101–108.
Sassen, S. (1991). *The Global City: New York, London, Tokyo.* Princton, NJ: Princton University Press.
Scherer, K.R. (2003). *A Cross-Cultural investigation of Emotion Inferences From Voice and Speech: Implications for speech Technology.* University of Geneva, Emotion Research Group.

Schutte, H. (1999). Asian Culture and the Global Consumer. In: Dickson, T. & Hawcock, N. (Eds.), *Financial Times Mastering Marketing*, (pp.37-43). London: Financial Times & Prentice Hall.

Semler, R. (1994). *Maverick!: the success story behind the world's most unusual workplace*. London: Arrow.

Senge, P. M. (1990). *The Fifth Discipline: The Art and Practice of the Learning Organization*. New York: Doubleday.

Severin, W.J., & Tankard, J.W., jr. (1988). *Communications Theories: Origins, Methods, Uses*, 2nd edition, New York & London: Longman.

Sharma, S. (1996). *Applied Multivariate Techniques*. Wiley.

Sharma, S., Niedrich, R.W., & Dobbins, G. (1999). A Framework for Monitoring Customer Satisfaction: An Empirical Illustration. *Industrial Marketing Management*, 28, 231-243.

Shaver, P., Schwartz, J., Kirson, D., & O'Conner, C. (2001). Emotion Knowledge: Further Exploration of a Prototype Approach. In: Parrott, W.G., (ed.), *Emotions in Social Psychology: Essential Readings*. Psychology Press.

Sheth, J.N., & Sisodia, R.S. (1999). The Changing Nature of Retailing. In: Dickson, T. & Hawcock, N., (Eds.), *Financial Times Mastering Marketing*, (pp.201-207). London: Financial Times & Prentice Hall.

Skaggs, B.C., & Youndt, M. (2004). Strategic Positioning, Human Capital, and Performance in service organizations: A Customer Interaction Approach. *Strategic Management Journal*, 25: 85-99.

Smit, N.C., & Klein, J.G. (1999). Adding Ethics to the Marketing Mix. In: Dickson, T. & Hawcock, N., (Eds.), *Financial Times Mastering Marketing*, (pp.59-63). London: Financial Times & Prentice Hall.

Solomon, M.R. (2002). *Consumer Behavior*, 5th edition. Prentice Hall.

Someren, T.C.R., van, (2005). *Strategische Innovationen:So machen Sie Ihr unternehmen einzigartig*, Wiesbaden: Gabler.

Sonnemans, M. (2002). De Customer Economy. In: Tricht, E. van (Ed.), *De Essentie van Customer Relationship Management*. F&G Publishing.

Sprigg, C.A., Smith, P.R., & Jackson, P.R. (2003). *Psychosocial risk factors in call centers: An evaluation of work design and well-being*. UK: HSE Books.

Stauss, B. & Friege, C. (1999). Regaining Service Customers. *Journal of Service Research*, 1, 4, 347-361.

Stevens, M. (2001). *Extreme Management: What They Teach You at Harvard Business School's Advanced Management Training Program*. London: Harper Collins Business.

Stone, M., Woodstock, N., & Wilson, M. (1996). Managing the Change from Marketing Planning to Customer Relationship Management. *Long Range Planning*, vol. 29, no. 5, 675-683.

Stubs, R., & Underhill G.R.D., (Eds.) (1994). *Political Economy and Changing Global Order*. London: Macmillan.

Sweeney, P. (2004). Telemarketing Curbs: Not a Boon to All. *Financial Executives International*, March/April, pp.37-39 (www.fei.org).

Tax, S., & Brown, S. (1998). Recovering and Learning from Service Failures. *Sloan Management Review*, 40 (1), 75-88.

Teerling, M., Gragg, S., & Bisgaard-Bohr, M. (2003). Beyond Consumerism – Know your customers Needs, before they do! In: Teerlink, M. & Bucnis, R., *Advanced Consumer Marketing,* Reader for International MBA Program, Rotterdam School of Management, Erasmus Graduate School of Business.

Teerling, M., Plagborg, L., & Gragg, S., (2003). Consumerism: Understanding the fickle behavior of the consumer as an individual"; In: Teerlink, M., Bucnis, *Advanced Consumer Marketing,* Reader for International MBA Program, Rotterdam School of Management, Erasmus Graduate School of Business.

Teerlink, M., & Bucnis, R. (2003). *Advanced Consumer Marketing,* Reader for International MBA Program, Rotterdam School of Management, Erasmus Graduate School of Business.

Tellis, G.J., & Golder, P.N. (2001). *Will and Vision.* The McGraw-Hill.

Terpstra, V., & Sarathy, R. (1999). *International Marketing*, 8th edition. Thomson & South-Western.

Terwogt, M. M., & Hoeksma, J. B. (1995). Colors and emotions: Preferences and combinations. *The Journal of General Psychology*, 122 (1), 5-17.

The Economist Intelligence Unit (2004). *Harnessing Innovation: R&D in a Global Growth Economy*

Thompson, P., Warhurst, C., & Callaghan, G. (2001). Ignorant Theory and Knowledgeable Workers: Interrogating the Connections Between Knowledge, Skills and Services. *Journal of Management Studies*, 38, 7, 923-942.

Timm, R. (1995). *Powerful Ideas to Keep Your Customers.* NJ: Career Press.

Treacy, M., & Wiersema, F. (1995). *The Discipline of Market Leaders*. Addison-Wesley Publishing.

Tricht, E. van, (Ed.) (2002). *De Essentie van Customer Relationship Management.* F&G Publishing.

Tripp, A. (2002). *Customer Management Excellence: Successful Strategies from Service Leaders.* UK: John Wiley & Sons.

VCN (2003). *Ontwikkelingen en Trends op Contactcenter Markt*, Vereniging Contactcenters Nederland, www.vcn.cc

Visser, M. (2004). *Deutero-learning in organizations: A review and a reformulation.* Nijmegen School of Management Working Paper Series on Research in Relationship Management, # RRM-2004-07-MGT

Vocalis, (2003). *Voice of Business Report*. Retrieved from contactcenterworld.com, accessed on 24-1-2005.

Waldez, S. (1993). *An Introduction to the Western Financial Markets*. London: Macmillan.

Walton, S. (2003). *Control and Agent Retention.* Retrieved from peoplepowerportal.com.au /current/03feature.html

Wassenhove, L. van, & Lapré, M. (2003). Conquering the Curve: Managing Learning Curves in Factories by Creating and Transferring Knowledge. *California Management Review*, Vol. 46, No 1.

Watzlawick, P., Bavelas, J.B., & Jackson, D.D. (1967). *Pragmatics of Human Communication: A Study of Interactional Patterns, Pathologies, and Paradoxes.* New York: W.W. Norton & Co.

Weiss, H.M. (2002). Conceptual and Empirical Foundations for the Study of Affect at Work. In: Lord, R.G., Klimoski, R.J., & Kanfer, R. (Eds.), *Emotion in the Work Place: Understanding the Structure and Role of Emotions in Organizational Behavior*, (pp.20-63). San Francisco: Jossey-Bass.

Wetzels, M. (1999). *Service Quality in Customer Employee Relationships: An Empirical Study in the After-Sales Services Context*, Summary Dissertation submitted to European Award for Theses on TQM.

Wilk, S., & Rothbard, N. (2004). Call Centers: How to Reduce Burnout, Increase Efficiency. *Knowlede@ Wharton*, June 16. http://knowledge.wharton.upenn.edu/

Wilk, S.L. (2002). Telephone Call Centers: The Factory Floors of the 21st Century, Knowledge@wharton, http://knowledge.wharton.upenn.edu/ Published: April 10, 2002.

Winer, R.S. (2001). A Framework for Customer Relationship Management. *California Management Review,* Vol 43, No 4, 89-105.

Wing, R.L (1986). *The Tao of Power: Lao Tzu's Classic Guide To Leadership, Influence, And Excellence*. New York: Dolphin Books.

Wing, R.L. (1988). *The Art of Strategy: A new Translation of Sun Tzu's Classic The Art of War*. New York: Broadway Books.

Wolfe, M., & Raaen, D. (1999). *How Much Are Customer Relationship Management Capabilities Really Worth? What Every CEO Should Know*. Retrieved from www.accenture.com.

Womack, J., Jones, D., & Roos, D. (1990). *The Machine That Changed the World*. New York: Rawson.

World Retail Banking Report (2004). ING, EFMA, Cap Gemini Ernst & Young. Retrieved from www.efma.com.

Zaleznik, A. (1977). Managers and Leaders: Are they different? *Harvard Business Review*, May-Jun, 67-78.

Zapf, D., Vogt, C., Seifert, C., Mertini, H., & Isic, A. (1999). Emotion Work as a Source of Stress: The Concept and Development of an Instrument. *European Journal of Work and Organizational psychology*, 8 (3), 371-400.

Zeithaml, V.A., & Bitner, M.J. (2003). *Services Marketing: Integrating Customer Focus Across The Firm*, International Edition, New York: McGraw-Hill / Irvin.

Zimmermann, P., Guttormsen, S., Danuser, B., & Gomez, P. (2003). *Affective Computing – A Rationale for Measuring Mood with Mouse and Keyboard*, Swiss Federal Institute of Technology, Zurich.

Zmud, R.W. (1990). Opportunities for Strategic Information Manupilation Through New Information Technology. In: Fulk, J. & Steinfield, C., (Eds.), *Organizations and Communication Technology*. London: Sage Publications.

# 13 SAMENVATTING

In de volgende paragrafen worden de theorieën aan de uitkomsten uit het ESCC (*Emotional Satisfaction of Customer Contacts*) onderzoek gekoppeld. Paragraaf 13.1 is een samenvatting van de introductie (Hoofdstuk 1). In paragraaf 13.2 worden de verschillende elementen en dimensies van klanttevredenheid en loyaliteit (Hoofdstuk 2) gekoppeld aan de onderzoeksuitkomsten (Hoofdstuk 5). In paragraaf 13.3 wordt de achterliggende theorie van de emotionele tevredenheid van klantcontacten (ESCC) (Hoofdstuk 3) gekoppeld aan de resultaten die uit de implementatie bij testbedrijven zijn gekomen (Hoofdstuk 6). In paragraaf 13.4, worden de stappen van ESCC-observaties naar loyaliteit (Hoofdstuk 4) gekoppeld aan modellen waarbij gebruik wordt gemaakt van ESCC informatie (Hoofdstuk 7). Ten slotte worden in paragraaf 13.5 enkele laatste terugblikken, implicaties en beperkingen samengevat.

## 13.1 Introductie

Hoofdstuk 1 benadrukt het groeiende belang van 'contact centers' en hun toenemende aanwezigheid in het dagelijkse leven van de consumenten in de 21e eeuw. Ondanks het groeiende aantal contact centers en hun toenemende belang, lijken zij en hun IVR (*Interactive Voice Response*) systemen een bron van frustratie te worden en mede daardoor krijgen zij regelmatig negatieve aandacht in de media.

Daarom is gesuggereerd dat een toename van het aantal positieve ervaringen van klanten in de contact centers nodig is. Verschillende studies tonen aan dat klanten persoonlijke aandacht (*Human Touch*) willen wanneer ze contact hebben met organisaties. De verwachte vergrijzing in de westerse wereld onderschrijft het belang van meer persoonlijke aandacht in de dienstverlening en van de contact centers in het bijzonder. *The Human Touch* is de positieve emotie die rondom de dienstverlening en de werkomgeving bestaat. In het proces dat de klant doorloopt van aankoopbeslissing tot en met de post-consumptiefase, hebben contact centers een cruciale rol bij door de klant positief ervaren van de dienstverlening en persoonlijke aandacht.

In dit onderzoek zijn vier partijen te onderscheiden als belanghebbenden van de contact centers: (1) *De directies* van veel organisaties zijn zich niet bewust van of houden zich niet bezig met de dagelijkse gang van zaken in de contact centers, terwijl zij wel eisen dat de contact centers meer verkopen en winst maken. (2) *De managers* van de contact centers lijken te worstelen met tegenstrijdige doelstellingen zoals het streven naar een betere kwaliteit, toenemende klanttevredenheid, het motiveren van werknemers en een toenemende winst, terwijl zij van de directie weinig hulpmiddelen krijgen om dit te waar te maken. Daarom wordt het werk in contact centers vaak gezien als 'lopende band werk ' en de centers bestempeld als de hedendaagse *'high tech sweat shops'*. Ondanks het grote belang wordt het werk van (3) de CSR's

(*Customer Service Representatives*) vaak als van laag niveau en routinematig beschouwd. Niet verbazingwekkend hebben CSR's vaak meer last van werkgerelateerde depressies of stress en zijn zij minder tevreden over hun baan dan andere werknemers. Hierdoor blijken de CSR's vaak de achilleshiel van de contact centers. (4) *Klanten* zijn vaak gefrustreerd over hun contacten met het contact center. Gegeven de verschillende mogelijkheden in een zeer concurrerende markt kiezen ze en - kunnen dat dus ook- soms zelfs voor een andere organisatie. Niettemin blijken organisaties zich daar vaak niet bewust van te zijn.

Eén van de oorzaken voor deze onwetendheid is vermoedelijk de traditionele manier van onderzoek naar klanttevredenheid. Die manier is namelijk niet geschikt om de frustraties van klanten naar boven te krijgen omdat het aantal benaderde klanten beperkt is, de respons onder ontevreden klanten laag is, respondenten ernaar neigen om vragenlijsten positiever in te vullen dan hun werkelijke ervaringen en het onderzoek een positieve invloed heeft op respondenten. Bovendien lijken klachten ook niet geschikt om de vele ontevreden klanten te identificeren. Kort samengevat gaan ontevreden klanten liever naar de concurrent in plaats van vragenlijsten of klachtenformulieren in te vullen. Organisaties lijken niet in staat om hiermee om te gaan. Het proactief identificeren van de ontevredenheid van klanten is dus een noodzaak, niet alleen in de marketingliteratuur maar ook in de marketingpraktijk.

De ontevredenheid van de klant neemt toe, in het bijzonder over contact centers, maar bedrijven zijn niet in staat om deze informatie te vergaren. De CSR's daarentegen merken voortdurend of de klanten al dan niet tevreden zijn. Het is daarom voorzien dat medewerkers van contact centers de tevredenheid van de klanten kunnen observeren, evalueren en direct registreren. Voorbeelden uit de literatuur en de praktijk tonen aan dat het zowel gewenst als realistisch is om '*frontline*' personeel, zoals CSR's, te betrekken bij het klanttevredenheid (onderzoeks) proces.

*In dit onderzoek wordt daarom getracht de klanttevredenheid en het loyaliteitproces te analyseren en wordt een model voorgesteld dat in de contacten met klanten kan worden gebruikt om klanttevredenheid te laten observeren door de CSR's. Omdat klantencontact een bron van frustraties (negative emoties) kan zijn en het noodzakelijk is gebleken om de positieve ervaringen (positieve emoties) te verhogen, is dit onderzoek toegespitst op emotionele aspecten van klanttevredenheid en de emotionele tevredenheid van de klantencontacten (ESCC) in het bijzonder. Het is te verwachten dat deze observaties tijdig tastbare informatie opleveren over zowel ontevreden als tevreden klanten. Hierdoor kunnen fouten in de dienstverlening hersteld worden door actie te ondernemen naar aanleiding van de ontevredenheid van de klant. Tevens kan de verkoopproductiviteit stijgen door gebruik van de kennis over de tevredenheid . De verbeteracties die ondernomen worden naar aanleiding van de informatie dragen bij aan het leerproces van de organisatie (organizational learning). Het is ook te voorzien dat door deze acties de interne en externe kwaliteit en tevredenheid zullen toenemen. Hierdoor stijgen de klantenloyaliteit (en winstgevendheid), zoals beschreven in "the service profit chain" door Heskett et al. (1997).*

## 13.2 Elementen, Dimensies en Correlaties in Klanttevredenheid en Loyaliteit

Naar aanleiding van de gelezen literatuur zijn er in Hoofdstuk 2 zes basiselementen van klanttevredenheid geselecteerd: prijs, product, gemak, de kwaliteit van dienstverlening, de manier waarop klanten zijn behandeld en positieve gevoelens over het bedrijf of het merk. Er zijn ook vier dimensies in het klanttevredenheidproces vastgesteld, namelijk de emotionele, de cognitieve, de transactionele en algemene tevredenheid. De cognitieve tevredenheid vertegenwoordigt de verstandelijke kant van de tevredenheid, terwijl de emotionele tevredenheid betrekking heeft op gevoelens. Met algemene tevredenheid wordt de globale tevredenheid van klanten bedoeld en bij transactionele tevredenheid gaat het om de laatste transacties, de tevredenheid over het laatste contact met de organisatie. Ten slotte is de loyaliteit van klanten onderzocht, met de vraag of zij de intentie hebben om klant te blijven.

In Hoofdstuk 5 worden de uitkomsten van onderzoeken beschreven die uitgevoerd zijn bij vier verschillende Nederlandse testbedrijven: een boek- en muziekhandel, een verzekeringsmaatschappij, een pensioenfonds en een bank. Uit deze onderzoeken blijkt dat de klanten het minst tevreden zijn over de volgende elementen: prijs, gemak en kwaliteit van dienstverlening. Deze uitkomsten geven aan dat de klanten lagere prijzen, meer gemak en betere dienstverlening verwachten. De negatieve uitkomsten bij dienstverlening en gemak bevestigen ook het oorspronkelijke idee dat dit onderzoek inspireerde: klanten zijn niet volledig tevreden over de dienstverlening. Klanten blijken echter loyaler te zijn dan hun tevredenheid aangeeft. Dit geeft aan dat klanttevredenheid niet direct vertaald kan worden in klantenloyaliteit.

Bijna alle tevredenheidelementen,[121] die gebruikt zijn in zowel dit onderzoek als verscheidene andere onderzoeken, werden matig geassocieerd met algemene tevredenheid, nog minder met de transactionele tevredenheid en ten slotte zwak met de loyaliteitsintentie. De geselecteerde elementen en concepten schijnen dus meer geschikt te zijn om algemene tevredenheid te meten dan de transactionele tevredenheid of loyaliteitsintentie. Deze uitkomst bevestigt zowel de effectiviteit van de toevoeging van het transactionele dimensie in het klanttevredenheidsonderzoek als de noodzakelijkheid om de loyaliteit te analyseren met meer specifieke *constructs* (cf. Reichheld, 1993:71; 1996:58).

De relatief positieve antwoorden op de surveyvragen bij de klanten uit de testgroep met name over hun laatste contact, geven aan dat organisaties in feite in staat zijn om de klanttevredenheid te verhogen als zij een omgeving creëren

[121] Prijs, product, gemak, kwaliteit van dienstverlening, de manier waarop klanten behandeld zijn en positieve gevoelens over het bedrijf of merk.

die hetzelfde is als tijdens de ESCC onderzoeksdagen, waarbij de klanttevredenheid continu geobserveerd en bewaakt wordt. Het werd echter ook duidelijk dat bij een – klein- deel zeer ontevreden klanten uit de testgroep extra aandacht tijdens contactmomenten de ontevredenheid over andere tekortkomingen van de organisatie niet volledig kan wegnemen .

Hieruit volgt dus dat contactmomenten een sterk *momentum* vormen om een uitgesproken mening te formuleren over de organisaties. Dit feit lijkt echter niet volledig erkend te zijn door veel organisaties wier klanten regelmatig gefrustreerd zijn door –het gedrag van - de contact centers.

Er is echter geen verschil gevonden in loyaliteitsintenties tussen de testgroep klanten en de controlegroep. Dit zou erop kunnen wijzen dat de omstandigheden van de onderzoeksdagen met ESCC het potentieel hebben om de tevredenheid te verhogen, maar gemiddeld geen directe invloed hebben op de loyaliteitsintenties, met uitzondering van extreme gevallen waar de klanten erg ontevreden zijn.

Uit het onderzoek komt naar voren dat de elementen product, de manier waarop klanten behandeld zijn, de positieve gevoelens en de loyaliteitsintenties significant verschillen bij de testbedrijven. Er is echter geen significant verschil geconstateerd bij algemene tevredenheid, prijs, gemak, de kwaliteit van dienstverlening en transactionele tevredenheid en dus blijken zij gemeenschappelijke kenmerken bij verschillende bedrijven te zijn.

Gebaseerd op de *'principal component'* analyse vallen de kwaliteit van dienstverlening, de manier waarop klanten behandeld zijn en de positieve gevoelens voor een organisatie onder de dimensie emotionele tevredenheid en vallen prijs en product onder cognitieve tevredenheid (Onderzoeksvraag 1).

Kruistabel analyses van de verschillende dimensies van tevredenheid tonen aan dat de emotionele dimensie consequent een sterkere rol speelt dan de cognitieve dimensie in de transactionele tevredenheid, in de algemene tevredenheid en in de loyaliteit (Onderzoeksvragen 2a, b, c). Ondanks het aangetoonde belang van emotionele aspecten, is het echter opvallend dat veel bedrijven in hun marketingstrategieën nog steeds de cognitieve aspecten zoals prijs en product benadrukken.

Uitkomsten uit onderzoek tonen aan dat loyaliteit meer afhangt van algemene tevredenheid dan van transactionele tevredenheid (Onderzoeksvraag 3). Met andere woorden, wanneer klanten over het algemeen tevreden zijn, lijkt een eenmalig transactioneel incident, zoals een teleurstellend klantencontact, acceptabel. Daar staat tegenover dat een eenmalig transactionele tevredenheid geen grote invloed heeft op algemene ontevredenheid. Deze uitkomst zou echter niet het belang van de transactionele tevredenheid moeten ondermijnen, daar de totale tevredenheid het gevolg is van een reeks transactionele tevredenheidsmomenten. Als bewijs hiervoor toont het ESCC onderzoek aan dat transactionele en algemene tevredenheid met elkaar zijn verbonden en elkaar nodig hebben om een sterker effect aan beide kanten te genereren. De onderzoeksuitkomsten wijzen ook uit dat hoe positiever de klantencontacten met een bedrijf zijn, hoe groter de algemene tevredenheid en loyaliteit intenties van de klanten zijn (Onderzoeksvraagen 4a, b).

De duur van de relatie met bedrijven lijkt geen significante rol te spelen in het proces van algemene tevredenheid van de klant, maar wel in de loyaliteitsintentie van de klant. Het blijkt dus dat klanttevredenheid een kwestie is die een continue en duurzame rol speelt tijdens *'customer lifetime'*. Daarentegen blijkt de loyaliteit sterker te worden naarmate er meer tijd verstrijkt. De uitkomsten uit het onderzoek tonen ook aan dat het beeld van de klant over het laatste contact met de organisatie in de loop van de tijd vervaagt en vervlakt (Onderzoeksvraag 5). Hieruit blijkt dat de klantcontactevredenheid bijzonder belangrijk kan zijn vlak voor (herhalings-) aankoop momenten.

## 13.3 Emotional Satisfaction of Customer Contacts (ESCC)

In Hoofdstuk 3 zijn de definitie, de meting en de rol van emoties in klanttevredenheid en in de contact centers onderzocht. De emoties van klanten zijn verbonden met de emoties van de CSR's terwijl de emoties van CSR's verbonden zijn met kwesties zoals het emotionele klimaat in de organisatie, de emotionele arbeid en emotionele intelligentie. Deze verbanden geven aan dat de situatie in een organisatie de emoties en stemmingen van de werknemer beïnvloedt en als gevolg daarvan ook de emoties van de klant.

In Hoofdstuk 3 wordt een simpele methodologie voorgesteld om (emotionele) klanttevredenheid te laten observeren door CSR's wanneer zij in contact zijn met klanten. In het ESCC model wordt een reeks kleuren gebruikt, van rood-oranje-geel-groen-blauw. Deze kleurenreeks vertegenwoordigt de observaties van de CSR's over de emotionele gemoedstoestand van klanten, die uiteen kunnen lopen van zeer negatief tot zeer positief. Er zijn twee richtlijnen opgesteld om de CSR's te ondersteunen bij het toekennen van een kleur aan een contactmoment met de klant. De eerste richtlijn geeft aan dat rood staat voor het ene uiterste, de meest onplezierige en problematische gesprekken en blauw voor het andere uiterste, de meest plezierige en soepel verlopende gesprekken. Volgens de tweede richtlijn worden de *energy* (intensiteit) en *pleasantness* (plezierigheid) van de gesprekken verdeeld over hoge en lage categorieën in een tabel met enige specifieke emoties vergelijkbaar met het *'affect circumplex'* model. Deze groep emoties is verbonden aan de ESCC- kleuren. Het was echter niet de bedoeling om de evaluaties van de CSR's door richtlijnen te beperken. Deze kleuren, die de transactionele tevredenheid weergeven, zijn verbonden met zowel de emotionele en cognitieve dimensie als met *churn* (het weglopen van klanten naar een andere aanbieder) en loyaliteit als cumulatief effect.

Tijdens de onderzoeksdagen hebben geselecteerde CSR's alle inkomende gesprekken geëvalueerd aan de hand van de ESCC methodologie, terwijl zij ook hun gewone dagelijkse taken uitvoerden. Het model en de onderzoeksmethode zijn kort uitgelegd aan de CSR's, die nog geen ervaring hadden met dit soort evaluaties.

In Hoofdstuk 6 wordt de basis implementatie van de ESCC methodologie in de testbedrijven beschreven, de nauwkeurigheid van de ESCC observaties onderzocht en de relatie tussen de geobserveerde ESCC, klanttevredenheid en loyaliteit intenties bestudeerd. De uitkomsten tonen aan dat de contacten het meest positief ervaren werden door de klanten uit de testgroep. De klanten uit de controlegroep ervoeren deze als redelijk positief en de CSR's ervoeren de contacten neutraal. (Onderzoeksvraag 6). Als de ruwe gemiddelden van de CSR's, de controle- en de testgroep in overweging worden genomen, blijkt dat ongeveer 10% van de klantcontacten negatief en zeer negatief werd beoordeeld, ongeveer 20% neutraal, ongeveer 50% positief en 20% zeer positief. Desalniettemin blijken er duidelijke verschillen wanneer specifieke steekproefgroepen geanalyseerd worden. Het percentage negatieve en zeer negatieve beoordelingen in de testgroep van de verzekeringsmaatschappij was 23,6%, terwijl dat percentage in de boek- en muziekhandel slechts 2,4% was.

Het kritieke punt was echter of CSR observaties wel accuraat zijn. De nauwkeurigheid wordt berekend door het verschil tussen 'klanten evaluatie' over het laatste contact (Surveyvraag 9) en de 'ESCC observatie' van de CSR over datzelfde contact uit te rekenen. In een-op-een vergelijkingen, was de gemiddelde nauwkeurigheid *34%*. Als dezelfde gegevens opnieuw gegroepeerd werden in drie klassen (zoals 1&2, 3&4, 5), nam de gemiddelde nauwkeurigheid toe tot *60%*. En als '*one-scale-differences*' - waarbij de klanten één score positiever zijn dan de CSR's - als accuraat werden beschouwd, dan steeg de nauwkeurigheid van de observaties naar bijna *80%*.

Cohen's Kappa Statistieken, de Boxplot grafiek, kruistabellen, $\chi^2$ analyse en correlatie- coëfficiënten duiden de ESCC eerder als een 'redelijk indicator' aan dan als een 'nauwkeurig instrument' om tevredenheid in klantencontacten te beoordelen (Onderzoeksvraag 7).

De nauwkeurigheid varieert tussen de testbedrijven onderling. Ze waren nauwkeuriger bij de boek- en muziekhandel en de verzekeringsmaatschappij en minder nauwkeurig bij het pensioenfonds en de bank. CSR's waren nauwkeuriger in extreme gevallen en zelfs nog nauwkeuriger in negatieve gevallen. Met andere woorden, hoe intensiever de klantencontacten hoe nauwkeuriger de evaluaties van de klanttevredenheid door de CSR's. Er zijn geen significante aspecten gevonden die het nauwkeurigheidsniveau van ESCC observaties mogelijk kunnen beïnvloeden. Toch blijkt dat de nauwkeurigheid groter wordt wanneer de ESCC observaties gedurende een langere tijd worden uitgevoerd en gekalibreerd door ze regelmatig te vergelijken met de evaluaties van de klanten. Een voorbeeld: in een Nederlandse financiële organisatie stegen de nauwkeurige observaties in één maand tijd van 30 tot 45%.

Er zijn positieve correlaties ontdekt tussen de eigen emoties van de CSR's en hun ESCC beoordelingen, dus hoe de CSR's de emotie van de klant ervaren. Het bleek ook dat ESCC significant samenhangt met hoe CSR's zich voelen direct na een telefoongesprek, maar niet met hoe zij zich voelen na diverse verschillende gesprekken (Onderzoeksvraag 8).

Zoals de correlatie en de $\chi^2$ analyse aangaven, was de samenhang tussen de ESCC observaties en emotionele tevredenheid sterker dan tussen ESCC observaties en cognitieve tevredenheid (Onderzoeksvraag 9a). Met andere woorden, in de ESCC observaties komen de volgende elementen van de klanttevredenheid meer naar voren: gemak, kwaliteit van dienstverlening, de manier waarop klanten behandeld zijn en positieve gevoelens over het bedrijf. Prijs en product komen minder naar voren. De statistische sterkte van deze samenhang bleek echter tussen zwak en gematigd te liggen.

Het verband tussen ESCC en transactionele tevredenheid, algemene tevredenheid en loyaliteit intenties zijn onderzocht met behulp van correlatie coëfficiënten, *correspondence* analyses, kruistabellen en $\chi^2$ analyses. De uitkomsten tonen aan dat ESCC matig wordt geassocieerd met transactionele tevredenheid; zwak met algemene tevredenheid en enigszins gematigd met loyaliteitsintentie (Onderzoeksvraagen 9b, c, d).

Daarnaast maken de ESCC observaties een effectief onderscheid tussen klanten die de intentie hebben om weg te gaan en klanten met een loyaliteitsintentie. Met andere woorden, de CSR's waren in staat om redelijk nauwkeurig de transactionele tevredenheid te observeren en vast te stellen tijdens contacten met de klant. Deze observaties zijn een redelijke indicator van loyaliteitsintenties van klanten. Specifieker: Hoe positiever de ESCC, des te groter de klanttevredenheid en loyaliteit!

## 13.4 Het inzetten van ESCC

Hoofdstuk 4 gaat uit van de veronderstelling dat informatie waardevol is als er actie op ondernomen kan worden en stelt de volgende stappen in ESCC proces voor aan de hand van gelezen literatuur. Hoofdstuk 7 beschrijft deze stappen in het kader van het ESCC raamwerk en gaat in op enig, zij het beperkt, empirisch bewijs. De beschreven stappen behelzen het opvolgen van positieve ESCC om zo meer verkoop te genereren, het opvolgen van negatieve ESCC om de dienstverlening te verbeteren en te herstellen, het leren van fouten en verbeteringen en vervolgens de toename van de klanttevredenheid en loyaliteit (Onderzoeksvraag 10).

Onderzoeken tonen aan dat positieve ervaringen van de klant leiden tot meer verkoop en er wordt voorgesteld dat de ESCC informatie over de ervaringsniveaus van klanten gebruikt kan worden om de verkoop te verbeteren, één van de '*hot topics*' in de contact center branche.

In contact centers wordt er voornamelijk verkocht door gebruik te maken van binnenkomende gesprekken of het initiëren van verkoopgesprekken aan de telefoon (*telesales*). Desalniettemin waarderen de meeste klanten een overdreven '*sales push*' niet wanneer zij zelf contact opnemen met het bedrijf en willen ze ook niet benaderd worden voor telefonische verkoop door organisaties. Bovendien kan de '*sales push*' klanten zelfs irriteren als de organisaties niet in staat zijn om hun klanten in eerste instantie behoorlijk van dienst te zijn.

De ESCC methodologie richt zich daarom op het identificeren van de beste klanten en de beste momenten waarop verkoop geïnitieerd kan worden. Dit is samen te vatten in drie mogelijkheden. Ten eerste is te verwachten dat door positief emotionele ervaringen met de dienstverlening de klanttevredenheid zal toenemen en daardoor de neiging tot een (herhalings-)aankoop. Ten tweede is gesuggereerd dat speciale acties ontworpen kunnen worden voor (zeer) tevreden klanten met een zeer positieve ESCC. De derde mogelijkheid is om teleurgestelde en boze klanten met een (zeer) negatieve ESCC uit te sluiten van direct marketing acties, dit bespaart kosten waardoor de verkoopproductiviteit toeneemt.

Het literatuuronderzoek bevestigde zowel de noodzaak als de effectiviteit van proactief herstel van de gemaakte fouten om de klanttevredenheid en de loyaliteit terug te winnen. De ESCC methodologie tracht de leemte 'hoe het operationeel te maken' te vullen. Daarom is voorgesteld dat de geregistreerde ESCC informatie geanalyseerd kan worden en dat de teleurstellingen van klanten waarop actie ondernomen kan worden eruit gefilterd worden, zodat deze klantproblemen proactief hersteld kunnen worden. Het beperkte empirische bewijs gaf aan dat verbeteracties zeer effectief zijn om klanttevredenheid en loyaliteit te herstellen en het bewees dat ESCC een betrouwbare constructie is voor het uitvoeren van het herstelproces van de dienstverlening.

Het proces om fouten te achterhalen en te corrigeren is onderzocht onder '*organizational learning*'. Studies stellen voor van fouten te leren en deze te vertalen in verbeteringen en daardoor klanttevredenheid en loyaliteit te creëren. Daarnaast zijn er ook drie 'learning loops' vastgesteld: *'single-loop learning'*, waarin fouten worden ontdekt en gecorrigeerd; *'double-loop learning'*, waarbij processen en producten worden verbeterd en *'triple-loop learning'*, waarbij systemen leren hoe ze moeten leren en waarbij normen, uitgangspunten en gerelateerde waarden worden aangepast.

Het ESCC model schrijft richtlijnen voor aan de praktische kant van het leerproces van de organisatie en stelt een simpele methodologie voor die in ieder geval de '*single-loop learning'* kan ondersteunen bij het ontdekken en corrigeren van fouten. De metafoor waarin de organisatie de pan is en de klanten het water vormen, illustreert het ESCC proces binnen het leerproces van de organisatie. In deze metafoor vangt het deksel (ESCC model) de stoom (informatie over klanten ontevredenheid) op en gebruikt deze om herstelacties op te zetten, om klanten vast te houden, om de processen te verbeteren voor het leerproces van de organisatie en voor meer klanttevredenheid.

Het onderstreept het belang van het gebruik van de ESCC-informatie en het boeken van vooruitgang naar een volgende *loop* in het leerproces van de organisatie. *Empowerment* (meer bevoegdheden geven aan werknemers), *team learning* en een verschuiving in managementstijl van controle naar zorg worden gezien als enkele basisfundamenten van een lerende organisatie.

Tenslotte bevestigen het literatuuronderzoek en de onderzoeksuitkomsten de verbanden tussen verbetering van dienstverlening en de toename van de klanttevredenheid; maar wat er na de tevredenheid gebeurt is echter niet bevestigd. Loyaliteit en winstgevendheid wekken de schijn een redelijke aanvulling te zijn op klanttevredenheid, maar zonder garanties.

## 13.5 Enkele Laatste Terugblikken, Implicaties en Beperkingen

Als laatste terugblik zijn er nog wat uitgangspunten opgesteld. Het ESCC model is ten eerste beschreven als een middel dat informatie verzamelt over elk klantencontact door de CSR's bij de processen van klanttevredenheid, loyaliteit en de lerende organisatie te betrekken en hen hierin een actieve rol te laten spelen. Ten tweede blijkt de ESCC benadering een instrument te zijn dat een volledig beeld van de transactionele tevredenheid in een klantencontact omgeving kan schetsen.

Het ESCC model stelt echter niet voor om (emotionele) relaties op te bouwen met de klanten en is niet bedoeld om de uitkomsten te generaliseren zodat CSR's, organisaties of klanten veroordeeld kunnen worden. Daarnaast is ook niet geïmpliceerd dat het ernstige kwaliteitsgebreken van het product of grote prijsverschillen met de concurrent kan compenseren.

Verschillende bevindingen in dit onderzoek, zoals "klanttevredenheid kan niet direct vertaald worden naar loyaliteit", "loyaliteit is meer afhankelijk van de emotionele dimensie dan van de cognitieve dimensie" en "verbeteracties na een onbevredigende dienstverlening kunnen voorkomen dat de klant wegloopt en zelfs de loyaliteit vergroten" zijn in lijn met bestaande literatuur. Dit onderzoek openbaarde ook de relatie tussen de dimensies transactionele tevredenheid en algemene tevredenheid, die met elkaar verbonden blijken te zijn en elkaars aanwezigheid nodig hebben.

Eerdere studies onderzochten de emoties van klanten en '*frontline*' medewerkers aan de hand van bijvoorbeeld '*critical incident*' technieken. Dit onderzoek hanteert echter een praktische methodologie voor het vaststellen van de emotionele tevredenheid over de klantencontacten en voor het vergelijken van de kijk van de werknemers op de tevredenheid over het klantcontact met de kijk van de klanten.

Als implicatie voor het management schetst dit onderzoek een eenvoudig observatie- en registratieproces in het vaststellen van emoties die naar boven komen tijdens contacten met de klant door de ogen van de CSR's. Door deze observaties zijn organisaties in staat om vele ontevreden klanten te identificeren. Normaal gesproken zouden die onbekend blijven, omdat ontevreden klanten over het algemeen klagen bij vrienden en familie en niet bij de betrokken organisaties. Dit onderzoek doet ook meerdere voorstellen over het verhogen van de verkoop(productiviteit) door het gebruiken van de naar boven gekomen

ESCC informatie, maakt een opzet voor een praktisch en proactief herstelproces van de dienstverlening en stelt een '*organizational learning cycle*' voor. En, *last but not least*, zoals Rust, Zeithaml and Lemon (2000: 34) al stelden, om de continuïteit van een organisatie nauwkeuriger in te schatten, dienen bedrijven zich niet alleen op huidige prestatie van hun producten te concentreren maar ook op de toekomst van hun klantenrelaties. Het ESCC model lijkt al het potentieel te hebben om precies die informatie te leveren.

De beperkingen van dit onderzoek hebben voornamelijk te maken met het lange termijn effect van het ESCC model. Dit onderzoek richtte zich op de '*inhouse*' contact centers van commerciële organisaties die te maken hebben met inkomende gesprekken van particuliere klanten. '*Outsourced*' contact centers, non-profit organisaties, uitgaande verkoopgesprekken (*telesales*) en zakelijke klanten zijn onderwerp voor toekomstig onderzoek. Ten slotte zijn de emoties in dit onderzoek verdeeld over een reeks die uiteenloopt van zeer negatief tot zeer positief en ging het dus niet om specifieke emoties. Toekomstig onderzoek zou de relaties tussen contacten met de klant en specifieke gevoelens, zoals woede, verrassing of blijdschap kunnen onderzoeken.